Rekindling the Sacred Fire

Rekindling the Sacred Fire

Métis Ancestry and Anishinaabe Spirituality

CHANTAL FIOLA

University of Manitoba Press

University of Manitoba Press
Winnipeg, Manitoba
Canada R3T 2M5
uofmpress.ca

Printed in Canada
Text printed on chlorine-free, 100% post-consumer recycled paper

19 18 17 16 15   1 2 3 4 5

Cover image: Christi Belcourt, "The Métis and the Two Row Wampum" (detail),
acrylic on canvas, 48 x 72 in., 2002
Cover design: Frank Reimer
Interior design: Jess Koroscil

Library and Archives Canada Cataloguing in Publication

Fiola, Chantal, 1982–, author
Rekindling the sacred fire : Métis ancestry and Anishinaabe spirituality
/ Chantal Fiola.

Includes bibliographical references and index.
Issued in print and electronic formats.
ISBN 978-0-88755-770-5 (pbk.)
ISBN 978-0-88755-478-0 (PDF e-book)
ISBN 978-0-88755-480-3 (epub)

1. Métis—Prairie Provinces—Rites and ceremonies. 2. Métis—Prairie
Provinces—Religion. 3. Métis—Prairie Province—Ethnic identity. 4. Métis—
Colonization—Prairie Provinces. 5. Ojibwa Indians—Prairie Provinces—
Religion. 6. Ojibwa Indians—Colonization—Prairie Provinces. 7. Prairie
Provinces—Ethnic relations. I. Title.

E99.M47F55 2015   971.2004'97   C2014-903277-3
                                              C2014-903278-1

The University of Manitoba Press gratefully acknowledges the financial support
for its publication program provided by the Government of Canada through the Canada
Book Fund, the Canada Council for the Arts, the Manitoba Department
of Culture, Heritage, Tourism, the Manitoba Arts Council,
and the Manitoba Book Publishing Tax Credit.

FSC
www.fsc.org
MIX
Paper from
responsible sources
FSC® C016245

Contents

This book is dedicated to all the Métis Anishinaabeg ancestors who worked tirelessly to ensure that we would still have our sacred teachings to guide us today. It is also dedicated to all those Métis Anishinaabeg who are now rediscovering our rightful place in the sacred circle and picking up our work, and to all those Métis Anishinaabeg who will come after us and continue this good work.

Note on Terminology

An indirect translation of "Anishinaabe" can be understood in English as "the original people." I learned from Eddie Benton-Banai, Grand Chief of the àr ee Fires Midewiwin, that while the term Anishinaabe is often associated with Ojibwe/Saulteaux/Chippewa people, in its broader meaning it can encompass all Indigenous peoples and their spiritualities. My preference is to use the term Anishinaabe in this book; however, I sometimes use the terms Indigenous, Native, and Aboriginal interchangeably to mean Anishinaabe in its broader sense. As in the 1982 Constitution Act, I also use the term "Aboriginal" to refer to the First Nations, Métis, and Inuit. As much as possible, I point out when I am using the more specific meaning of the term Anishinaabe (as belonging to the Ojibwe/Saulteaux/Chippewa cultures). Also, the double-vowel writing system for Anishinaabemowin (Ojibwe language) is used in this book except when referring to sources that use the phonetic system.

CHAPTER 1

Seven Fires Prophecy and the Métis: An Introduction

Many years ago, seven prophets came to the Anishinaabeg. Each foretold a prediction of what the future would bring. Each prophecy was called a Fire, and each Fire referred to a particular era of time that would come in the future....

The first prophet said to the people, "In the time of the First Fire, the Anishinaabe nation will rise up and follow the Sacred Shell of the Midewiwin Lodge. The Midewiwin Lodge will serve as a rallying point for the people and its traditional ways will be the source of much strength."...

The Fourth Fire, given by two prophets who came as one, told of the coming of the Light-skinned Race. It was said that the future of our people will be known by the face of the Light-skinned Race. If they come wearing the face of brotherhood, there will follow a time of wonderful change and the two nations will join to make a mighty nation.... But, if they come wearing the face of death, there will follow a time of great suffering....

The seventh prophet said to the people, "In the time of the Seventh Fire an Osh-ki-bi-ma-di-zeeg' (New People) will emerge. They will retrace their steps to find what was left by the trail. Their steps will take them to the elders who they will ask to guide them on their journey.... The task of the New People will not be easy.... If the New People will remain strong in their quest, the Waterdrum of the Midewiwin Lodge will again sound its voice. There will be a rebirth of the Anishinaabe nation and a rekindling of old flames. The Sacred Fire will again be lit.

"It is at this time that the Light-skinned Race will be given a choice
between two roads. If they choose the right road, then the Seventh
Fire will light the Eighth and Final Fire—an eternal Fire of peace,
love, brotherhood and sisterhood. If the Light-skinned Race makes
the wrong choice of roads, then the destruction which they brought
with them in coming to this country will come back to them and
cause much suffering and death to all the Earth's people."
— Edward Benton-Banai, *The Mishomis Book*, 89–93

The Seven Fires Prophecy (above) was given to the Anishinaabeg in the
distant, pre-contact history by a series of prophets and triggered a great
migration among the Anishinaabeg who would heed its warnings. Some
Anishinaabe Elders believe that each of the fires (or eras of time) that were
predicted has come to pass and that we are currently in the time of the
Seventh Fire. They believe that the two paths mentioned in the *Neesh-wa-
swi' ish-ko-day-kawn* (Seven Fires Prophecy) are interpreted as the path of
technology and the path of spiritualism—the former representing the rush
to technological development (devoid of spirit) leading to destruction,
and the latter representing the slower path of the traditional spirituality of
our ancestors, which many are seeking anew and which does not lead to a
scorched earth (Benton-Banai, 93). Our traditional teachers are encouraging
us to recognize modern challenges to *mino-bimaadiziwin* (good, balanced
life) and the ongoing importance of our ancestral ways of seeing, sometimes
termed *360-degree vision*, a holistic, interdependent world view (Dumont
1979, 11). A return to traditional spirituality among Anishinaabe people
today represents one form of contemporary agency, as well as the unfolding
of an ancient prophecy. As foretold in the prophecy, such a return is not easy.

Many Aboriginal families today, including Métis people, are disconnected from our ancestral spiritual ways as a result of colonization. Métis
people have sometimes been referred to as the "New People"—for instance,
in Jacqueline Peterson and Jennifer Brown's 1985 book, *The New People:
Being and Becoming Métis in North America*, which remains one of the most
seminal academic sources on Métis studies to date.[1] However, most Métis are
unaware that we are included in the Oshkibimaadiziig (New People) spoken
of in the Seven Fires Prophecy and that we are welcome, to name just two examples, at the Sundance and in the Midewiwin Way, a spiritual society based
on ancestral Anishinaabe teachings and ways of life (Gaywish 2008, 1).[2] It
would likely come as a shock to many to learn that Louis Riel—arguably the

most famous Métis leader, the Father of Manitoba and a devout Catholic—
was, according to oral history, adopted by a Midewiwin family and became
Midewiwin himself (Chapter 2). The Seventh Fire speaks of the importance
of the work of the Oshkibimaadiziig as contributing to the potential for an
Eighth (and final) Fire, an eternal fire of unity to be lit by all humans (Simpson
2008b, 14). Métis people can contribute significantly to this work in contemporary times. Hence the title of this book; it refers to Métis participation in
the work of the Oshkibimaadiziig (rekindling our sacred ancestral ways)
spoken of in the Seven Fires Prophecy.

The colonial agenda of assimilating Anishinaabe peoples into dominant
European settler ways dates back to early contact and continues to this day.
European religions have played a central role in this assimilative agenda,
the history and consequences of which have played out in both similar and
unique ways across Aboriginal groups in Canada. In this book, I illustrate how
Christianity was encouraged among (often forced upon) Aboriginal peoples,
including the Métis, in many ways—missionary efforts, the residential school
system, and the child welfare system—and has greatly influenced Métis relationships, or lack thereof, with Anishinaabe spirituality. Given this history, it
is not surprising that so many Métis people today are Christian, including especially high rates of Catholicism among Red River Métis families. It is not my
intention to discourage Métis people (or anyone) from pursuing Christianity;
rather, I am providing an opportunity to learn about the Anishinaabe ways of
our ancestors that historically (and contemporarily) we as Indigenous people
living in a colonial world have not been free to choose. A consequence of this
history is that many Métis (and other Aboriginal) people who are disconnected from these ways worry that we "don't have the right" to participate in
ceremonies and feel unsure about seeking them out. This book is an effort
to expose and counter this history and these all-too-common worries; it is
a reminder that Anishinaabe spirituality is a legitimate option that remains
open to us. Our ancestors worked hard to ensure that these ways would still
be here for us today, and, despite all odds, they succeeded. You are welcome
to respectfully seek out these ways. In these pages, you will also learn about
this journey, the challenges, and insights learned by others who have found
meaning and fulfillment in Anishinaabe spirituality.

Anishinaabe perseverance and the will to survive have always existed
alongside assimilative pressures. Contemporary examples abound, including
increasing numbers of people "newly" identifying as Aboriginal and Métis
(reasons for not self-identifying in these ways in the past may have to do
with persecution by the government and internalized racism, as discussed in

Chapters 2 and 3). From 1996 to 2001, according to Statistics Canada (2003a; 2003b), while the Canadian population grew by 3 percent, the population self-identifying as Aboriginal grew 22 percent. In the same five-year period, the Métis population increased by an astounding 43 percent (with the highest populations in Alberta, Manitoba, and Ontario) (Statistics Canada 2010).[3]

Agency and resistance are also found in court cases where Aboriginal people are demanding acknowledgment and protection of our rights. In March 2013, in *Manitoba Métis Federation (MMF) v. Canada*, the Supreme Court of Canada ruled in favour of the Métis by declaring that the Government of Canada failed to uphold its constitutional obligation to the Métis under section 31 of the Manitoba Act of 1870 (Chartrand 2013, para. 1). The court case, launched by the MMF in 1981, argued that due to unscrupulous government and surveyor tactics, the 1.4 million acres of land promised to the Métis in section 31 was swindled from us. As a result, many Métis argue, any supposed extinguishment of Aboriginal title to land and rights that went along with the "land exchanges" are null and void. Therefore, contemporary Manitoba Métis, as descendants of the historic Métis Nation whose ancestors received scrip, should be compensated (financially and/or otherwise) for the massive theft of our land. Two months before this decision, the Federal Court ruled, in *Daniels v. Canada*, that "Métis and Non Status Indians are defined under the term 'Indian' for the purposes of Section 91(24) [para. 619]" of the Constitution Act, 1867 (Henry 2013; *Daniels v. Canada* 2013). Yet another case—*Alberta (Aboriginal Affairs and Northern Development) v. Cunningham*—played out in 2011 involving members of a Métis family whose membership in an Alberta Métis settlement was revoked when they obtained registered Indian status. This case is controversial among Métis people themselves, with some supporting the Cunninghams' plight and others siding against them. These court cases, discussed at length in Chapter 3, illustrate Métis resistance to ongoing colonial control over the lives of Métis people.

Then, at the end of 2012, the Idle No More movement seemingly came out of nowhere, commanding media attention throughout Canada and abroad. This grassroots movement birthed and led by (mostly young) Aboriginal people (especially Nina Wilson, Sylvia McAdam, and Jessica Gordon) with non-Aboriginal supporters (notably Sheelah McLean), began with extreme discontent over the Canadian government's proposed omnibus Bill C-45 (Jobs and Growth Act), which received assent on 14 December of that year. Controversy over this Act included its size (over 450 pages), its inclusion of many disparate issues, and an overall lack of consultation with Aboriginal peoples. Many argued that the government was trying to sneak harmful changes into law, hiding them in the massive document and hoping no one would notice. Such harmful changes include those made to the Navigable Waters Act (only a fraction of Canadian bodies of water are now protected), the Indian Act, and the Environmental Assessment Act. In contrast, "Idle No More calls on all people to join in a revolution which honours and fulfills Indigenous sovereignty which protects the land and water" ("9 Questions about Idle No More" 2013). Attawapiskat Chief Theresa Spence went on a six-week hunger strike (ending on 24 January 2013) to raise awareness about First Nation issues including poverty, substandard housing, and unsafe drinking water on reserves, as well as to protest Bill C-45 and raise awareness about the Idle No More movement. In no time, and thanks in part to communication via social media, thousands of people were participating in a National Day of Action; flash mob round dances in shopping centres, airports, and intersections; sit-ins and teach-ins; rallies, marches, and protests; and road, bridge, and mine blockades across Canada and in other countries. The prime minister agreed to a meeting with a delegation organized by the Assembly of First Nations (AFN) on 11 January 2013, but many criticized the meeting as lip service with no concrete outcomes and because the Governor General did not participate (except in a "ceremonial" manner afterwards). Treaties were signed between First Nations and the reigning monarch of Canada; as a representative of the Queen, the Governor General should participate in such meetings. While Idle No More is no longer in the headlines every other day, it is still very much ongoing, often taking the form of smaller local events and projects aimed at cultural, linguistic, and spiritual resurgence and regeneration. Idle No More did not spring forth from nowhere; it is the latest grassroots movement in a history of Indigenous resistance to colonization that is as old as contact itself.

Another example of contemporary agency, one likely less obvious to non-Aboriginal Canadians, is occurring on a spiritual level. More and more Aboriginal people (Métis included)—newly identifying or not—are becoming curious about Anishinaabe spirituality or strengthening their commitment to it. Increasingly, Elders and spiritual teachings are being sought out and participation in ceremony is on the rise. Some spiritual teachers are becoming more vocal and visible in an attempt to reach out to more of our people and to encourage them to come to ceremony. A noteworthy example occurred recently; Spruce Woods Sundance Chiefs David and Sherryl Blacksmith, with the blessing of Sundance Elder "Grandpa Joe" (Esquash)—Sherryl's grandfather, by whom they have been given the right and responsibility to conduct Sundance—gave permission to Aboriginal Peoples Television

Network (APTN) reporter Shanneen Robinson and a camera crew to film
segments of the Sundance and create a three-part documentary about the ceremony, which aired on APTN National News in mid-August 2013 (Robinson
2013a).[4] Reaction to the controversial documentary has been strong and
mixed, with some condemning and vilifying the Blacksmiths for filming
a sacred ceremony, accusing them of contributing to the commodification
of ceremony for personal gain, and arguing that to participate in ceremony
requires soul-searching and spiritual work including approaching Elders
and participating in person. Others praise the Blacksmiths' efforts to show
positive images of healthy Aboriginal people on the news (instead of the
usual negative images that promote stereotypes) and gratitude for helping
more Aboriginal people find their way to ceremony as a result of seeing the
documentary.[5] It is my belief that these concerns are important and can help
protect ceremonies, but we must also take care not to be so "protective" and
secretive that we fail to pass on the ceremonies to subsequent generations
for whom they are intended.

It is important to keep in mind that the Canadian government, through the
Indian Act, effectively made Indigenous ceremonies illegal for approximately
a century (Chapter 3), and as a result ceremonies had to go underground and
were practised in secret by brave souls who risked persecution if they were
caught. Most purposely did not pass the teachings on to their children in an
effort to spare them further persecution. I personally attended the Sundance
in question and saw the documentary crew filming throughout the weekend,
and I listened to the Sundance Chiefs David and Sherryl Blacksmith explain
to everyone present that they had been called by spirit to reach out in this way.
They reminded us that our ceremonies are no longer illegal, yet the secrecy,
once needed for survival, persists. But we no longer need to hide; we can be
open and inviting again, which also amounts to "protecting" ceremonies and
ensuring they will continue into the future (not through film recordings and
books for preservation, but through the increase in participation that may
result from such efforts). Anishinaabe Professor Tara Williamson (2013)
wrote a blog post, "Of Dogma and Ceremony," in response to the backlash
surrounding the Blacksmiths' decision to allow the documentary, wherein
she states, "without context our practice as Indigenous peoples becomes a
dogmatic religion that can no longer adapt and survive the way we have so
far through the onslaught of colonialism, nation-statehood, Christianity,
and so much more." She reminds us of the importance of context, and that
for Indigenous peoples, "surviving (and, indeed, thriving) involved bending
rules," including learning to whisper in residential schools so that Indigenous

languages were not lost and so that "we still have ceremony because we hid ourselves so well that nobody noticed" (Williamson 2013). She comments on how times have changed and how Aboriginal people, especially urban Aboriginal people, have to make decisions that our ancestors never did (including how to give an offering while living in the city). Williamson suggests that using clips from Sundance to reach out to those who are lost (our youth especially) must be considered in context, which includes overwhelmingly negative portrayals of Aboriginal peoples in the media, disconnection from ceremony overall due to colonization, the agreement among the leaders of this Sundance lodge to allow the documentary, and, most importantly, direction from spirit. Sherryl Blacksmith teaches that "change is inevitable, you can fight the process or you can go with it; the most beautiful teachings come from adversity. Accepting that culture changes, like the seasons, helps us to accept growth within ourselves and our Nations" (pers. comm.). We are still here because we learned to adapt.

Long ago, the Seven Fires Prophecy foretold that Anishinaabe people would forget our original ways in favour of those of the light-skinned race, but that we would eventually remember our original ways (Benton-Banai 1988, 93). While this may not yet be reflected in scholarly literature (exceptions include Simpson 2008 and Anderson 2011), the examples of contemporary Anishinaabe agency discussed above, as well as the return to Anishinaabe identities and spiritualities among the participants in this study, suggest that this is indeed happening.

My own spiritual journey is a reflection of this. I share some of this with you now because it explains how I arrived at the topic for this book, but more importantly because introducing myself in this way is customary in Métis Anishinaabe cultures and fosters connections with the reader (for example, through the clan system), but also allows readers to form their own opinions of me and my motivations. I am a descendant of the historic Red River Métis Nation with Anishinaabe, Nêhiyaw, and French-Canadian ancestry.[6] On my maternal grandmother's side, our ancestors include Pierre "Bostonnais" Pangman Jr.[7] and Marie Wewejikabawik, one of four founding families of the historic Métis community of St. Laurent, Manitoba. Bostonnais was a skilled Métis bison hunter who was asked to provide food for Lord Selkirk's settlers so they would not starve during their first winter in Pembina.[8] He also participated in Métis resistance to European settler encroachment, playing a key role in the Pemmican Wars leading up to the Battle of Seven Oaks (1816), and was recognized as one of four "Chiefs of the Halfbreeds" (or "Captains of the Métis") by the North West Company along with Cuthbert Grant Jr. (Gordon

2005; St. Onge 2004; Fiola 2010).[9] My mother grew up in a Michif-speaking family in St. Laurent, with three younger brothers and three older brothers. My two sisters and I are the first generation within our family that did not grow up in St. Laurent and cannot speak Michif (an Indigenous language consisting of mostly Cree and/or Saulteaux verbs and French nouns), and the third generation that cannot speak Anishinaabemowin (Saulteaux/Ojibwe) and Nêhiyawêwin (Cree).

On my father's side, our ancestors began coming (predominantly from France) to Quebec in the early 1600s; we can trace our genealogy back to France in the early sixteenth century.[10] At the turn of the twentieth century, three Fiola brothers moved from Quebec to Manitoba: one stayed in Winnipeg, one established a farm in the parish of La Broquerie, and the other (my great-grandfather Ferdinand Fiola) was given two side-by-side, 160-acre plots of land in Ste. Geneviève, Manitoba, for free by the government, which was common at the time as part of their incentive to settle the West.[11] He farmed the land with his wife, my great-grandmother Noëllie Brisson, and their eighteen children (three of whom died in infancy). Their third-youngest child, my grandfather, eventually bought the land and the farm in 1955. My father, the eldest of eight, was raised French Catholic and was no stranger to difficult farm labour. He was given two acres of the land as a wedding gift. After marrying, my mother moved away from her home community to live in a house that my father built on his two acres; my sisters and I were raised there.

I went to school in the neighbouring community of Ste. Anne, which until relatively recently I thought to be a rural, French Catholic community. As an adult, I was shocked to learn that it was in fact an historic Métis settlement.[12] Sadly, by the time I got there it was heavily assimilated, with most of its residents self-identifying solely as "French-Canadian" and non-Aboriginal, and much of its Métis history denied or silenced. Shortly after I left, the atmosphere began to shift with the election of a Métis mayor, who has now been active with the Manitoba Métis Federation's Southeast Local for more than a decade. Almost every second weekend, from my birth to graduation from high school, my family drove two hours north to spend time with my maternal relatives; those long car rides and visits remain some of my fondest childhood memories.

Like many Red River Métis people, I was raised Roman Catholic. Around age thirteen, I stepped away from the church due to growing theological disagreements, and in high school and university I found empowerment in feminism (Fiola 2004). My undergraduate degree in Women's Studies encouraged me to explore my social locations and identity; I began doing family history research and asking myself "What does it mean to be "Métis?"[13] However, I felt a growing spiritual void in my life. During my master's studies, I began taking Native Studies courses and, for the first time, had a professor openly self-identify as Métis (Fiola 2006). I am indebted to Professor Judy Iseke for helping me to begin to reconnect with the spiritual ways of my ancestors. She introduced me to smudging, sharing circles, women's drum circles, full moon ceremony, and sweat lodge ceremony. Then, during my doctorate, I met third-degree Mide-Kwe Rainey Gaywish, who quickly became my mentor, spiritual advisor, and trusted friend. She brought me to my first Midewiwin ceremony (and many thereafter), introduced me to that community, and has been invaluable to my spiritual development.[14]

I connected deeply and began to identify with these teachings and ceremonies. I learned that my spirit was starving for the knowledge and ways of my ancestors (as with many others, due to colonization) and I eagerly participated in ceremony at every opportunity. Reconnecting in these and other ways is a priority in my life. In my family history research, I have uncovered that twenty-one of my ancestors were issued scrip for land or money (resulting from section 31 of the Manitoba Act, 1870) in Saulteaux, Cree, French, and unspecified "Indian" languages (Chapter 3). I have taken several Anishinaabemowin courses over the past few years. I am developing relationships with land and people by participating in ceremony regularly, especially in the First Nations of Roseau River and Hollow Water, Manitoba, and Bad River, Wisconsin.

I carry two spirit names—Miskwaadesiins (Little Red Turtle) and Zaagaate Kwe (Red Rays Appearing [Shining] Woman)—and have been ceremonially adopted as a daughter by Mizhaakwanageezhik, Charlie Nelson, Chief of the Minweyweywigaan Midewiwin Lodge. As the clan is passed down through the father's line among the Anishinaabeg, I am recognized as belonging to the Biizhew Doodem (Lynx Clan) through my adoptive father. Prior to my adoption, I was welcomed as a member of the Waabizhayshii Doodem (Marten Clan) because my biological father is non-Aboriginal; according to Three Fires Midewiwin teachings, it was the Marten Clan who stood up to recognize the children from such unions during early colonial contact (Benton-Banai 1988, 105). I am learning to understand my names and clan, including recognizing my gifts, responsibilities, and relationships in creation.

In 2011, I initiated as first-degree Midewiwin of the Three Fires Midewiwin. I have been taught that, as Midewiwin, all of creation recognizes that I have reconnected and re-established my family's Midewiwin line.[15]

Midewiwin philosophy and spirituality resonate within me and help me understand who I am in creation (a spirit being living a physical existence) and how I relate to all beings. It offers me a set of values and "Original Instructions," which help me live a good, balanced life (*mino-bimaadiziwin*). I have committed myself to the life-long pursuits of *mino-bimaadiziwin*, decolonization, healing, and self-determination among the (Métis) Anishinaabeg; this is what Anishinaabe spirituality means to me personally.

Over the years, it seemed I was the only one from my family who was interested in reconnecting in these ways. In retrospect, I ended up distancing myself from my family and traditional homeland of southeastern Manitoba—the historic birthplace of the Métis Nation—and went all the way to downtown Toronto, Peterborough, and Wisconsin to find my way home to my ancestors and our spiritual ways. At times I felt lonely and confused, and wondered if this experience was unique to my Métis family. I began to search for role models: Métis people who pursue Anishinaabe spirituality. This population seemed almost non-existent. Most Métis people I met were either Christian (especially Roman Catholic) or secular, and made hard distinctions between Métis and First Nation cultures and spiritualities. Slowly, I did find some people with Métis ancestry who had found what they were searching for in life in Anishinaabe spirituality (but did not necessarily self-identify as "Métis"). I would come to learn that this sort of experience is not unique to me; in fact, this *search* and the complications brought about by assimilation were also foretold in the Seven Fires Prophecy. All this left me with questions, which, along with direction from spirit through ceremony (Chapter 4), led me to undertake the study that forms the basis of this book.

In this book, I uncover experiences and factors that influence people with Red River Métis ancestry to pursue Anishinaabe spirituality and explore how this relationship influences identity. With the exceptions of Ghostkeeper (1986) and Préfontaine, Pequin, and Young (2003), I have found no academic literature focusing on this topic. With some digging, I have gleaned pieces of relevant information through oral history, literature on identity theories and spiritual journeys, and texts on early efforts to Christianize the Métis, which offer insight into our relationships with Anishinaabe spirituality. Also, an examination of the impacts of Christianity and colonial policies and systems (such as the Indian Act and residential schools) is necessary for understanding the historical and colonial context of contemporary Métis identities and spiritualities. A consequence of such colonial legislation has been the creation and solidification of divisions between Métis and "Indians" (or First Nations people) where no such divisions existed before, or where boundaries were much more flexible. This book also seeks to expose how some of these divisions have been created and encourages contemporary Aboriginal people to recognize and reject these colonial divisions, while embracing and celebrating our differences, in order to heal our relationships.

At the core of my study are interviews I conducted with eighteen participants of Métis ancestry (or with a historic, familial, and geographic connection to the Red River Métis Nation) who follow Anishinaabe spirituality; an equal number were female and male, status and non-status, and they ranged in age from twenty-five to seventy-six. Participants were asked to discuss an array of topics in an effort to learn more about the relationship between Métis ancestry, Anishinaabe spirituality, and identity. Topics include family history, relationship with Aboriginal and dominant Euro-Canadian cultures, self-identification, experiences with racism, and relationship with (Anishinaabe) spirituality, especially key factors in spiritual development.

I focused primarily on the Red River Métis in Manitoba because Métis consciousness coalesced into the development of the Métis Nation in the early nineteenth century here in central Canada (J. Peterson 1985, 64). Manitoba— or, more specifically, The Forks in Winnipeg where the Red and Assiniboine rivers converge—is referred to as the "birthplace of the Métis Nation." Also, my Red River Métis ancestry, personal experience, and familial knowledge provide me with a good starting place.[16]

I use the term *Anishinaabe spirituality* because it emphasizes that teachings and ceremonies come from specific nations. I was hesitant to use the term "traditional" because some traditions have been corrupted by colonization and are now used to oppress Aboriginal women and other marginalized groups like two-spirit people (J. Green 1997 and 2007; Deerchild 2004; Allen 1992; Martin-Hill 2004). Moreover, I use it in its singular form to promote consistency and good flow; it is not meant to imply a monolithic culture or spirituality. Finally, my choice of this term reflects an effort to use our original spirit languages.

Anishinaabe people are taking up the challenge spoken of in the Seven Fires Prophecy—the work of the Oshkibimaadiziig—in various ways. Nêhiyaw Métis author Kim Anderson is motivated by the words of Elder Danny Musqua: "It will be up to these young people ... that are just digging up and going around—they've got to *dig up the medicines*, to heal the people. And the medicines, in this case, are the teachings. They've got to dig them up! You've got to find them" (Anderson 2011, 3). The late Elder Peter O'Chiese spoke with Maria Campbell about our lives as Indigenous people before colonization as an intact puzzle; that puzzle, however, has been shattered by colonization, and we are now picking up the pieces and fitting them back together to find wholeness (Campbell 2011a, xix).

This book is my humble effort to contribute to the work of the Oshkibimaadiziig—to pick up the pieces, dig up the medicines, decolonize ourselves—and help our peoples find wholeness again. It is my hope that this book encourages more Métis (and other Aboriginal) people to retrace the steps of our Anishinaabeg ancestors and rediscover what has been left for us. It raises awareness about barriers that inhibit Métis (and other Aboriginal) people from meaningfully connecting with Anishinaabe spirituality, and shares the stories of some of us who have overcome these barriers and are walking this path in life. It breaks down colonial divisions between Métis and First Nations peoples, and encourages healing and reconnection within our communities and nations; we are, after all, family. It begins to fill the gap in literature on this important topic. Within these pages, you will find role models encouraging pride in Métis Anishinaabe identities and spiritual reconnection.

Métis people are being called to pick up our sacred bundles and do our work to ensure that *mino-bimaadiziwin* will continue at least seven generations into the future. The more of us who reconnect in these ways, the more moccasin tracks we leave upon the earth. These tracks remain visible long after we have gone home to the spirit world, ensuring that those who come after us will also have this path of *mino-bimaadiziwin* to follow. I believe that by rekindling the sacred fire in these ways, and working to light the Eighth Fire, the work of the Oshkibimaadiziig can better the lives of Aboriginal and non-Aboriginal peoples alike.

CHAPTER 2

Spirituality and Identity

The Métis are first peoples of Canada, recognized as Aboriginal people in the Canadian Constitution and they are a unique Indigenous group.... The Métis are under-represented in the literature and research. Often coupled with the First Nations and Inuit, the Métis often fall victim to forms of academic homogenization.

—Tricia Logan, "We Were Outsiders," 7–8

Bawdwaywidun Benaise (Grand Chief of the Three Fires Midewiwin Lodge, Eddie Benton-Banai) shared with me that, while Louis Riel was in America after having been exiled from Canada by the Canadian government, he was adopted by a Midewiwin family and became Midewiwin himself.[1] This is not common knowledge; rather, Riel is remembered for being a key Métis leader, the Father of Manitoba, and a fervently devout Catholic. Yet, Riel's interest in Anishinaabe spirituality should not come as a surprise given his well-known encouragement to honour the ways of our Aboriginal *and* European ancestors. In Riel's own words: "It is true that our savage origin is humble, but it is meet that we honor our mothers as well as our fathers. Why should we concern ourselves about what degree of mixture we possess of European or Indian blood? If we have ever so little of either gratitude or filial love, should we not be proud to say, 'We are Métis!'" (quoted in Howard [1952] 1974, 44–45). Maggie Siggins (1995), author of *Riel: A Life of Revolution* (one of the most extensive and thorough books ever written on Riel), explains that "He was a devout Catholic, yet his heart-felt religion was laced with *Indian spiritualism*, and he didn't hesitate to thumb his nose at meddling clergy, who promptly labelled him a heretic" (3, emphasis added). Riel's boyhood had been filled with "the dramatic and imaginative spirituality that was *the Métis religion*. As one anonymous poet described it, 'A nervous tic, a flight of birds, a strange, new sound, all had importance and prophecies were built from these signs'" (254, emphasis added). Not only did the Catholic Church and the entire Judeo-Christian tradition (which so influenced the Riel family) have a long history of acclaiming such supernatural occurrences (254), Anishinaabe

spirituality also recognizes that spirit is everywhere and supernatural occurrences are not uncommon; this, too, likely influenced the Métis religion
Siggins speaks of and Riel's own spirituality. By the time Riel was helping to
form the second Métis provisional government, this time in Saskatchewan
in 1885 (the first was in Manitoba in 1869–70), many surrounding Métis had
rejected the Oblates[2] as too-closely associated with the Canadian government,
which continued to ignore the Métis plight. They turned to Riel, as Diane
Payment writes, "whose creative doctrine had succeeded in indigenizing
the Christian message and presenting it in a form that was meaningful and
relevant to the Métis and the crisis they were facing" (Payment 2009, 108).
Riel was certainly not the only Métis whose spirituality was indicative of
syncretism between the world views, spiritual beliefs, and traditions of both
parent cultures. While oral history in select families has quietly passed on
stories such as the one in Benton-Banai's family, these stories have often not
made their way into written records.

I have found only two sources that touch directly upon Métis relationships with traditional Indigenous spirituality: *Spirit Gifting: The Concept of
Spiritual Exchange* by Elmer Ghostkeeper (1986) and *Métis Spiritualism* by
Darren Préfontaine, Todd Paquin, and Patrick Young (2003). Ghostkeeper's
short book is derived from work he did on his master's thesis, which looks
at major shifts in livelihood that occurred in his community (Paddle Prairie
Métis Settlement in Alberta) between 1960 and 1976. In Chapter 2, he
shares his understanding of a Métis world view (in his case, with Cree- and
English-speaking influences), including the belief that the universe is alive
and contains three worlds: the spirit world, the world humans live in, and
the evil world (9). According to Ghostkeeper, the challenge for humans is to
keep spirit, mind, emotion, and body in harmony through *gifts* from all three
worlds. In his words: "Food for the body consists of gifts in the form of the elements of air, water, meat, fruit, and grains. Food for the mind consists of gifts
of experience and knowledge, and comes in the form of creating, thinking,
learning, and teaching. Food for the emotion consists of gifts, which come in
the form of love, happiness, anger, and pain. Food for the spirit consists of gifts
of spirituality, both good and bad, and comes in the form of giving, receiving,
sharing, stealing, hoarding, and greediness. One acquires these gifts through
the activities of ceremony (*wuskawewin*), ritual (*isehchikewin*), and sacrifice
(*kamekith-kmiteochi*)" (Ghostkeeper, *Spirit Gifting* 9–10). Collectively, these
exchanges are known as "Spirit Gifting" (10). Ghostkeeper's brief chapter appears to be unique in the published record as it focuses on a Métis world view;
Indigenous and Western syncretism are clearly visible within his descriptions.

Préfontaine, Paquin, and Young (2003) provide the only other source I found that touches directly upon Métis relationships with traditional Indigenous spirituality. Theirs is even shorter than Ghostkeeper's; it appears to be a brief chapter (titled "Métis Spiritualism") written for students on behalf of the Gabriel Dumont Institute and accessible through their website called "The Virtual Museum of Métis History and Culture." According to the authors, "it is impossible to discern a common Métis religion and spiritualism. For instance, many Métis orient themselves towards traditional Aboriginal spiritualism, while others are adherents of Roman Catholicism and various Protestant denominations; and still others blend Christianity with Aboriginal spiritualism" (Préfontaine, Paquin, and Young 1). However, they argue that, historically, the Métis adhered either to "Aboriginal Spiritualism" or to Catholicism, Anglicanism, Methodism, or Presbyterianism, with Michif-speaking Roman Catholics having the most favourable opinion of Aboriginal spiritualism. This was because of the many parallels between the folk Catholicism of their French voyageur fathers and the "Anishinabe (Ojibwa) and Nehiy(n)awuk (Cree)" traditions of their mothers (1–2); these parallels included a penchant for frequent prayers, ceremonial liturgy, frequent religious feasts, one God (Kitche Manitou), angels and saints (spirits), evil spirits (Satan or Windigo), and a life of charity (communalism). After identifying characteristics of First Nations spirituality, the authors briefly highlight aspects that influenced the traditional Métis belief system: consensus, interconnectedness, sharing and communalism, time, respect for elders, symbolism, and death, and treatment of the dead. The remainder of the chapter narrows its focus on the beginning relationships of the Métis with Christianity and eventually the permanent establishment of Christian religious infrastructure in the religious life of the Métis, especially in Manitoba. This focus on Métis' relationships with Christianity is common to most sources on early Métis spirituality; it is exceedingly difficult to find historical and contemporary published sources focusing on Métis' relationships with Anishinaabe spirituality. Complicating the issue further is the fact that the Métis have had many different names, and indeed the metis are not homogeneous, resulting in different experiences.

Historically, our Indigenous relatives had names for us (that some of us continue to use today). Among the Nêhiyawak (Cree), names include *âpihtawikosisân,* meaning "half sons" (Teillet 2013, 1–3; LaRocque, "Métis and Feminist" 57) or "half people" (Teillet 1–3); O-tee-paym-soo-wuk, meaning "their own boss" (Harrison 12) or "the independent ones" (Teillet 1–3); Êka ê-akimiht, meaning "not counted" in the treaties;[3] and, even a specific sign made with the hands that means "half wagon, half man" (Alberta Federation of Métis Settlement Associations 22). Names given to us by the Anishinaabeg (Saulteaux/Ojibwe/Chippewa) are aay-*aabtawzid* or *aya:pittawisit*, meaning "one who is half" (Teillet 1–3), and Wiisaakodewikwe(g) and Wiisaakodewinini(wag), meaning "half-burnt woodswoman (women), woodsman (men)" respectively and referring to their lighter complexion in comparison to full-blooded Native people.[4] French European settlers adopted this translation and also referred to us as Chicot (Teillet 1–3), or Bois brûlés, meaning "burnt-wood" people (Harrison 11).

It is difficult to say with certainty exactly when individual families and communities began referring to themselves as "Métis." In the early nineteenth century, in many regions, the categories of "Métis," "Halfbreed," and "Indian" were still mutable. Written sources from that time employed such colonial labels, which were based on a civilized/savage dichotomy and do not necessarily indicate any actual cultural and biological difference. To the European gaze, anybody who did not live a life of "pure" savagery was considered a "Halfbreed," so that, to some eyes in some regions, the same group of people was alternately considered "Indian" or "Halfbreed" by different viewers. In other words, according too much meaning to such labels from that time risks projecting different categories in areas where they may not have had much meaning to the Indigenous inhabitants themselves. Likewise, it is important not to project contemporary divisions backward as immutable and naturalized.[5]

It is important to keep in mind that, historically (and contemporarily), not everyone with Indigenous and European blood would automatically be considered "Métis." Some of the earliest examples of the recognition (by the Métis themselves and by settlers) of a distinct Métis identity and the growing sense of nationhood occurred among the Métis in Red River around 1811, with the foundation of the Red River Colony (a.k.a. the District of Assiniboia or Selkirk settlement); with Governor of Assiniboia Miles Macdonnell's infamous Pemmican Proclamation in 1874, which restricted the export of pemmican (the Métis's source of livelihood and sustenance); and with the tensions between the Hudson's Bay Company, the North West Company, and the Métis thereafter, which resulted in a Métis victory at the Battle of Seven Oaks in 1816. These and other events would contribute to the emergence of the Métis Nation in central Canada.[6]

Thinking of the metis more broadly, they are not a homogeneous group and have had different experiences in different regions; however, there are also similarities among the experiences of metis people. For example, the experiences of metis in northern Michigan, Wisconsin, and Minnesota, with their Chippewa (Anishinaabe) relatives, can be compared with the Métis of Red River, with their Saulteaux (Anishinaabe) and Cree (Nêhiyaw) relatives; both appear to have nurtured stronger ties with Anishinaabe spirituality in the early years of the European colonization of North America.[7] The Roman Catholic Church became a definitive presence in the lives of the Red River Métis, while the metis of northern Michigan, Wisconsin, and Minnesota remained closer to Anishinaabe influences for longer.

Several factors influenced such spiritual development. In Michigan, Wisconsin, and Minnesota there was no large, centralized settlement like the one at Red River, where the Métis formed a majority population. Red River provided a focal point for Métis identity in the face of European discrimination against the Métis, especially during the first half of the nineteenth century (Widder 1999, 133). In contrast, the metis of the Great Lakes region would instead experience what Keith Widder calls "Americanization" (134). Before this, however, these metis would live in the relative safety of the woods and lakes of northern Wisconsin and Minnesota, where they continued their traditional lifestyle. As Widder writes, this "simply delayed the consequences. Shut out of American society, many of the Métis moved closer to their Chippewa kin, who were even more alienated from the Americans" (134). Another reason the Wisconsin and Minnesota metis remained closer to their Chippewa relatives for longer was because the missionaries did not perceive the metis as a unique people and were unable to incorporate them into the developing American society.

Before this, while European fathers would have influenced the lives of their biracial children, most children would have followed the ways of their mother's people simply because their father's family was still living in Europe. Mothers influenced the daily lives of their children, who grew up knowing their maternal grandparents who lived next to them, other Aboriginal relatives, and Chippewa ways quite well (Widder 10). Moreover, gendered divisions of labour led to girls being closer to their Chippewa ways, while boys were trained by their European fathers (15).

Yet another important factor was the official French colonial policy of encouraging intermarriage between French and Indigenous people in order to assure good trade relations (Dickason 1985, 21–22). Oral history confirms these early good relationships between the Anishinaabeg and French men, with many French men adopted into the Marten Clan (Benton-Banai 1988, 105). Rather than the hoped-for outcome—that Anishinaabe women and their biracial children would voluntarily become members of the "one French nation"—many French men were choosing to stay and live among their wives' people. In fact, so many chose this option that French colonial policy changed to official disapproval of intermarriage in the hopes of discouraging this trend (Peterson and Brown 1985, 8; Dickason 1985, 25–26).

The role played in the fur and bison trade by the European (or later Métis) male head of household influenced the family's relationship to Anishinaabe culture. "Traders and clerks," writes Widder, "retained a stronger sense of their French-Canadian identity, especially Catholicism, than did the voyageurs, who adopted more Indian customs and manners" (Widder 1999, 18). However, both European and Anishinaabe cultures were significant influences in the lives of the Métis and contributed to the synergetic development of "their own distinctive belief system" (16). Furthermore, Widder writes, "in Métis families, Native spiritual beliefs, Roman Catholicism, Indian and French names, among other things drawn from both Native and French cultures, all gave meaning to the lives of family members" (xviii). Chippewa women and European-American men "made room for the ways and beliefs of each partner" including marriage rites, naming ceremonies, lodgings, language, trade relations and whether to choose nomadic or sedentary life (3). And as Payment notes, "Métis spirituality was syncretic or incorporated elements from both parent cultures. The Métis believed in God and the Great Spirit and in miracles or divine intervention, as well as in spirit helpers and foretelling" (Payment 2009, 93).

In his research on the Mackinaw mission, Widder found that the traditional clan system of the Chippewa influenced metis spirituality during and after the fur trade era. He writes: "Although many of the Métis children who came to the Mackinaw mission may have belonged to a clan, it is not known whether the missionaries knew or cared about this" (Widder 1999, 11).

Widder offers two more examples that shed light on the Chippewa spiritual influence over the metis. Me-sai-ainse, a French-metis girl raised by her mother of Chippewa descent, apparently without her natural father, grew up near Lac Court Oreilles, Wisconsin, before attending the Mackinaw Mission in 1825 when she was fifteen years old. Me-sai-ainse was in the final stages of initiation into the Midewiwin "as a full priestess or conjuress" when her uncle (who was also her namer) had a dream that she should not initiate (Widder 17). She abided by his suggestion and eventually converted to Protestantism. Her experience "illuminates Chippewa religious practices which Metis children could choose to follow" (17).

Another example, this time without an absent father, is also telling. Historian Francis Parkman asked his canoe pilot, Joseph Gurnae (a

French-metis who was a former student at the Mackinaw Mission), about local "Indian myths" and concluded that "he evidently believed much of them himself, and cautioned me against letting an Ind. [sic] girl, to whom I might become attached, get possession of one of my hairs, as she would then have in her power to do me mischief. He boasted to have once defeated a spell cast on a man by a conjuror" (quoted in Widder 15).

Like the metis of the Great Lakes region, the Métis of Red River had similar influences from their French-Métis fathers and Saulteaux, Cree, or Métis mothers during early contact (Lussier 1985). For instance, in Duck Bay, Manitoba—a traditional fall gathering place for First Nation and Métis people—Father Simonet described the population as consisting of Saulteaux, Métis, and some Swampy Cree (McCarthy 1990, 113). While it appears that many of these people were converted to the Catholic religion, Simonet lamented that "nearly half of them had abandoned their Catholic religion and renewed their Native beliefs and practices" (113). By 1858, when Henry Youle Hind visited the area, "he found forty to fifty 'halfbreed indians' living there. This would seem to indicate that the original Sauteux [sic] and Cree evangelized by Belcourt and Darveau had been absorbed into or replaced by Métis, but by Métis who lived a life very similar to that of the Sauteux [sic]" (112).[8] Ten years later, Père Camper visited Duck Bay and witnessed a large number of Aboriginal people who had gathered there: "Their purpose was to make 'la Grande medicine' and consequently the drums sounded the night and day. A large lodge was erected and the Natives all painted their faces red. Camper spent his time baptizing the children of the Catholic Sauteux [sic] but realized that their faith was somewhat uncertain. They sometimes attended his services and sometimes those at the medicine lodge" (114). Belcourt, a predecessor to Camper, was similarly frustrated when he witnessed 200 Saulteaux families gather at Manitoba House (en route to Duck Bay). McCarthy writes that "this large number had gathered for the Midewiwin ceremony, the type of native religious practice which was abhorred by the missionaries because it posed such an obstacle to the inculcation of Christianity" (103–4). Most missionaries could not distinguish between Indians and Métis (Logan 2007, 98); indeed, differences between them may have been so few that distinguishing between them may not have been necessary. Or, they may not have distinguished amongst themselves. Whatever the case may be, it is probable (especially given Simonet's assessment of the Duck Bay residents) that Métis families were included among those participating in ceremonies at Manitoba House.

The complexity of conversion to Catholicism must also be considered to understand relationships between Métis people and Anishinaabe spirituality. Huel notes that "it is obvious that testimonials of missionaries concerning the remarkable conversion of Indians, statistics on baptisms, confessions, communions and other outward signs of religious conformity are not accurate barometers of true spirituality" (Huel 1996, 270–1). From the perspective of the missionary, conversion was motivated by Christianity's supposed superiority and the desire to be redeemed. However, writes Huel, "for Indians, the motives for conversion were far more complex and rooted in the 'elemental fact of ethnic survival' in the face of social, cultural and economic challenges" (xiii). Aboriginal people's motivations for conversion included disease, anxiety brought about by social change, and/or the generosity of the missionary with indispensable articles (57, 270–71).

Aboriginal communities often appeared divided in their acceptance of Christianity. Mizi-Epit (Joseph-Constantin), the Chief of the Duck Bay mission, was baptized in 1843 and asked for a more regular mission at Duck Bay. However, McCarthy writes that "old Agaskokat, who had considerable influence, affirmed that Native beliefs were as valid as Christianity, and that religion was like a double-barreled gun, each shot carrying with the same accuracy to the same end" (McCarthy 1990, 109). Huel notes, "the Saulteaux would convert or allow their families to convert only with the consent of the tribal elders ... [and had] strong indigenous spirituality that allowed them to radically interpret certain segments of the Christian message much to the dismay of the missionaries" (Huel 1996, 18). Often, "the Saulteaux resisted or refused to listen to the Christian message because they realized that the acceptance of Christianity would entail significant changes to their culture through the substitution of the values, traditions and morality of western European civilization" (19).

Throughout the life of the Mackinaw Mission, only twenty or thirty students converted to Evangelical Christianity because the teachings went counter to those held by their parents (Widder 1999, 125). Missionaries, writes Widder, "presumed that the young converts would renounce Roman Catholicism as well as Chippewa religion ... to disavow all belief in *manitoes* [spirits] and to discontinue participation in Chippewa religious ceremonies" (Widder 1999, 125). However, conversion did sometimes happen. This was the case with Me-sai-ainse, who converted to Protestantism in 1828, despite her Midewiwin upbringing. She gave an account of her conversion experience in Chippewa to Reverend Ferry through an interpreter; it reveals that she was under extreme pressure from the mission and family members to assimilate to Christianity coming from the mission and family members (126).

Many Aboriginal people around the Mackinaw Mission who converted brought together tenets of Chippewa religion, Protestantism, and Catholicism (125). This is evidenced by missionaries who claimed that "virtually all French-Canadian and French-Metis men identified themselves as Roman Catholics, but most exhibited little evidence that they followed the Church's dictates" (Widder 16). Protestant missionaries at the Mackinaw Mission determined that "since the Roman Catholic French-Métis seemed to have adopted or accepted much of what they found in Indian society, the missionaries often relegated many of them to an 'uncivilized' status as well," Widder writes (44). Similarly, in the Red River area, those Aboriginal converts who attended the Pilgrimage at Lac Ste. Anne in Alberta had appropriated it on, in Huel's words, "terms consonant with native modes of thought and relevant to perceived needs" (Huel 1996, 270–1). Payment provides the example that "Métis believed in the immortality of the soul as well as some 'form' of the body and that 'the two would go to the happy hunting ground.'" Also, the persistence of "customs such as serial monogamy, polygamy, conjuring rituals, and casting of spells by the Métis" frustrated the missionaries who condemned the practices as "'pagan' and 'savage'" (Payment 2009, 95; Lussier 1985).

During these early times, the spirituality of Aboriginal families and communities in these regions ran the gamut from Anishinaabe spirituality, to syncretism and unique blends of Anishinaabe and Christian spirituality, to Christianity. Those for whom conversion to Christianity was sincere had to accept the Western values and traditions that were inherent in that faith; in Payment's words, "they became Latinized and westernized" (Payment 2009, 267). Despite the influence of Anishinaabe spirituality during early contact, Christianity would come to hold a dominating place in the lives of many First Nations and Métis people, especially among the Red River Métis, often at the expense of adherence to Anishinaabe spirituality (see Chapter 3).

Spiritual Journey Literature

Unlike literature on the relationships between Métis people and Anishinaabe spirituality, literature on *spiritual journeys* in general is prolific. This literature is often very personal and written in narrative and autobiographical form across cultural traditions, but can also be written from academic, research, and mental health perspectives; common perspectives include Christianity, Eastern religions, and Goddess- and nature-based spiritualities. This literature reveals endless topics, including love, family, illness, aging, sexuality, self-help, and awakening. There is also a substantial body of literature coming from Aboriginal perspectives on healing with the purpose of decolonization.

One topic that is relevant to my own research is personal spiritual journey narratives on healing from abuse and addictions. Articles like "Stories of Spiritual Awakening: The Nature of Spirituality in Recovery," by Lesley Green (1998), and "Recovery from Alcoholism: A Spiritual Journey," by Jeanne Bowden (1998), discuss how some people recovering from addictions experience life-altering transformations as a result of embracing a higher power, which can lead to intense spiritual journeys and maintained sobriety. Similarly, a few participants in my study speak of the importance of Anishinaabe spirituality in recovering from addictions and in their own sustained abstinence from alcohol (see Chapter 8).

Literature on spiritual journeys often speaks of these life-altering transformative experiences either resulting from spirituality or leading to a life of spirituality. One example can be found in experiences by adventure athletes who participate in extreme sports with high personal safety risks. Amy Crawford's (2011) dissertation, "Pursuit of Higher Self: Stories of Personal and Spiritual Transformation shared by Adventure Athletes," uncovers five key themes regarding such personally and spiritually transformative experiences, including the desire to give back and inspire. This desire to give back is a theme that also arises among my interviewees (see Chapter 8).

Other spiritual journey literature is autobiographical, discussing the author's life path and their relationship with spirituality, highlighting challenges, significant experiences, and personal beliefs. Christian perspectives are perhaps the most frequently published; a non-Christian example can be found in Alison Leonard's (2003) "Journey towards the Goddess," wherein she tracks her life journey from the void left by her dismissal of Christianity, her subsequent search through earth-based spiritualities, and her reverence for the ancient Goddess and a non-Christian sect within the Quaker religion. A more recent example is *My Spiritual Journey: The Dalai Lama*, wherein the fourteenth Dalai Lama shares his own spiritual journey from boyhood, to his life as a monk in a monastery, to his life in exile and as a world leader.

Aboriginal perspectives within spiritual journey literature often speak of healing from colonization and traditional forms of healing as processes of decolonization. Such literature includes academic and research discussions on traditional Aboriginal healing ways, as well as personal narrative accounts. For example, Hawai'ian Indigenous author Poka Laenui (2000) takes us through five stages of colonization, and then into the processes of decolonization, in his article "Processes of Decolonization." Laenui suggests five phases of a people's decolonization: rediscovery and recovery, mourning, dreaming, commitment, and action (2000, 152–59). He explains that during the processes of decolonization, one is reunited with the languages, music, literature, and other cultural knowledge (presumably including spirituality).

Aboriginal voices take aim at the commodification and appropriation of Aboriginal spiritual items, practices, and ceremonies by non-Aboriginal (and sometimes by Aboriginal) people. Andrea Smith (2005) makes this connection in her chapter titled "Spiritual Appropriation as Sexual Violence." She points out several negative consequences for Native (and even non-Native) people when non-Native people appropriate Native spiritual traditions. For example:

> When the dominant society disconnects Native spiritual practices from their landbases, it undermines Native peoples' claim that the protection of the landbase is integral to the survival of Native peoples and hence undermines their claims to sovereignty. Such appropriation is prevalent in a wide variety of cultural and spiritual practices—from New Agers claiming to be Indians in former lives to Christians adopting Native spiritual forms to further their missionizing efforts. The message is that anyone can practice Indian spirituality anywhere, so that there is no need to protect the specific Native communities and their lands that are the basis of these spiritual practices. (A. Smith 2005, 122–23)

Moreover, "this practice of taking without asking, and the assumption that the needs of the taker are paramount and the needs of others are irrelevant, mirrors the rape culture of the dominant society" (126). Smith goes on to say that "spiritual appropriation is hazardous to your health" and that "something bad will happen if ceremonies are not performed correctly" (131). One tragic example of this is the case of James Arthur Ray, a White "self-help guru" found guilty of three counts of negligent homicide but acquitted of manslaughter when three people died in his "abomination of a sweat lodge" ceremony at his so-called "Warrior Society" retreat in Arizona. According to BBC News (2011), Ray was charging up to $9,000 per participant for the retreat. He was sentenced to two years in an Arizona State prison and released in July 2013.

There is also a large body of literature on traditional Aboriginal healing ways and practices. For example, in his article "Mind, Body, Emotions and Spirit: Reaching to the Ancestors for Healing," Métis author Glen McCabe (2008) writes about turning to our ancestors for help in healing, including use of the Medicine Wheel, storytelling, and sacred medicines. Some of this literature also highlights specific spiritual practices and their impacts on healing. Authors Lawrence Berger and Eric Rounds (1998), Jeanette Schiff and Kerrie Moore (2006), and David Smith (2005) have all written articles on sweat lodge and its impact on Aboriginal health and healing. Still other literature emphasizes traditional Aboriginal healing for Aboriginal peoples as groups, communities, and nations. Works by Eduardo Duran and Bonnie Duran (1995), RodMcCormick (1997), and Cynthia Wesley-Esquimaux and Magdalena Smolewski (2004) discuss the spiritual healing journey of Aboriginal peoples overall. In addition, the extensive work done by the Aboriginal Healing and Wellness Strategy (2006) in Ontario also promotes healing of Aboriginal communities through mainstream and traditional ways.

Yet another theme within Aboriginal spiritual journey literature is personal narratives of healing journeys; for example, Roxanne Struthers's and Valerie Eschiti's (2005) article "Being Healed by an Indigenous Traditional Healer: Sacred Healing Stories of Native Americans." In their article, Struthers and Eschiti share stories of spiritual healing journeys by people who have been profoundly impacted by participation in ceremonies such as Sundance, shake tent, and Yuwipi, a healing ceremony practised by the Dakota and others.

There are also many stories of spiritual journeys of healing from residential schools, often written by residential school survivors. Madeleine Dion Stout and Gregory Kipling's report, "Aboriginal People, Resilience, and Residential School Legacy" (2003), highlights traditional Aboriginal spirituality as one key way of healing from the legacy of residential schools. In addition, the Aboriginal Healing Foundation (AHF) has an entire research series dedicated to learning about, discussing the effects of, and healing from residential schools, including the importance of traditional spirituality in such healing.

Parallels within this literature that complement my own work include the fact that some participants in my study arrived at Anishinaabe spirituality after personal crises or transformative experiences, or during recovery from addictions or abuse. Moreover, several participants also discussed significant events and practices, such as receiving a spirit name or participating in a sweat lodge ceremony, as being highly influential on their personal spiritual journeys.

Theories on Identity Relevant to Métis People and Spirituality

Theories on identity form another body of literature relevant to Métis people and spirituality. Especially useful are discussions of group identity among mixed-race people, such as work by Janice Acoose (1992, 1994, 1999, 2008), Devon Mihesuah (1999), and Maria Root (1992). Self-identification strategies for survival—including silence, *passing*, and internalized colonization, as well as traditional definitions of identity—are important for understanding Métis identities. While many of these theories affect First Nations and Métis people alike, some ignore Métis realities.

Post-colonial theorist Edward Said (1978) argued that the colonizer is largely responsible for creating the identity of the "Other." This does not mean that the people in question did not have an identity before the colonizers gave them one; rather, the colonizers are responsible for creating stereotypical identities, which then become popular knowledge. According to Said, "cultural identity of the 'other' (in this case of Aboriginal peoples), or the non-European, was largely an artifact of European colonialism" (quoted in Coates 1999, 24). Said continues, "Through paintings, poetry, fiction, history, anthropology and government reports, the argument goes, the 'Indian' was defined in ways that both explained the nature of indigenous life in terms that Europeans could comprehend, and rationalized the occupation and confiscation of their traditional lands" (25). European colonizers found it necessary to justify, to themselves as well as to the Natives, their heinous and genocidal treatment of the Native peoples of Canada. Coates argues that this construct has changed over time depending on the social, political, and economic influences at the time, as well as the needs and desires of the colonizers.

Coates offers what he believes is a healthier way to define and measure First Nations identities. He lays out three stages for such identification, involving self-identification, identification with a small-scale group and recognition from this group, and pan-Indigenous identification. According to Coates, the first level is "intensely personal, and requires the First Nations person to see themselves as an indigenous individual. The second stage 'involves the effort to establish a connection between the individual and the cultural or political group.' On the third level, indigenous people readily identify with other First Nations in Canada, often even if they are facing difficulties at the local level" (36).

Social constructionists offer another approach to understanding Métis identity. Fontaine argues that "identity is a social construct that is continual, fluid, always in transition and that there is no one Aboriginal identity" (Fontaine 2001, 11). Following this line of thought, social constructionists also believe that "meaning is constructed through language" (Weaver 2001, 242). These two traits are characteristic of most, if not all, social constructionists. However, not all social constructionists are exactly alike in their views. Hilary Weaver (2001) argues that difference (from other individuals and communities) is a prerequisite in the formation of identity, going as far as arguing that "identity is always based on power and exclusion" (244).

Weaver suggests that identity is likely a combination of self-identification and the perceptions of others. She contends that the extent to which one can choose to self-identify as *Indigenous* is limited by various factors, including phenotypical appearance. Moreover, Indigenous identity is inseparable from community, whereby membership and integration are key factors. Both Weaver's and Coates's theories on Indigenous identity emphasize self-identification and recognition from community members.

Some literature on identity, such as the works of Janice Acoose, is helpful in understanding unique challenges and issues faced by people who are multiracial or have multiple heritages. Acoose's ancestry and heritage is Nêhiyaw-Métis-Nahkawè. As she writes, she "grew up nurtured by both the Metis and Saulteaux cultures; my communities—situated in Saskatchewan's beautiful Crooked Lake area—were both the Marival Metis community and the Sakimay Indian Reserve" (Acoose 2008, 4). She explains that when her parents married, they "brought with them the strengths, beliefs, values and traditions of both their cultures. As is our right as human beings, my five brothers and five sisters inherited both those cultures" (4). She continues, "I know who I am because I know my relations. Having had my life enriched by both Metis and Saulteaux relatives…. Understanding how my personal strength comes from being rooted to the earth through my ancestors, I have to honor all my relations" (4).

Acoose has been publishing on the topic of identity for many years. Her master's thesis, "Iskwekwak—Kah' Ki Yaw Ni Wahkomakanak: Neither Indian Princess Nor Squaw Drudges," analyzes stereotypes of Aboriginal women in Canadian literature, as well as Aboriginal literature which has the potential to resist and challenge these stereotypes (Acoose 1992). In a later article, Acoose explores whether Beatrice Mosionier's book, *In Search of April Raintree*, enables readers to learn something about Métis culture, and comments on the relationship between assimilation, stereotypes, culture, and identity within the text and its historical and contemporary Canadian contexts. She argues that "the term 'Native' is problematic because it simultaneously suppresses the Métis culture specific voice of both author and narrator. With its protagonists seduced by popular terms like 'Native' and 'Halfbreed,' and confused by colloquial terms like 'Native' and 'mixed-blood' and 'part-Indian,' the text does not successfully illustrate the Métis cultural identity" (Acoose 1999, 228). On the other hand, Acoose believes the text "makes clear that identity and culture are inextricably intertwined in the processes of formation and influenced by numerous mitigating factors (229). Acoose theorizes that Mosionier struggles to portray Métis culture because she herself was removed from her family and placed in White foster homes at a young age. She continues, "Those experiences left her struggling to bring into sharper focus a culture specific voice.... [The same is true for] Native people growing up in urban Canada today ... there is a lot of pressure on you to assimilate and forget totally what you are as a person, what your heritage is" (230).

It is Acoose's (2008) article, "Honouring *Ni'Wahkomakanak* (all my relations)," that I find most interesting in its negotiation of multi-heritage identity and spirituality in contemporary life. She discusses Aboriginal writers who simply identify as "Native," "Aboriginal," or "full blood" (as opposed to naming their specific cultural heritage) as suffering from "perplexing identity crises" because they have "ceded not only vast territories of land, but also the territories of imagination and of voice" (Acoose 2008, 219). As someone with multiple heritages, Acoose explains her passion for "'honouring my relations' whose spiritual presence continues to influence my life and work" (219). She does this by always naming her cultures and including "medicine words" from her Indigenous languages, as well as by speaking from a *Koochum* (grandmotherly) place, among other techniques. She writes, "When I name and place in this written text my Nêhiyaw-Métis-Nahkawè cultures, ceremonial traditions, ancestors, and present system of relations, I perform an 'honouring' cultural ritual" (220–1). Furthermore, she explains that by doing so, just as is done through "Nêhiyaw-Métis-Nahkawè ceremonial traditions, [she] invokes the spirit-presence of ancestors, as well as the living presence of 'all my relations'" (ibid. 220). Acoose's work illustrates how one Nêhiyaw-Métis-Nahkawè woman successfully negotiates her identity and spirituality in a contemporary context.

Another identity theory relevant to mixed-raced peoples is Devon Mihesuah's (1999) use of William Cross's "Cycles of Nigrescence" in combination with Maria Root's theories of identity resolution for biracial people. William Cross developed a "life stages" paradigm for African Americans, calling it "Cycles of Nigrescence," meaning the process of becoming "Black." This cycle comprises four stages: pre-encounter, encounter, immersion-emersion, and internalization. In the pre-encounter stage, the individual realizes they are Black, but does not give much thought to it. During the encounter stage, the individual experiences a "shocking event that jolts them into considering that their frame of reference for forming their identity is inadequate. The person then decides to develop his [sic] black identity" (Mihesuah 1999, 15). In the third stage, immersion-emersion, the individual has an intense and enthusiastic interest in everything pertaining to blackness; however, they remain insecure about their identity and often criticize others who embody unattractive aspects of the person's old self (16). Finally, the fourth stage, internalization, "comes when the person attains a sense of inner security and self-confidence about his black identity [and possesses] ideological flexibility, psychological openness, and self-confidence [and] is at peace with himself [sic] and is able to express feelings of dissatisfaction about racism and in-equality through constructive, non-violent means" (16).

According to Mihesuah, "if we substitute American Indians for blacks and figure in social, economic, and political influences, it is possible to use the Nigrescence outline to logically consider the various elements that influence the identity choices of persons who claim to be racially and/or ethnically American Indian" (14). During the pre-encounter stage, she argues, Native individuals occupy a range of feelings regarding the awareness of their "Indianness," including identification with White culture, denying Indianness in favour of simply identifying as a human being, having little knowledge of their tribal history and culture, or fulfillment with their place in the world (17). In the encounter stage, Mihesuah declares there are three basic goals of individuals who have an Indian encounter: Becoming an Indian, Becoming More Indian/Rediscovering Indianness, and Becoming Less Indian (20–23). It is during this stage that Mihesuah turns to sociologist Maria Root's theory of identity resolution for biracial people.

Sociologist Maria Root's theory of identity resolution for biracial people outlines four possible types of resolution. Resolution one—acceptance of the identity society assigns—occurs when, as Mihesuah writes, "multiheritage people who are part White, who do not appear to be Caucasian, and who are reared in racially oppressive parts of the United States will have little choice about their racial identity" (Mihesuah 1999, 23). In other words, despite your racial makeup and the way you self-identify, if you look stereotypically African American, society perceives you as African American. Resolution two—identification with two or more racial or cultural groups—involves a "positive resolution only if the persons are able to retain their personal-ity across groups and they feel welcomed in both groups" (24). Mihesuah explains that "the challenge for multiheritage Indians wishing to live in two worlds is to construct strategies for coping with social resistance to their membership in both groups" (24). Identification as a new racial group—identity resolution number three—has been the route taken by the Hapa Haole in Hawaii and the Métis of Canada. Mihesuah claims that "many mul-tiheritage Indians prefer this type of classification either because they know little about their racial heritages or because they cannot decide which one to designate as the primary racial reference group" (25).[9] Finally, resolution four—identification with a single racial and/or cultural group—"is different from the first one because the person actively seeks identification with one group regardless of what society thinks, the choices made by one's siblings, or one's physical resemblance to the group" (25). Several factors influence which identity a person can realistically pursue, including negative and positive stereotyping, self-identification that differs from how others perceive the individual, tribal membership, and appearance (25–28). Mihesuah also explains that "acceptance of these resolutions depends on the social, political, economic, and environmental situations the person encounters. Therefore, the person may change resolutions more than once in a lifetime, or may settle on two resolutions at once" (23).

After mobilizing Root's identity resolution theory, Mihesuah returns to an application of Cross's final two stages onto Aboriginal experiences. During stage three—immersion-emersion—the African American "attempts to develop a thorough black frame of reference" (Mihesuah 1999, 28). This stage is often characterized by volatility, depression, and frustration, as the individual deconstructs old perspectives and tries to construct a new frame of reference. Cross's final stage—internalization—involves the individual developing "inner security about her identity" (29). Mihesuah points out that this occurs on an individual basis and requires the development of "strategies for coping with resistance to their proclaimed identities" (30). While neither Cross, Root, nor Mihesuah focuses on the issue of spirituality, if spirituality were considered it would seem likely that in the final stages of identity resolution the individual may also seek to reconnect with their ancestral spiritual traditions in meaningful ways, or at least to decide consciously not to follow them.[10]

Other relevant literature on identity involves self-identification strategies that have been used as survival tactics. Generations of internalized colonization, silence, and passing as White have impacted the relationship between Métis people and Anishinaabe spirituality, perhaps even to the extent of individuals and Métis families rejecting all association with their Anishinaabe heritage. Also influential are self-identification strategies for resistance, such as politicizing terminology, the creation of new identity theories, and traditional definitions of identity.

Internalized Colonization

Internalized colonization occurs when colonized peoples believe in the superiority of the dominant culture while criticizing their own culture and (sometimes forcefully) encouraging other colonized peoples to adopt these

values. Post-colonial theorists Paulo Freire and Albert Memmi have popularized the notions of internalized colonization and the "colonized mentality."
In his book, *The Colonizer and the Colonized*, Memmi ([1957] 1965) explains
"colonized mentality" as a state of mind whereby the colonized person feels
contempt toward the colonizer, mixed with "passionate" attraction toward
him. In *Pedagogy of the Oppressed*, Freire ([1970] 2006) suggests that such a
colonized mentality comes about through self-deprecation, "which derives
from their internalization of the opinion the oppressors hold of them. So often
do they hear that they are good for nothing, know nothing and are incapable
of learning anything—that they are sick, lazy, and unproductive—that in the
end they become convinced of their own unfitness" (63). Similarly, in *The
Wretched of the Earth*, Franz Fanon (1963) argues that at an individual level,
violence frees the oppressed person from an inferiority complex in a confusing restoration of self-respect (94). Existing in this type of environment can
also lead to, in Freire's words, "horizontal (or lateral) violence" whereby "the
colonized man will first manifest this aggressiveness which has been depos-
ited in his bones against his own people," for it is too dangerous to strike out
against the colonizer (Freire [1970] 2006, 62).

In his book, *Prison of Grass*, Métis scholar Howard Adams (1989) points
out an example of internalized colonization when Aboriginal leadership
becomes co-opted by European values, corrupted by greed and bribery, and
is merely a puppet in the hands of Western culture. Another example of internalized colonization occurs when Aboriginal people police other Aboriginal
people in terms of degree of supposed authentic Aboriginal identity (Chapter
4). Most of the time, such internalized colonization is unhelpful. However,
some argue that at times it can be helpful or at least demonstrative of agency,
such as in band-enforced blood quantum membership criteria; this remains
controversial because membership can also be used to externalize minorities,
such as those with Bill C-31 status (Chapter 3).

Silence

Silence can be viewed as a self-identification strategy whereby the indi-
vidual/family self-identifies as anything but Métis or Aboriginal as a survival
mechanism. This can be viewed as choosing to, or succumbing to pressure to,
assimilate. For example, this was the case with the tremendous silence around
Métisness resulting from the massive disenfranchisement of Métis families
brought about by the Manitoba Act of 1870, the scrip system, and the effects
of the Northwest Resistance of 1885 (Chapter 3). As Lawrence writes, "the
number of individuals in Western Canada who identified as 'Indian or Métis'

dropped by half in the 20 years between 1881 and 1901, to about 26,000" (Lawrence 2004, 77). Moreover, she adds, "in the years after 1885, Metis identity virtually went underground in most of Western Canada" (77). This was due to Métis people being labelled "traitors" and actively persecuted. Since it was dangerous to be Métis, many Métis people learned to hide their identity, downplay their Aboriginal heritage, and emphasize their Euro-Canadian heritage.[11] Many Métis parents were increasingly silent about their Métis heritage, for example, by not teaching their children how to speak Michif. Lawrence writes: "The price of this silence, however, particularly when it has been accompanied by the removal of people from the communities which hold their history, has been the rupturing of many connections with the past, a sense of alienation from other Native people, and in some cases deep levels of shame or discomfort about their Native identity" (196).

Silence as a coping strategy has often been "tactical and usually partial" (Lawrence 197). The parents in Bonita Lawrence's study had passed down enough pride about Nativeness for their children to reclaim their identity when it became safe to do so. Several participants' comments echoed Lawrence's description of parents who had "passed Native values on to them without overtly naming them as values from a specific culture. Humour, the importance of kindness, habits of avoiding direct questions, attitudes about the importance of family and respect for the sacred—these and other aspects of family behavior were attributed by several participants to the Native values they had learned from their parents, in French or English rather than a Native language, and without having them named as such" (198). Sometimes parents openly resisted being silent about their Nativeness (201).

Passing

A common self-identification strategy open to those with lighter skin is the phenomenon known as *passing*. Linked to silence as a strategy, passing is similarly not always seen as healthy or well-adjusted, but can be nonetheless demonstrative of agency. G. Reginald Daniel's (1992) article "Passers and Pluralists: Subverting the Racial Divide" provides a useful discussion of this phenomenon. According to Daniel, "individual resistance has taken the form of 'passing,' a radical form of integration whereby individuals of a more European phenotype and cultural orientation make a clandestine break with the African American [or other visible minority] community, temporarily or permanently, in order to enjoy the privileges of the dominant White community" (91–92). Passing means to shift one's racial reference group to that of another group (including other groups of colour) perceived to be less marginalized in the existing racial hierarchy (92).

Daniel explains that there exist varying degrees of passing, from the more common scenario of simply not saying anything about one's racial identity in order to enjoy White privileges, to "continuous passing, which involves a complete break with the African American [or other marginalized] community" (93). He argues, further, that passing is Eurocentric in nature because it is "generated by racist pressure that has rewarded Whiteness and punished Blackness" (107). "Passing," then, is but one tactic in a range of tactics in dealing with a multiracial identity in a country that praises monoraciality. Daniel also discusses collective efforts at integration, such as "blue vein societies" and "triracial isolates," which are pluralistic and live apart from both Black and White communities; for example, "on the fringes of villages and towns, or in isolated rural enclaves" (98).

Historically, in Canada the settler government has felt threatened by mixed-race individuals who can pass as White. According to Renisa Mawani (2005), "Differentiating between Indian-ness, whiteness, and everything in-between was necessary for protecting the identity, privilege, and property of whites.... If mixed-race people would *pass* as white, officials feared they would gain illegitimate access to these rights and disrupt Euro-Canadian dominance. Protecting the boundaries between 'Indians' and mixed-race people was essential to asserting white superiority" (53–54). She explains that racial ambiguity is an obstacle to securing White superiority, which is why so much time and energy has been spent on legislating Halfbreed/Métis and Indian as separate legal and racial categories; the consequences of this are an erasure of identity, rights, and territorial claims as well as "struggles by mixed-race people to reclaim their Native ancestry and their real and symbolic space in the nation" (63, 69).

On one hand, passing as White may have tangible results for marginalized peoples. In her article, "A Room without a View from within the Ivory Tower," Aboriginal scholar Angela Jaime (2003) discusses the difficulties she had in being the only Native person in her class, and then the only Native professor in the faculty. As a way of dealing with racism, she at times hid behind her light skin and let people think she was Caucasian. Other times, she was vocal about her identity as a Native woman. She attests that her students resisted her less and accepted her authority more when she "passed" as White (260). On the other hand, continuous passing, denying one's identity, and disconnecting from one's culture(s) may result in psychological distress, identity crises, spiritual imbalance, and strained family relationships.[12]

Complicating the matter further, passing as White can sometimes be forced upon mixed-race people despite our wishes, and some people are engaged in a constant struggle to assert and maintain their Indigeneity. In her article "My Life in Pieces," Métis scholar Jennifer Adese (2010) shares her emotional journey in this regard, and her efforts to feel comfortable in her own skin. Adese explains that while she is proud of her heritage (Caucasian mother and Cree father), she feels her identity is challenged constantly, especially by White people. Even well-meaning White people tell her they "'couldn't tell [she] was Native' and that [she] could 'pass for white'" (240). Adese has come to the following conclusion: "I had been given tacit acceptance based on my appearance, however in order to pass *fully*, I needed to stop opening my mouth and *telling* about my Native-ness. Not looking it and not speaking it would apparently allow for my total transgression into whiteness and signal the death of my Indian-ness" (241). She chooses to remain "in between and out of place" (241). Adese comments, "As an urban 'mixed-blood' I am at no loss for a connection to the markers of whiteness. It is the 'Other' side, my Indigeneity, that daily I fight tooth and nail to hold on to" (241).

Politicizing Terminology

Other types of self-identification strategies involve pride, reclamation, and redefining Native identity.[13] One such strategy is the politicization of terminology. In explaining his choice of the term "mixblood," as opposed to the more common "mixed blood," for the title of his book, Penn (1997) concludes that the former connotes "the unified and inseparable strands of their heritage and experience" (9). He also rejects the term "cross blood" because of its association with the term "mixed blood." In the same volume, Craig Womack (1997) challenges both the terms "mixed blood" and "mixblood," insisting that such terms diminish sovereignty because they lack reference to tribal specificity (23). Spencer (1997) argues that biological races have never existed, that everyone is always already mixed, that there is no identity but rather identities, and that we must focus on what is positive about the identities one has (128, 132–33). When asked, "What part Indian are you?" Inez Petersen (1997) responds, "I think it is my heart" (86).

Métis scholar Chris Andersen (2014) challenges the "Métis-as-mixed" misconception and argues that a racialized understanding of Métis (as opposed to one rooted in nationhood) enables anyone with Aboriginal and European ancestry to claim Métis identity (even those without a connection to the historic Métis Nation), thereby inhibiting Métis political self-determination. Andersen encourages these individuals to assert an Aboriginal identity rooted in their tribal ancestry, such as Inuit (Andersen 2014, 195, 215–216n35). He agrees with former leader of the Métis Nation of Ontario Tony Belcourt's suggestion that such individuals might be "grandfathered" into the Métis Nation via citizenship codes (Andersen 2014, 24; Belcourt 2013), thereby, maintaining the integrity of the Métis Nation while resisting identity politics of exclusion based on colonial divide and conquer tactics. I focus on an aspect of Métis nationhood that has been neglected in scholarship and politics: Red River Métis had a complex relationship with Anishinaabe spirituality but the sustained agenda of colonial assimilation has Chrisitanized most Métis; this does not preclude Métis from reconnecting with Anishinaabe spirituality today. It is this reconnection, and the ways it influences self-identification, that I am exploring.

Hybridity and Mestiza/o Consciousness

Still others are claiming (and reclaiming) *hybrid* identities. These people refuse to adhere to unhelpful stereotypes or to be restricted to only one identity. They are claiming labels and identities that challenge the notion, in Bonita Lawrence's words, of "cultural homogeneity of Native communities" (Lawrence 2004, 285). It has been argued that some people decouple appearance from identity, and those who self-identify as "hybrid" find it easier to accept their White appearance than those who adhere to rigid boundaries of Nativeness (289).

Perhaps the most well-known form of hybridity comes from Gloria Anzaldúa's work around the concept of "mestizo/a" in her book *Borderlands/ La Frontera: The New Mestiza*. Interested in physical, psychological, sexual, and spiritual borderlands as places of contradictions and possibilities, Anzaldúa (1987) claims that for multi-race/multi-heritage people, "the lifeblood of [at least] two worlds merg[es] to form a third country—a border country" (25). Anzaldúa creates a paradigm (*mestiza consciousness*) for people who live in, and migrate across, such borderlands. The new mestiza is one who realizes she has internalized the borderland conflict, but one day her inner struggle will cease and a true integration will take its place (85).

Anzaldúa was influenced by Mexican philosopher José Vasconcelos's envisioning of a fifth race, a cosmic race, embracing the four major races of the world (99). She added onto his theory, arguing that things will not get better for marginalized peoples, nor for the dominant, unless people of European descent "take back their collective shadow [aspects of themselves they would prefer not to admit] and the intra-cultural split will heal" (108). She further argues that the false rational/spiritual dichotomy is the root of all violence, and emphasizes the spiritual nature of mestiza consciousness (59). I am struck here by the parallels between these beliefs and the Seven Fires Prophecy: the joining together of all peoples to form one global nation, the importance of the Europeans making the right choice to enable such a global nation of unity, and the Midewiwin belief that humans are spiritual beings living a physical existence.

Anzaldúa rejects that people of mixed race are forced to choose an either/ or identity, or a supposedly poorly adjusted hybrid identity; instead, she argues for the possibility of incorporating all aspects of one's identity (including contradictory aspects) into a well-adjusted whole. The person who is successful in this incorporation is the *new mestiza*. Such a position meshes well with experiences among Red River Métis people in that they often assert a unique identity that comprises European and Aboriginal heritage/ancestry and reject the suggestion that such an identity is necessarily poorly adjusted, inauthentic, or not whole. However, some may find the term "hybrid" offensive with its animal husbandry connotations. Self-identification strategies of resistance enable marginalized individuals and communities to assert pride in their identities and may be useful to people with Métis ancestry wanting to reconnect with the spiritual traditions of our Native ancestors.

Traditional Criteria for Self-Identification

Traditionally, Aboriginal nations had many avenues for group membership and self-identification, including genealogy, marriage, adoption, loyalty, and community recognition. Community recognition, especially for urban Aboriginal people, can follow from community participation or participation in Aboriginal organizations. But can these values be mobilized to determine identity and membership (especially for non-status First Nation and Métis people) in contemporary times? Since each of these methods is still used in one way or another in contemporary times, the answer seems promising.

Bonita Lawrence's (1999) dissertation research provides examples of contemporary community involvement and participation as being influential upon identity; these include helping to start an Aboriginal organization, leading an organization, working in one, or even using such an organization's services (404). Participants in her study were also finding and strengthening community recognition through ceremonial life, teaching circles, healing circles, activism and jobs in the community, art, film, theatre, traditional hand drumming, and volunteering (407, 410). In the Métis context, some scholars believe that participation in an organization such as the Manitoba Métis Federation (MMF), along with an increase in Métis numbers in Winnipeg, may re-establish the centre of the Métis Nation (Shore 1999, 78).

Re-Traditionalization and Reclaiming Native Heritage

Reclaiming Anishinaabe heritage, or "re-traditionalization," is another way of determining cultural identity in contemporary times. LaFramboise, Heyle, and Ozer (1994) explain that re-traditionalization is about integrating traditional and contemporary demands "in a positive and culturally-consistent manner" whereby the "structure of the cultural system remains intact, but the specific jobs are modernized in accordance with social change" (481). This is especially useful in countering the often cited argument that it is impossible to get back to "the old ways." These authors further discuss re-traditionalization specifically in relation to women; they argue for a return to the spiritual source of women's strength and a re-traditionalization of the roles of Aboriginal men and women (ibid. 481).

Lawrence also focuses on the reclamation of Native heritage and includes Métis people in her discussion. She explores some of the complexities involved in this process and highlights that it would be most difficult for those who are "White-looking," urban and/or non-status. She explains, "The mixed-race people who can pass as white who decided that they do not want to participate in the obliteration of their Native heritage are thus forced to declare themselves as Native, regardless of their appearance.... This can be extremely difficult, especially if they have been brought up to consider themselves white—either because of silence around Indianness in their family, because of extremely white appearance, or because they were adopted" (Lawrence 1999, 267–68); furthermore, "Declaring themselves as Native, for these individuals has meant challenging the racial identity they grew up with—a deeply disorienting process which some of the participants nonetheless have undertaken in order to reach a self-definition that more accurately describes who they are—or at least one that is not premised on the denial of part of who they are" (268–69). Light-skinned Natives also face denials of their Nativeness by other Natives who think their light-skin privilege renders their Nativeness meaningless (273).

Lawrence discusses ways that non-status, landless, and Métis people can strengthen collective identity, including tracing lineage to/in a community (360). Another option would be to give treaty status to those Métis whose families were given scrip; the scrip system may lead the way to rebuilding an Indigenous Métis nation. Lawrence explains this as follows:

> Individuals could demand that the numbered treaties (with the exception of Treaty Three which already includes the Métis) be renegotiated so that the descendants of individuals who received

halfbreed scrip could be included into treaty. These individuals could then be considered 'treaty Métis,' or could be admitted as status Indians who were Métis—and could thus begin to negotiate sovereignty in conjunction with treaty Indian groups—in particular, the acquisition of a land base.... This approach should be seen as an interim one, a means of obtaining the maximum leverage out of the fiduciary relationship which the *Indian Act* has signified, before entering into new forms of Indigenous sovereignty. (470)

Jeffrey Murray (1993) makes a comparable argument, stating that the scrip system amounts to "primary evidence of the federal treatment of this indigenous group and will eventually constitute a basis for which the Métis can begin building a renewed relationship with the federal government" (14).

Yet another potential interim strategy for Métis people is to work (with the support of First Nations organizations) toward assuring legal rights of all non-status Aboriginal people under an organization like the Métis Nation (without emphasis on Red River settlement and homogeneous national culture). In her dissertation, Lawrence (1999) suggests "individuals who receive their legal rights as Native people under the Métis Nation could then seek out ways of *culturally* affiliating with the First Nations—through adoption by Elders, through forms of clan affiliation—a number of possibilities exist" (470).

Lawrence also discusses the importance of language and spirituality as ways that mixed-race people can reclaim Native heritage. Learning the language is helpful because it shapes thought and custom, and therefore behaviour (361). Along with learning the language comes learning traditional teachings and the importance of spirit names (362, 433). She notes that family bonds, family beliefs about spirituality and connection to nature, and ties to ancestors "were some of the few things left about being Native that [participants] still had access to on a daily basis, as people from extremely acculturated and diasporic families" (363).

Returning to traditional values and world views is a way of understanding existing identity categories available to Métis people. Advocates of this view are often concerned with traditional definitions of identity, re-traditionalization, reclaiming tribal heritage, strengthening collective identity, community recognition and participation, participation in Aboriginal organizations, and reclaiming traditions, including ceremony.

CHAPTER 3

Understanding the Colonial Context of Métis Spirituality and Identity

*Métis people have been forgotten in too many areas of Canadian
and Aboriginal history. They are a First People of Canada with
Aboriginal rights entrenched in the Canadian Constitution, 1982.
It is unfortunate that the battle for recognition continues today.*

—Tricia Logan, "Lost Generations," 62

Examining the historical and colonial experiences of Métis people is
paramount in order to understand contemporary Métis identities and relationships with spirituality. Much has already been written on Métis history
and heterogeneity; therefore, I will not repeat it here, but instead focus on
various aspects of Métis experiences that remain largely ignored.[1] It is crucial,
for example, to analyze colonial policies and legislation (such as the treaties
and the Indian Act) and their effects upon Métis identity and relationships
(especially forced divisions) between Métis and First Nations, as well as their
effects upon spirituality. In addition, an in-depth exploration of historical
efforts to convert and Christianize Aboriginal people reveals significant and
ongoing impacts upon Métis identity and spirituality. Moreover, examining
colonial systems, such as the residential school and child welfare systems,
reveals their intergenerational impacts upon Métis identity, relationships, and
spirituality. While differences between "Indians," "Halfbreeds," and "Métis"
were likely mutable early on, colonial legislation and systems had momentous
implications in terms of solidifying them as distinct categories in Canada.
These systems also had huge impacts on the ways in which the spirituality
of Métis people has unfolded historically, as well as the ways it is lived in a
contemporary context.

Legal Context of American Indian Identity

Before discussing these Canadian colonial systems and legislation in depth,
I would like to point out that the colonial context that shaped Indigenous
identity played out differently in the United States. In Canada, "half-breed

and Métis" people have been largely excluded from legislation pertaining to "Indians and First Nations" people; in the U.S., people of mixed Aboriginal and European heritage were never *legally* "non-Indian." While distinct Métis identities developed in central Canada, they did not arise as such in the U.S. because their legal "Indianness" was primarily defined as being on a blood continuum whereby mixed-bloods and full-bloods were all considered Indian; however, divisions would nonetheless be encouraged among them through government rolls and tribal membership.

During early contact in the Americas, European pseudo-scientific concepts of "blood" and "race," existing on a savage/civilized continuum, led to hierarchical classification systems whereby European characteristics and culture were deemed superior to so-called primitive cultures and peoples (i.e., Indians and Africans) (Schmidt 2011, 2; Hamill 2003, 267). According to Melissa Meyer, the term blood "presages modern conceptions of 'race'" (quoted in Schmidt 2011, 3). The concept of race was used, in Meyer's words, for "the conquest of indigenous peoples, their domination and exploitation, and the importation of a controllable population from Africa to serve capitalistic needs of the dominant European society" (2).

Schmidt's (2011) division of American history into the treaty period (1817–1871), the reservation period (1871–1887), and the allotment period (1887–1934) is helpful for our discussion. Virginia came to a legal definition of "mixed-blood" in 1705 by coining the term "mulatto" for individuals with at least one-eighth-blood African ancestry or one-half Indian ancestry; several states followed suit with similar definitions in order to restrict and limit civil and property rights (4). When the United States became a nation-state with constitutional authority, treaties became the preferred means of negotiating with tribes as sovereign political entities, especially regarding the cessation of tribal lands (4). American Indian status was not defined during the treaty period; instead, reference to blood quantum differed from treaty to treaty with regard to land entitlement but not to tribal membership. As Schmidt writes, "one of the earliest references to treaties with language of 'half-bloods,' 'half-breeds,' or 'quarter bloods' began in 1817 to grant various benefits, usually land and money, to mixed individuals" (4). During the treaty period, the U.S. government decided that "a mixed-blood was a citizen of the United States under virtue of his or her white ancestry and therefore not an Indian; however, the mixed-blood was also an Indian if he or she was a tribal member" (4). Then with the reservation period came judicial and legislative attempts to define Indian identity and individuals with mixed ancestry: "Most notably was the patrem rule (patrilineal descent) that stated all those with a non-Indian paternal ancestor were non-Indian, no matter the amount of 'Indian' blood" (4). This did not lead, however, to the same outcome as the Indian Act in Canada, with massive and long-term disenfranchisement of Aboriginal women and their children.

During the allotment period, blood quantum became officially integrated into the legal status of Indian identity in order to divide communal tribal lands into individual parcels called allotments, to promote Indian self-sufficiency, to break up tribal governments, and to end financial drain on the federal government (Schmidt 2011, 4; Ellinghaus 2008, 81). With the General Allotment Act (the Dawes Act) of 1887, Indian nations had to be enumerated and listed on census rolls using blood quantum as a determinant of tribal affiliation (Schmidt 2011, 5); rolls were used to calculate and allocate parcels of land (Ellinghaus 2008, 82). Between 1880 and 1920, the federal government placed thousands of names of these first rolls (Harmon 2001, 178). Importantly, tribal authority to determine enrollment policies was upheld in 1905 in *Waldron v. United States* and in the 1934 Indian Reorganization Act (the Howard-Wheeler Act). However, the federal government would continue to influence who should and should not count as "Indian."

Felix S. Cohen, the main architect behind the Indian Reorganization Act, wrote the *Handbook of Federal Indian Law* in 1941; in it, "American Indians are descendants of the original peoples of the New World who have 'no known mixture of other races,' whereas mixed-bloods are defined as descendants of those Indians who 'inter-married with other races'" (Haas, quoted in Bizzaro 2004, 63). Also, the Federal Acknowledgment Act of 1978 prescribes that most federally recognized tribes require a certain level of blood quantum. While the federal government does not *force* tribes to implement blood quantum criteria, the Bureau of Indian Affairs (BIA) provides a step-by-step process for guiding tribal enrollment (Schmidt 2011, 5; Bizzaro 2004, 66) and must certify this process (TallBear 2003, 89).

By 1934, 118 out of 213 reservations had been allotted, resulting in the loss of nearly 90 million acres of tribal lands (Schmidt 2011, 5; Hamill 2003, 269) from 138 million acres in 1887 to 48 million acres (Ellinghaus 2008, 81–82). "In 1906 and 1907 Congress added [Clapp] riders to the Indian Appropriation acts that removed restrictions to the sale, incumbrance, or taxation of allotments held by adult 'mixed-bloods' of the White Earth Reservation," writes Ellinghaus (2008, 92). Since the federal government prevented full-blood Indians from controlling their land, many Anishinaabeg simply called themselves "mixed blood" to gain control of it (92). Fraud ensued, and while some mixed-blood Anishinaabeg did facilitate land being taken away from other Anishinaabeg, it is also true that "a vast majority of the people who found themselves landless in such a short time were also of mixed descent, particularly as the Clapp amendments defined a person of mixed descent according to a virtual 'one-drop rule'" (93).[2] When people of mixed descent were given tribal benefits, they received fewer protections and thus were far less likely to hold onto them (83). The federal government tried to bring such people to court and promoted "the myth of light-skinned mixed bloods being largely responsible for the major land loss" that persists in Indian communities today (83).

There are currently 565 federally recognized tribes in America ("Tribal Directory"). Contemporary American Indians must be enrolled members in one of these tribes to receive benefits from the tribe or the federal government. Each tribe has criteria that must be met in order to be considered enrolled members; these often appear in tribal constitutions approved by the US Bureau of Indian Affairs (Thornton 1997, 35). Once recognized as members, individuals are given registration numbers and cards—known as a Certificate of Degree of Indian Blood (CDIB), issued by the BIA—specifying blood quantum (36). According to Ellinghaus (2008), about "two-thirds of all federally recognized tribes are required to specify a minimum blood quantum in their legal citizenship criteria" (85). More recently, some tribes are discussing genetic DNA testing to determine Indian identity as a means of supporting or denying claims to cultural and political rights (TallBear 2003, 82).

Though people of mixed descent were never legally "non-Indian," the U.S. federal government (and the tribes themselves) has created divisions based on blood quantum and government rolls. The exclusion of unenrolled individuals leads to loss of identity, connection to traditional ways (including spirituality), opportunities for self-determination, and, in Bizzaro's words, "psychological debilitation and fragmentation of unacknowledged mixed-bloods, who are consistently excluded from being Indians" (Bizzaro 2004, 66, 70). When a non-Indian meets an Indian, the first question is often "how much Indian are you?" Any response less than 100 percent blood quantum is met with satisfaction that "real Indians" no longer exist (71). According to Bizzaro, arguments that weaken an individual's claims to membership in an Indian nation also undermine the collective personhood of all Indian people (71). American Indigenous scholars like Bizzaro and TallBear argue that tribes must find some way to acknowledge the more than 4 million mixed-blood people in America, and that this will strengthen Indian nations overall; this makes sense, considering that tribes with higher blood quantum criteria have shrinking populations because of urbanization and intermarriage (Thornton 1997, 40). There is, writes Schmidt, one "inevitable fact if blood quantum requirements are allowed to run their course: termination" (Schmidt 2011, 7)—the termination of Indians, their rights, and lands.

The colonial context shaping Indigenous identity has been different in Canada; however, on both sides of the border, the federal governments have created divisions among Indigenous peoples that persist to this day and have influenced self- and group identity, belonging, and spirituality.

Colonial Legislation Influencing Métis Spirituality and Identity in Canada

Various colonial, federal, and provincial legislation and systems pertaining to Indigenous peoples have influenced "Halfbreed" and Métis experiences in Canada. After 1885, the Canadian government stepped up its long-standing attempt to use legislation to eliminate Aboriginal cultures (Dickason and Newbigging 2010, x). In 1920, deputy superintendent of the Department of Indian Affairs Duncan Campbell Scott told a special parliamentary committee, "I want to get rid of the Indian problem.... Our objective is to continue until there is not a single Indian in Canada that has not been absorbed into the body politic, and there is no Indian question, and no Indian Department" (Burnett and Read 2012, xxi–xxii). The Métis were not spared the devastating consequences of such legislation. Below, I discuss some of the legislation with far-reaching effects that has greatly impacted the definition(s) of Métis/Halfbreed, as well as Métis experiences in relation to Anishinaabe spirituality. Examples of such legislation include the treaties, the Manitoba Act (1870), the scrip system, the Indian Act(s) including Bill C-31 and Bill C-3, and section 35 of the Canadian Constitution Act, 1982. I also discuss important recent court decisions affecting the Métis: *Manitoba Métis Federation v. Canada* (the Dumont Case); *Daniels v. Canada*; and *Alberta v. Cunningham*.

The Treaties

Treaties—such as the Robinson-Superior, Robinson-Huron, and numbered treaties—were signed across Canada and are supposed to signify an agreement between specific Aboriginal Nations (almost entirely First Nations) and the federal government of Canada, wherein the rights and responsibilities of all parties are defined. According to Gilbert (1996), a former registrar at Aboriginal Affairs and Northern Development Canada (AANDC), "From the beginning of treaty-making in Canada, First Nations have assumed the right to determine who is treaty according to the customs of those peoples" (3).

Unfortunately, motivated by limiting the number of people who could claim treaty, the federal government consistently made the final decision about who could and could not be included, ignoring the wishes of the Indigenous peoples themselves. While there are exceptions for individuals, in the end almost every treaty (numbered or otherwise) externalizes and excludes Métis people as a group. Métis peoples often resisted such externalization and with the help of First Nations family, friends, and allies tried hard to be included in the treaties.

The issue of "half-breed rights" arose during discussions for the Robinson treaties, eventually signed in 1850. That First Nations and Métis were working together to protect the land against White settlement can be seen in the Mica Bay Incident. Surtees (1986) explains that a band of Indians, including Chief Shingwaukonse (better known as Chief Shingwauk) and several Métis travelled 200 miles from Sault Ste. Marie to Mica Bay, there disrupting, in November 1849, the mining installations of the Quebec Mining Company. Two Anishinaabe chiefs (Shingwauk and Nibina-goo-ging) and two (un-named) Métis leaders were arrested but later released and pardoned. In the treaty discussions that followed, Chief Shingwauk tried to secure reserve land for "Halfbreeds" at 100 acres per head, but Robinson refused because he was given instructions to deal with "Indians not whites"; Métis were considered "white" according to the government's assimilation agenda. Both Robinson treaties contained a clause stating that reserves could not be sold or leased without the consent of the Chief Indian Superintendent; therefore, the question arose of whether treaty Indians could give reserve land to Halfbreeds "by permitting persons of mixed blood to join the band and/or to share in the annuity money" (ibid.). Robinson himself suggested this could be done, and the matter was resolved by requiring that "half-breeds declare themselves as *either* Indian or non Indian" (ibid., emphasis added). Surtees argues that, "by requiring this choice, the government effectively prevented the development of Métis communities in Ontario similar to those that grew in Western Canada" (ibid.). I would add that this differential treatment of "half-breeds and Indians" by the Canadian government worked to solidify divisions between First Nation and Métis kin who did not recognize such divisions among themselves. In this way, the Robinson treaties set the stage for the treaty-making period that followed, including the numbered treaties.

During the 1870s, on the prairies, bureaucrats and politicians decided that treaty entitlement was limited to a certain class of Indians (Gilbert 1996, 3). Evidence suggests that the Government of Canada had difficulty distinguishing between Indians and persons of mixed blood for reasons including "the nomadic way of life shared by both populations, identical clothing, intermarriage, sharing of language and sometimes customs" (Gilbert 1996, 39). Indeed, distinguishing among themselves in these ways may not have been a priority for the Indigenous peoples in question. At that time, writes Gilbert, "the Treaty Commissioners were giving the Indians and the half-breeds a choice. Everyone had the option of having their territorial rights extinguished by taking treaty and annuity as treaty Indians or taking scrip as persons of mixed blood" (39). As Lawrence notes, treaty commissioners in each location would set up tables "where potential 'Halfbreeds' were to present themselves, individual by individual, to be judged by white officials as to what they were" (Lawrence 2004, 81). This was a biased, racist, and arbitrary process; Native families and entire bands not present during signings became de facto "Halfbreeds" (81).[3]

Treaties 1 and 2 cover southern and central Manitoba, and were signed in 1871 with Saulteaux, Cree, and other nations. One year earlier, the Manitoba Act, 1870, was signed between the Métis and the Government of Canada, which created the province of Manitoba and brought it into confederation. The government was trying to extinguish Aboriginal title from the Métis through the Manitoba Act and the scrip system (more on these later), and from the First Nations through treaties. For Treaties 1 and 2, "Mixed blood members of Ojibway and Cree bands who regarded themselves and were regarded as Indians were included in the Indian treaties, with the provisio that they were relinquishing any rights as half-breeds" (Lawrence 2012, 199). Whenever possible, the government did not want "half-breeds" accepting treaty (199).

The issue comes to a head with the signing of Treaty 3 in 1871 by the Saulteaux tribe of southwestern Ontario, overlapping into southeastern Manitoba. As was the case in the Robinson treaties, "it was clear that the Saulteaux viewed Canada's desire to segregate mixed-bloods from full-bloods as a strategy to divide Indigenous resistance" (199). In 1873, some Métis groups sought adhesion to this treaty; in 1875, this was granted, and the Métis of Rainy River were given distinct treaty land and rights. The Memorandum of Agreement reflecting this, titled *Adhesion by Halfbreeds of Rainy River and Lake* (AANDC 2008b), reads "Whereas the Half-breeds above described, by virtue of their Indian blood, claim a certain interest or title in the lands or territories in the vicinity of Rainy Lake and the Rainy River, for the commutation or surrender of which claims they ask compensation from the Government." Moreover, the agreement states that Halfbreeds "shall receive compensation in the way of reserves of land, payments, annuities and presents, in manner similar to that set forth in the several respects for the Indians in the said treaty." For subsequent treaties, the government was sure to tighten its grip and inhibit as many Métis as possible from signing; the fewer treaty signatories, the fewer responsibilities for the government.

With the passage of the Indian Act, 1876, Manitoba "Halfbreeds" were prohibited from being counted as "Indians," and this was used as further justification for excluding Halfbreeds from subsequent treaty-making (Lawrence 2004, 80). The government's response to Métis persistence to be included in treaties was to amend the Indian Act again in 1880 "to specifically exclude 'halfbreeds' outside Manitoba from coming under the provisions of the Act, and from any of the treaties" (Dickason 1992, 279). The 1880 Indian Act introduced the rule that Halfbreeds in treaty could voluntarily withdraw from treaty and take scrip. With the 1888 Indian Act, such withdrawals were deemed to include the Halfbreed's minor, unmarried children, who were withdrawn from treaty with their father (Gilbert 1996, 40). In the 1927 Indian Act, it was explicit that the wife and minor, unmarried children of such a Halfbreed would be included in the withdrawal (40).

Despite these increasing restrictions, there is evidence that Métis people nonetheless continued to try to be included in discussions for Treaties 4 (1874), 6 (1876), 8 (1877), and 11 (1921), but with even less success. While some Métis made it into Treaty 6 (Nicks and Morgan 1985, 176), the government did not systematically deal with Alberta Métis land rights until the Métis Population Betterment Act, 1938.

During Treaty 8 discussions, the Dene people (referred to by Euro-Canadians as Chipewyans) recommended Pierre Beaulieu—a well-known and respected local Métis leader—as their *chief*. However, the government rejected their choice (Lawrence 2004, 80). Some Métis who had adopted the Aboriginal way of life were able to adhere to Treaties 8 and 11 on an individual basis but the majority were excluded from the treaty process (Aboriginal Self-Government in the Northwest Territories n.d.). Then again, in the 1970s, a number of Dene and Métis communities from the area in question (Northwest Territories) sought a comprehensive treaty agreement with Ottawa. After rejecting the final agreement offered by Ottawa, these communities went forward with regional negotiations that were eventually signed by the Gwich'in, Tlicho and Sahtu Dene, and Métis.

A similar pattern of Métis seeking inclusion into treaties but for the most part being denied is also apparent in the history of the Pembina Band of Chippewa Indians, who eventually signed treaties in Manitoba, Minnesota, North Dakota, and Montana. When the government was trying to decide who to include in the Pembina Band—and by extension who could live on reserve and receive treaty rights—Métis once again sought inclusion. Indian agent John Waugh appointed a hand-picked thirty-two-member commission to transact with government, in this regard, comprising sixteen "Full Bloods" and sixteen Métis. They immediately struck from the treaty rolls 112 families, comprising 525 individuals, many of whom were Métis (Dusenberry 1985, 129). Chief Little Shell and his assistant Red Thunder were outraged, and tried to get their Métis relatives back on the list. Red Thunder had this to say to the commissioners: "'When you (the white man) first put your foot upon this land of ours you found no one but the red man and the Indian woman, by whom you have begotten a large family.' Pointing to the metis present, he added, 'These are the children and descendants of that woman; they must be recognized as members of this tribe'" (129–30). The commissioners did not listen. Instead, they went ahead with the infamous "ten cent treaty." While individual Métis made it into treaty with the Turtle Mountain Band of Chippewa; many more were excluded throughout the twenty-five-year ratification process, becoming landless, dispossessed, and shunned to this day by Whites and enrolled band members.

Throughout the treaty-making eras, the government tried to limit the number of people owed treaty responsibilities and rights, and increasingly tightened its grip on who could and could not enter into treaty, taking aim specifically at people of mixed blood. One constant throughout the history of treaty-making is the government's refusal to recognize the Métis as an Aboriginal group, as well as their continual disregard for the views and wishes of the Indigenous peoples themselves, often dividing kinship networks when some family members were accepted into treaty and others refused, with others accepting scrip only to be told that this made them ineligible for treaty. These divisions persist today.

At the same time that the government was negotiating treaties with First Nations, the Red River Métis were also organizing themselves in direct opposition to the flood of White settlers continually encroaching upon their land. Under the leadership of Louis Riel, among others, Métis people demanded that Canada also legally protect Métis rights. In July 1870, the Métis successfully forced "Canada to accept Western terms for the Confederation of Rupert's Land as the Province of Manitoba," writes Fred Shore (Shore 1999, 74). The Manitoba Act—created by the Métis Provisional Government and the result of negotiations between the peoples of Red River and the Canadian government—was ratified, and the Métis people won statutory protection for their language, religion, and laws (76).[4] As Milne describes,

"Section 31 set aside 1.4 million acres of land for distribution among the children of Métis heads of families residing in the province, while section 32 guaranteed all old settlers, Métis or White, 'peaceable possession' of the lots they occupied in the Red River settlement prior to 15 July, 1870" (Milne 1995, 30). Unfortunately, the policy for distributing land in Manitoba was altered by legislation eleven times between 1873 and 1884; more than half of these "supplementary" laws were amendments to sections 31 and 32. As a constitutional amendment, the Manitoba Act was supposed to adhere to Section 6 of the Canadian Constitution which states "it shall not be competent for the Parliament of Canada to alter the provisions" of the Manitoba Act; therefore, the amendments, it is argued, were illegal (as cited in Milne 1995, 32). With the first amendment, the number of people eligible for allotments under section 31 was reduced from approximately 10,000 to less than 6,000 by excluding "partly Indian heads of families from sharing in the allotments," writes Douglas Sprague (Sprague 1980, 418–19). With the second amendment, these parents were instead promised "a form of personal property, a scrip, which was supposed to be redeemable for land" (419). Rather than include Métis people in the treaty-making process, the government of Canada decided to create the scrip system in order to divide and administer the land promised to the Métis.

Scrip was designed to extinguish Métis Aboriginal title and was implemented in three phases: in the 1870s in Manitoba, through the Manitoba Act; in the Northwest through the North-West Halfbreed Commissions, 1885–1889; and in conjunction with Treaty 8, through the Scrip and Treaty Commission of 1899, and Treaty 10, through the Scrip Commissions of the early 1900s (Augustus 2008). Under the Dominion Lands Act of 1872, the federal government arbitrarily valued farmland at one dollar per acre, and this was still in effect during the scrip period. This Act offered plots of 160 acres of land for free (except for a small registration fee) to White settlers in order to populate the prairies and secure Canadian sovereignty in the face of American expansion. This was the same land that had been promised to the Métis via the Manitoba Act. Métis people were coerced into "giving up" their Indian title and rights in exchange for scrip notes, as Murray describes, "printed by the Canadian Bank Note Company in denominations of $80, $160 and $240; and in 80, 160 and 240 acres" (Murray 1993, 13).

The history of the scrip system is filled with corruption on the part of the federal and provincial governments, as well as European land survey-ors and bankers who swindled the largely illiterate Métis out of land and money. Countless examples of such dishonesty and trickery exist regarding the history of scrip in Manitoba (Sealey 1978, 21). Land allotments were always purposely far from Métis settlements to prevent Métis solidarity and resistance. If the land could be located, it was found to be unsuitable for agriculture (Sealey 1978, 22). Most Métis were not aware that a patent would be issued and that they had to formally register their land to obtain title (22). As Sealey writes, "the easiest way for the Half-breed to solve the problem was to sell the land to someone" (22). Fillmore (1978), a scrip buyer at the time, gives us a firsthand account of the disgusting corruption: "I was told that the practice was for the holder of a scrip to pick out some local Indian or half-breed and take him to the Dominion Land Office and present him as the person named in the scrip. The holder of the scrip, pretending to be the agent of the half-breed, would designate the land. The patent to this land would then be issued, and the scrip holder would then have to get title. Presumably, this was done by completing and registering the Quit Claim Deed" (35).[5] As a result of such corruption, "By the turn of the century, 90% of the Métis were landless and destitute and a number of prominent [White settler] individuals and institutions had amassed considerable fortunes from scrip speculation, including the Bank of Montreal and Bank of Nova Scotia" (Lawrence 2004, 76).

The Métis of Red River were effectively pushed off their land through the corrupt scrip system and the constant influx of new settlers coming in from Ontario. Some headed south to the northern United States, or further north in Manitoba, and many went westward, deeper into Canada. Hopes were high that a new homeland could be forged in Batoche, Saskatchewan. Unfortunately, it would not be long before White settlers pushed further westward into the interior of the country. Again, Métis voices demanding protection over land and other rights were ignored by the Government of Canada. Disaffected by the lack of action (and outright swindling) by Canada to meet their demands, and fearful that they would once again be pushed out of their homeland, some Métis began to take up arms this time.

At that time, in addition to the onslaught of White settlers, bison numbers on the plains were dwindling, forcing a change from a hunting and fur trade economy to one of agriculture, and many people were literally starving. First Nations peoples were also feeling the consequences of these changes; in many communities, especially in the Plains, where the economy was dependent on bison, poverty and starvation worsened by broken treaty promises were becoming epidemic. The introduction of new diseases brought by settlers was also devastating Indigenous populations at that time. According to Daschuk, Hackett, and MacNeil (2006), in the early 1870s, a smallpox epidemic devastated central Alberta, spreading along the North Saskatchewan River, killing (by official accounts) almost 3,500 Blackfoot, Métis, and Cree (309). Conditions continued to deteriorate among many First Nations in the southern plains and by 1879, official correspondence of the Indian Department acknowledged deaths from starvation whereby "young men who a few months ago had been stout and hearty were reduced to perfect skeletons" (quoted in Daschuk, Hackett, and MacNeil 2006, 317).

It was around this time that Riel and other Métis stepped up their efforts to create a Native Confederacy (a Métis-First Nation alliance) in the hopes of having their voices and demands recognized by the Government of Canada.[6] Riel travelled to many First Nation reserves (if he did not go himself, he would send representatives—usually one Métis and one First Nation person) to drum up support (Stonechild and Waiser 1997, 79). At the same time, influential Chiefs such as Mistahimaskwa (Big Bear), Pitikwahanapiwiyin (Poundmaker), Minahikosis (Little Pine), and Kamiscowesit (Beardy) were trying to encourage a pan-Indian alliance. To this end, in the spring of 1884, Mistahimaskwa invited all plains First Nations to a thirst dance and council, but the North West Mounted Police quickly shut it down. Discontent with the government finally came to a head, and a series of battles ensued—with Métis, First Nation, North West Mounted Police, Canadian militia, government agents, and settler participants—which would come to be known as the Northwest Resistance of 1885.

There is ongoing debate regarding the extent to which First Nation and Métis people were working together around this time. According to Stonechild and Waiser (1997), "Indian involvement was isolated and sporadic, not part of a grand alliance with the Métis" (4); they go as far as arguing that the Métis *coerced* First Nation people to participate against their will (148). They do admit that individual First Nations men participated, including Mistahimaskwa's (Big Bear's) son Imasees and Wandering Spirit's warriors (109), some Dakota (156), and some Cree, especially Kamiscowesit (Beardy) and his Willow Cree men (69, 75), men from One Arrow (74), and some from the Petequakey reserve (80). Stonechild and Waiser also argue that Mistahimaskwa viewed the Métis as competition and had clashed with famed Métis buffalo hunter and leader Gabriel Dumont's family over the buffalo hunt (61).[7] On the other hand, while Siggins (1995) agrees there was no grand Métis-First Nation alliance, she argues that "support did come from the south branch of the Saskatchewan; *scores of warriors* arrived from the One Arrow, Beardy, Okemasis, Chakastapaysin and Petaquakey reserves" (361, emphasis added). In July 1884, Kamiscowesit (Beardy) called a council of plains Indians and invited Riel, who declined to participate; however, three weeks later Riel and Mistahimaskwa had a meeting where Mistahimaskwa pleaded with Riel that, "once the rights of Métis had been secured he [Riel] would help the Indians. It's not known whether Riel agreed" (Siggins 1995, 350). According to Siggins, dozens of First Nations men participated along with 200 Métis in the Battle of Duck Lake (348), and thirty Sioux and Cree participated along with 200 Métis in the Battle of Fish Creek (397); in each of these battles, the first casualty was actually a First Nation man. On 1 May 1884, a message of support from Pitikwahanapiwiyin arrived at Riel's camp promising reinforcements, but shortly after he became involved with his own bloody battle with Middleton's forces and no men could be spared; at that point, besides Chief White Cap and twenty Sioux, the Métis were left to fight the Battle of Batoche alone (399).

On 15 May 1885, under the orders of General Middleton, his army of approximately 550 troops and the new Gatling gun took the small group of Métis by surprise at 5:15 a.m. while the camp was still asleep at Batoche (Stonechild 1986, 102). Of all the battles that make up the Northwest Resistance of 1885, the Canadian government's militia were only victorious in one; the defeat at the Battle of Batoche would be the decisive battle that ended the Métis (and First Nation) resistance. By the end of November 1885, the great Métis leader Louis Riel was tried for "high treason" and executed by hanging. Fearing a First Nation and Métis alliance, Canada also imprisoned Cree leaders Mistahimaskwa and Pitikwahanapiwiyin, and eventually hung eight First Nations warriors for participation in the Resistance (ibid. 105). After 1885, First Nation participants in the Resistance and the Métis were branded "traitors" and "rebels"; twenty-eight reserves were identified as "disloyal" and more than fifty First Nation individuals were convicted of rebellion-related crimes (Stonechild and Waiser 1997). Consequently, First Nations and Métis were *further* denied full membership in the Canadian mainstream.

According to Sawchuk (2001), the Métis were ultimately forced to fight for their very existence and "they lost not only their territory, as did the Indians, but also their right to a legitimate status, which the Indians were at least allowed to keep; thus their population faced a cataclysmic decline" (70). Similarly, Harrison (1984) recognizes the effects of these dire circumstances: "to avoid discrimination from the white settlers some Métis changed their names to ones that would not reveal their ancestry, a practice that contributed to the decline in the numbers of identifiable Métis" (63–64). However, despite overwhelming odds, "the Métis also managed to organize themselves into small communities on the periphery of Canadian society or next to Reserves.

In these small communities, they kept alive their culture, language and customs and waited for a better day" (Shore 1999, 77–78).

Some historic Métis communities in the southern prairies survived as Métis communities, largely by maintaining a low profile about Indigenous identity (Lawrence 2004, 77). But this silence about identity had dire consequences. Between 1881 and 1901, the number of people identifying as "Indian or Métis" was halved and reflects people who fled for their lives after the 1885 Resistance, those who left due to White encroachment, and those who passed as White (Lawrence 2004, 77). Shore (1999) writes that "Canada successfully prevented most Métis land holdings in the Settlement Belt from being retained by their rightful Métis owners" and that, "abused, dispossessed and outnumbered, the frustrated, angry and disheartened Métis were dispersing to the far corners of their former homeland. In their eyes, Canada had broken what one of their leaders [Riel] had called the Métis Treaty" (76).

In 1981, the Manitoba Métis Federation (MMF) and the leaders of seventeen Métis families, representing the Métis Nation, launched a court case—*MMF v. Canada (Attorney General)*, also known as the Dumont Case—in which they sought a ruling stating that, "the governments acted wrongly in passing those [corrupt scrip] laws and that those laws should be declared *invalid* seeking an amount that would compensate for the lost use of the land and an award equal to the current value of the land" (Santin 2007). The price tag would exceed several billion dollars. In other words, these Métis argued that, since Métis land was stolen, *Indian title* was never lost; therefore, contemporary Manitoba Métis, as descendants of the historic Métis Nation whose ancestors received scrip, should legally continue to enjoy *Indian title* and rights and be financially compensated for the massive theft of our land. In December 2007, Justice Alan MacInnes "rejected the federation's claims that their ancestors had a treaty with Ottawa in 1870 over a 566,000-hectare stretch of land in the Red River Valley that includes most of modern-day Winnipeg" (CBC News 2008). MacInnes said, rather than a treaty or agreement, the case involved an act of Parliament and that too much time had passed between the signing of the Act and the lawsuit. The MMF appealed the decision, and on 13 December 2011 they took their case to the Supreme Court of Canada.

Finally, on 3 March 2013, the Supreme Court of Canada granted a declaration that the federal government failed to uphold section 31 of the Manitoba Act of 1870 (Chartrand 2013, para. 1) and that the delay in making land grants was a historical injustice: "They conclude that the Métis did not receive the benefit that was intended by the land grants, and they imply that this was a cause of the Métis' subsequent marginalization" (*Manitoba Métis Federation Inc. v. Canada (Attorney General) 2013*, 284). According to Chartrand (2013), "A declaration is not legally binding of itself but it declares what the law of the Constitution requires. In Canada, governments are expected to abide by the law of the Constitution and the rule of law. The declaration in the MMF case must lead to productive and good faith negotiations and must engage both the federal and provincial governments" (para. 2). It is too soon to comment on the consequences of this historic court case.

Sections 91(24) and 35 of the Canadian Constitution Act

The Canadian Constitution Act (1982) is the supreme law of Canada and includes the Canadian Charter of Rights and Freedoms, the Constitution Act, 1867 (formerly the British North America Act), and other acts and amendments. This legislation also greatly impacts First Nations and Métis people, especially sections 91(24) and 35.

Section 91(24) of the Constitution Act (1867) provides Parliament with exclusive jurisdiction for "Indians and lands reserved for the Indians"; however, Parliament "has largely chosen over the years to narrow its actual legislative role to 'Indians on lands reserved for the Indians'" (Morse and Groves 2002, 196). This excludes Métis people and other non-status Aboriginal people. Contrary to Parliament's narrowed focus, most scholars argue that the section in question does indeed apply to Métis people (ibid. 195; Gibson 2002, 263; RCAP 1996, 209).

In 1982, the Constitution Act would undergo amendments; of particular interest to Métis people is the amendment, section 35. "Section 35 of the Constitution Act (1982) expressly recognizes and affirms the existence of three *distinct* categories of Aboriginal peoples [Indians, Métis, Inuit], whose rights are protected by the Constitution. In contrast, the federal law and policy continues to be based largely upon the nineteenth century Indian Act, which contains a limited definition of 'Indian' that has not changed substantially since it was unilaterally drafted by federal officials in 1867" (Chartrand 2002a, 20, emphasis added).

Chartrand explains that one of the reasons for this inconsistency is that there exists "an apparent anomaly, which has yet to be given constitutional interpretation by the courts [until recently], between the category of 'Indians' in section 91(24), and the category of 'aboriginal peoples' in section 35" (ibid. 16). A growing number of scholars began arguing for the inclusion of Métis people in section 91(24); noteworthy examples include RCAP (1996, Vol. 4, Section 5.1) and Chartrand and Giokas (2002). Chartrand and Giokas (2002) contend that in defining who can be considered "Métis," the historic Métis Nation of Red River should form the "core" of the larger Métis population. Their reasoning emphasizes the fact that the Red River Métis are the only *nation* of Métis to have challenged the sovereignty of Canada and to have a history of legal recognition by the Manitoba Act, 1870, and the Dominion Lands Act, 1879; and who were in existence as a Nation at the time when treaties were being signed in western Canada (287).

Finally, on 8 January 2013, the Federal Court, in *Daniels v. Canada*, ruled that "Métis and Non Status Indians are defined under the term 'Indian' for the purposes of Section 91(24) [para. 619]" of the Constitution Act, 1867 (Henry 2013; *Daniels v. Canada* 2013). The decision did not go as far as declaring that the Crown owes a fiduciary duty to Métis and non-status Indians, nor that the Crown must negotiate and consult with those in question on a collective basis with respect to rights (Henry 2013). The Government of Canada promptly appealed the decision citing the need to be "fiscally sustainable" and because the case "raises complex legal issues" (Duncan 2013); the Federal Court upheld the original decision. While there are "no immediate expectations of changes to access for new programs and services from the Federal Government for Métis people in … Canada," it is nonetheless considered to be a landmark ruling in favour of the Métis in terms of moving Métis rights forward (Henry 2013).

Determining who is and is not included in the sections discussed above is of utmost importance to all Aboriginal peoples because so many other rights and legislation stem from them. Excluding certain Aboriginal groups from these sections effectively cuts them off from subsequent rights and protection, and creates divisions between Aboriginal peoples. When legal decisions enforce a definition of Métis that necessitates being *distinct* from "Indianness," Métis people are actively *encouraged* to separate themselves from Indians/First Nations. For example, while the 1982 Constitution amendment finally recognized the Métis as an Aboriginal group with rights, it also implied that Métis and First Nations are wholly distinct, forcing divisions that were not there before. Indeed, "the cost of recognition for Métis, then, has been permanent segregation from Indianness and a hardening of what was once a mutable and shifting identity" (Lawrence 1012, 203). If Métisness depends on being entirely distinct from Indianness, then it is almost certain that most Métis would react with negativity to any idea that Métis people could embrace so-called "Indian" spirituality and still be Métis. It is unclear whether such exclusionary legal definitions would mean that Métis people who practise Anishinaabe spirituality would therefore be ineligible for Métis rights (because we are not *distinct* enough).

The Indian Act(s), Bill C-31 and Bill C-3

The Indian Act was enacted in 1876 by the Parliament of Canada under the provisions of section 91(24) of the Constitution Act, 1867. The profoundly sexist Indian Act and its various amendments and manifestations have greatly impacted First Nations and Métis peoples, but in different ways. Bonita Lawrence (1999) explains that, "In 1876, the multiple statutes which had been created to define and control Indigenous peoples were codified into a body of laws known as the Indian Act. Almost immediately, a series of modifications were introduced to the Act which differentiated between 'Indians' and 'halfbreeds' in order that the latter could be excluded from the Act" (59). Métis people were denied status as "Indians" under the Act (Shore 1999, 77). The Indian Act was revised ten times between 1910 and 1930, mostly to curb Native resistance to it—for example, to make it illegal to use band funds for land claims (Lawrence 1999, 60).

Lawrence highlights the gender discrimination supported by the Act when she states that "the very notion of which Native people should be considered 'mixed race' is highly shaped by gender" (69). The Indian Act made it such that if a status Indian woman married a non-status man (Indian, Métis, or White), she and her children lost their Indian status; this has been termed the "marrying out rule" (Eberts 2010, 21). This was not the case for status men who married non-status women (Indian, Métis, or White); instead, the women (even White women) and their children gained Indian status (Lawrence 1999, 69). In addition, the "double mother rule" made it so that an individual "lost Indian status upon attaining 21 years if both their mother and their paternal grandmother had acquired status through marriage to an Indian" and could only confer status if they themselves had children before age twenty-one (Eberts 2010, 19). The Indian Act has led to the solidification of demarcations among various Aboriginal peoples and has led to Métis invisibility (Coates 1999, 30).

Joyce Green (1997) discusses the costs of such exclusion including loss of human resources, family solidarity, and contributions of community members (69). She goes on to highlight that the costs for the women and children who were excommunicated are even greater, including deprivation of cultural context significant to their identity; lost access to government programs for Indians (including education at all levels); health care and prescription drug coverage; housing programs; access to funds like the Indian Economic Development Fund; and certain Aboriginal and treaty rights, such as not being able to inherit property on reserves (69–70). Even if these women were divorced, widowed, or abandoned, they could not return home. Green is quick to point out that these are merely material losses; the psychological trauma is inconceivable (70).

The Indian Act was also openly discriminatory toward Métis people in that they were and still are excluded from "Indianness," particularly in western Canada. The Act contained a provision (section 3) that for the first time excluded anybody who was not *full blood*: "no half-breed head of family (except the widow of an Indian, or a half-breed who has already been admitted into a treaty) shall be accounted an Indian, or entitled to be admitted into any Indian treaty" (Green 79). According to Lawrence, the Indian Act has played the largest role in creating the separate category of 'halfbreed' in regions where no such concept existed and in "forcibly externalizing mixed-race people from Native communities" (Lawrence 1999, 79).

The Indian Act(s) also had devastating impacts on Anishinaabe spirituality. Amendments to the Indian Act resulted in "cultural institutions and spiritual practices, such as the potlatch on the West Coast, and the Sun Dance on the Plains, being banned" (J. Miller 1996, 191–95) and prohibitions against wearing ceremonial regalia and dancing (Dickason 1992, 326). The Indian Act essentially banned ceremonies from approximately 1885 to 1951, but the effects of this are still present today. Amendments to the Indian Act also made it illegal for three or more "Indians" to gather (except in Christian churches) without an Indian Agent present. Some Aboriginal peoples continued to practise truncated versions of these ceremonies, despite repression, in the decades afterward (Lawrence 2004, 35).

There has always been much resistance to the Indian Act by First Nation and Métis peoples, especially from women. After sustained resistance, the federal government passed Bill C-31 in 1982, which was supposed to eliminate the sexist section 12(1)(b) that had stripped Native women of their Indian status for marrying non-status men and excommunicated them since 1869 (J. Green 1997, 68). By 1995, Bill C-31 enabled approximately 100,000 individuals to regain their status by 1995 (Lawrence 2004, 59).

Despite the Bill C-31 amendment, sexist discrimination persisted in the Indian Act. Bill C-31 introduced the "two-parent rule." Eberts (2010) explains: "Now to get 'full' status a person must have two status parents, instead of only one. The child with only one status parent gets a 'life interest' in status, being unable in his or her own right to pass it to a child" (23). Another problem introduced by Bill C-31 has been termed the "second generation cut-off rule," which maintains that the grandchildren of reinstated women who are not 6(1) Indians will nonetheless lose their status (Giokas and Groves 2002, 62). Other problems caused by Bill C-31 include band resistance, as bands wish to decide their band membership for themselves, taking into consideration scarce resources (Lawrence 2004, 65). Many male-centred band councils are resistant to allowing newly reinstated women to live on their reserves, citing resources already spread too thin. Lawrence concludes that Bill C-31 creates more divisions among Aboriginal peoples and that the blatant sexism in many band councils continues to discriminate against Aboriginal women and their children (68).

For years, Sharon McIvor and her son Jacob Grismer (2010) have been battling the courts to eliminate some of the gender discrimination in the Indian Act. McIvor has two status grandmothers, but did not apply for status herself until after 1985. McIvor had her status restored under section 6(1) (c) of Bill C-31. Because she married a non-status male, their son Jacob had only one status parent, so he was registered under section 6(2) and could not confer status to his children (Eberts 2010, 27). They challenged the status hierarchy established in section 6(1) in the British Columbia Supreme Court, "so as to eliminate the differential impact of the two-parent rule on those tracing their descent through the female line. In particular, they sought to have included in s. 6(1)(a) all of those born before April 17, 1985, who were descended in either the male or the female line from a status Indian" (Grismer 28). In this way, both McIvor and her son would have "full" 6(1)(a) status, which would enable Grismer to pass his status to his children regardless of whether or not the other parent had status" (28).

At trial, Justice Ross agreed with McIvor and Grismer that section 6(1)(a) enabled "preferential treatment of patrilineal descendants over matrilineal descendants in the right to be registered as Indian" (Eberts 34) and ordered principles that would "nullify the result of the marrying out rules on female Indians…. [Consequently, a] population of status Indian women now able to confer status on their descendants has been brought into being" (34). However, Justice Groberman of the Court of Appeal responded by curtailing Justice Ross's suggestions by narrowly defining the extent of the wrongful discrimination. Based on Justice Groberman's inadequate judgment, Bill C-3, the Gender Equity in Indian Registration Act, was introduced into the House of Commons in March 2010 (Canada 2010). McIvor and Grismer were unsuccessful in seeking leave to appeal the Court of Appeal's decision to the Supreme Court of Canada. In November 2010, they aired their case to the United Nations (McIvor and Grismer 2010).

Bill C-3 introduces section 9, a "no liability" clause, which states, "[no] person or body has a right to claim or receive any compensation, damages or indemnity from Her Majesty in right of Canada, any employee or agent of Her Majesty, or a council of a band, for anything done or omitted to be done in good faith in the exercise of their powers or the performance of their duties" (Parliament of Canada, n.d.). According to the National Aboriginal Law Section (NALS), this "would remove the right of anyone to sue the federal government for not providing them with status as a result of the gender discrimination addressed by the Bill.... including such a provision could make the Bill vulnerable to further Charter challenges" (NALS 2010, 6).

The main amendment enacted through Bill C-3 is the new section 6(1) (c.1), which sets out four criteria that must be met before a person is eligible for registration under 6(1); a person is only eligible if all these criteria are met (NALS 2010, 5; Eberts 2010, 41). More specifically, for someone in Jacob Grismer's position, the four conditions for registration under section 6(1) are as follows: "his or her mother lost status because of the old marrying out rules or through marrying out plus enfranchisement; his or her father was not an Indian under the 1951 *Act* or a predecessor *Act*; the person was born after the marriage which deprived his or her mother with status; and lastly, the person must have had or adopted a child after September 4, 1951, when the double mother rule came into force" (Eberts 2010, 42). The fourth criterion may lead to "'family status' discrimination, in that some people will only be 'bumped up' from section 6(2) to 6(1) status if they parent a child. This may affect people whose band membership code denies membership to Indians registered under section 6(2) and also in communities where there is a certain stigma associated with having section 6(2) status rather than section 6(1)" (NALS 2010, 5). In addition, "Bill C-3 fails to provide additional resources to First Nations to address an influx of persons with status, particularly section 11 bands.... This may invite some First Nations to adopt more restrictive membership codes, as occurred after the passage of Bill C-31 in 1985" (7).

According to human rights activist Shelagh Day, "What the bill essentially corrects is the discrimination against the women who married out and their descendants, but it leaves in place the discrimination against the women who partnered in common-law relationships and their descendants" (quoted in Cole 2011). Most people resoundingly reject Bill C-3 because it affects at most 2,000 people, rather than addressing once and for all "the discrimination that has blighted the lives of tens of thousands that we know of, and probably many tens of thousands more whose stories remain untold" (45). Furthermore, "the large population of off-reserve and urban Indians, many *Bill C-31* reinstatees, lacks many essential services and supports because Canada's funding is keyed to reserves" (44), thus creating yet another site of contention.

Since some Métis people are gaining status through Bill C-31 and Bill C-3, they are also subject to the same areas of contention and sites of gender discrimination therein. These include gaining a type of status that cannot be conferred onto their children or grandchildren, and potentially becoming part of a band that has not been given extra funds to deal with new members as a result of these bills. On the other hand, many Métis are still not eligible for any type of status, specifically because the gender discrimination persists within the Indian Act and its amendments.

In addition, great numbers of Métis people could have been eligible for Indian status had Bill C-31 included scrip as evidence of "Indianness." According to Gilbert (1996), former Indian Registrar for AANDC, indeed, "scrip is simply proof of Indianness" (39). Gilbert explains that "scrip is a bar to entitlement because the former Act [pre-1985] specifically listed it as a basis for disentitlement whereas the present Act is silent on the matter. The Registrar interprets this legal framework as a basis for treating persons who received scrip as non-Indians" (39). He continues, "Sections 12(1)(a)(i) and (ii) of the *Indian Act* as it read immediately prior to April 17, 1985, provided (i) a person who has received or has been allotted half-breed land or money scrip, and (ii) a descendant of such a person, are not entitled to be registered in the Indian Register" (ibid. 40). Yet, a subsection was added stating that this did not apply to persons (and their descendants) registered as Indian on 13 August 1958, because this would have required the removal of several hundred families and each of their several generations (40–41). The reason for this was because there are "repeated examples of families taking scrip and then taking treaty" (41). This protects those registered as Indians who also took scrip, but discriminates against those "Halfbreeds" who took scrip and prevents them from also taking treaty. This is no accident; rather, Halfbreeds who took scrip are considered non-Indians because it suits the government's consistent policy of reducing the Aboriginal population of Canada (39). Gilbert agrees with fellow scholar Kent McNeil that there are "a number of grounds for challenging the department's treatment of descendants of scrip and in particular the descendants of those ancestors known as 'half-breeds,'" and that families with a history of scrip should research the details of the scrip transaction, which may "assist the applicant in proving entitlement to registration as an Indian and, where relevant, band membership" (41).[8] Had Bill C-31 explicitly included scrip as evidence of "Indianness," a great many Métis would likely be eligible for Indian status (including several participants in this study, my family, and me).

Alberta v. Cunningham

That colonial legislation such as Bill C-31 is directly impacting Métis people can be seen in a 2011 court case—*Alberta (Aboriginal Affairs and Northern Development) v. Cunningham*—which went to the Supreme Court of Canada (AANDC 2011). Members of the Cunningham family had their membership in the Peavine Métis Settlement in Alberta revoked when they registered as "Indians" under Bill C-31 of the Indian Act (Randall 2011). *Alberta Sweetgrass* author Shari Narine Sweetgrass (2011) writes that "Sect. 75 of the Métis Settlement Act prohibits anyone with Indian status from obtaining Métis settlement membership, while Sect. 90 calls for the removal of member-ship from the settlement for individuals who have voluntarily registered as Indians under the Indian Act." While the Alberta Court of Queen's Bench found no violation of rights, the Alberta Court of Appeal later found that the Cunninghams' section 15 equality rights were indeed violated and struck down sections 75 and 90 of the Act. However, on 21 July 2011, the Supreme Court overturned this decision and found that "the exclusion of Indians from the Métis Settlements is constitutionally sound and connected to the objects of the Métis Settlements which includes the establishment of a Métis land base, the protection of Métis culture and the creation of Métis self-government" ("Métis Nation Applauds" 2011). Essentially, the Supreme Court of Canada is saying that one cannot be *both* Indian and Métis.

Métis reactions to the decision appear to be split. Obviously the Cunninghams are not satisfied with the Supreme Court's decision. On the other hand, "Métis National Council President Clément Chartier applauded the decision as a further affirmation of the recognition of the Métis Nation as a distinct people, separate and apart from Indian and Inuit peoples" ("Métis Nation Applauds" 2011). It would appear that the Supreme Court is uphold-ing the right of Métis people to determine their own membership. Whether Métis and First Nation reactions to the decision are positive or negative, the fact remains that provincial and federal Canadian governments ultimately maintain the "right," in one way or another to determine membership and identity for Aboriginal groups to this day. The Cunningham decision also continues the government's work of creating and solidifying divisions be-tween First Nation and Métis people and families.

Through the colonial legislation discussed above, the provincial and fed-eral governments have created the legal categories of "Indian," "Aboriginal," "Métis," and "Halfbreed" with accompanying legislation regarding land rights for each group; in addition, the governments continue to determine who can claim membership within these and other categories. Such colonial legislation has many consequences for all Aboriginal people, including divisions between Métis and First Nation people and exclusion of some Aboriginal people from access to ceremonies due to geographic distance, loss of cultural and spiritual identity, and hierarchies of Nativeness wherein some people are seen as "more Indian" than others—for example, because they grew up on a reserve and have Indian status (see Chapter 4). Particularly damaging consequences for Métis people include internalized tensions surrounding identity as a result of being externalized from "Indianness," severed ties with our First Nations relatives, and a subsequent lack of opportunities to participate in the spiritual ceremonies and beliefs of our Anishinaabe relatives and ancestors.

Métis People and Christianity[9]

At the same time as policy and legislation were being drafted to facilitate the assimilation of Aboriginal peoples, ongoing missionary efforts with the purpose of converting the Métis were also occurring. These efforts have also drastically influenced Métis identity and relationships with Anishinaabe spirituality. This analysis clearly illustrates reasons why so many Métis are Christian (especially Roman Catholic) and have nearly severed their relationships with Anishinaabe spirituality today.

French orders of the Roman Catholic faith were the first to attempt to "Christianize" the Native population in the French colonies of the New World (beginning with Quebec in 1615). Unlike the Anglicans and Protestants who came later, the French Récollets and the Jesuits believed there was at least some good inherent in the Native population.[10] Perhaps this reflected the French desire to create "one French race/nation." Dickason (1985) points to the French settler prioritization of spiritual conversion of Native and Métis populations when she outlines the Company of New France's Article 17, which states: "The Savages who will be led to the faith and to profess it will be considered natural Frenchmen, and like them, will be able to come and live in France when they wish to, and there acquire property, with rights of inheritance and bequest, just as if they had been born Frenchmen, without being required to make any declaration or to become naturalized" (22).

This view of a degree of innate goodness, combined with the desire to create one French nation, according to the Jesuits, would be the foundation upon which a new form of Christianity could be built. Significantly, "the Jesuit missionary effort, therefore, was based on the premise that native tribal culture was to be left largely intact and become the context for a *new expression of Christianity*" (Moore 1982, xi, emphasis added). "To the Jesuits," Moore writes, "conversion to Christianity and Europeanization were *not* inexorably linked" (138). To this end, the Jesuits were open to learning the customs of the Native people. It was not uncommon for the Jesuit fathers to accept an "Indian name" from their converts after giving their converts a Christian name upon conversion. Evidence that the fathers took this seriously can be found in the use of their Indian names in official documents sent back to Europe. In accordance with their view that it was not necessary to Europeanize the Natives, the Jesuits accommodated themselves to the semi-nomadic lifestyle of the Native peoples they encountered. One way of doing this was to follow the Native people and preach to them while on their bison hunt (64).

By 16 July 1818, Catholic missionaries arrived permanently in the Red River region, and their first priority was to save the souls of "savages"; indeed, within days of their arrival Fathers Joseph Provencher and Sévère Dumoulin had already baptized more than 100 Métis and First Nation children (Siggins 1995, 22). Continuing the tradition of the bison hunt missions, or *missions ambulantes*, the Catholic Oblates in the Red River area accompanied Métis hunters *à la prairie*, lived with them, and instructed them in their camps (Huel 1996, 53). They were also known to winter with them (Payment 2009, 96). Huel outlines a typical bison hunt mission: "After a successful hunt, the camp was not displaced and during that time [the priest] could hold a regular mission with mass, hymns, catechisms and instructions for all. During a move, he could instruct the children when the caravan rested whereas adults were instructed at night" (Huel 1996, 54). For many hunters, this was the only time they saw a priest. Until 1833, the Catholic Church missions in the Northwest consisted only of these bison hunt missions and two establishments, one at St. Boniface and the other at St. François Xavier. Each served French-Canadians and Métis rather than Indians (McCarthy 1990, 15).

The linguistic skills of some of the priests were of considerable advantage to them in these bison hunt missions. Some of these early missionaries recognized the potential for more converts to Christianity if they learned to speak the Native languages and taught Christian teachings in the languages of the people they encountered. For example, around 1821, James Evans of the Wesleyan mission (northern end of Lake Winnipeg) is often credited with developing Cree syllabics and translating the Bible so that it could be printed in Cree and facilitate conversion of the Cree people with whom he worked (Woodley 1953, 53–54). However, it is more likely that he received help with these efforts from three other Methodist missionaries: Benjamin Sinclair (Cree from Norway House), Henry Steinhauer ("Indian"), and William Mason and his Cree wife Sophia (Mason 1996, 56, 59). Soon thereafter, word of this reached Europe, and Bibles, hymns, and schoolbooks were printed in Cree and then shipped to Canada via the Hudson's Bay Company. It was in this way that Cree syllabics came to be widely used throughout northern Canada. Similarly, in the Red River area, "The Métis preferred to hear [the priest] preach in Sauteux [sic], which they understood better than French [and English]" (McCarthy 1990, 18).

For various Catholic branches, denominational fights further motivated the use of Indigenous languages, for, the idea goes, if the Natives will not speak French, better they speak a Native language than English. As Huel writes, "this amalgam of race and religion produced a missiology that placed great value in the preservation of indigenous languages as a bulwark against Protestantization and subsequent Anglicization" (Huel 1996, xix). Catholic Oblates recognized that making use of the Indigenous languages facilitated presentation and comprehension of preaching and instruction; "if they fumbled their words weren't taken seriously; notes, dictionaries, grammars compiled by early oblates made it easier for those who came later to study the Indian languages" (ibid. 31). Moreover, some familiarity with the Indigenous language "provided the missionary with insights into the Indian character and culture, permitting oblates to tailor their ministry to accommodate certain traits in the Indian character and temperament" (33).

These early, relentless efforts by European missionaries to convert the Native peoples had a considerable impact on the spiritual lives of the Métis. Undoubtedly, some Métis would have willingly chosen to follow a European spirituality, especially given the presence of their European fathers and/or partial European ancestry. While it is difficult to determine when conversion was made willingly and when it was "accepted" due to mounting pressures of assimilation, European religion may have become a defining factor in the internalization of difference between Métis and First Nations people. For example, this is apparent in memoirs written by a Métis woman about life on the prairies around 1870: "While we roamed the prairies of western Minnesota and the Dakotas, we were always in the same company of people of part Indian blood, and travelled in many groups.... Just camping here and there without thought of settling permanently at any place, just following the buffalo trails. *You might think we lived the life of the real Indians, but one thing we had always with us which they did not—religion.* Every night we had prayer meeting and just before a buffalo hunt we would see our men on bended knee in prayer" (Dusenberry 1985, 124–25, emphasis added).

Increasingly, those who would have preferred to follow the spiritual traditions of their Native mothers were actively denied such an opportunity. As discussed previously, Aboriginal people were often ambivalent towards

Christianity and at times outright rejected it; when conversion did occur it was often motivated strategically rather than spiritually. The earliest (French) missionary efforts were satisfied to leave "Indian" cultures mostly intact while converting the people; priests learned and preached to us in our Native languages and followed us on our bison hunts to preach, rather than trying to force us to settle. Sadly, this degree of respect for our cultures did not last long.

As time went on, missionary efforts quickly became ever more determined to sever our spiritual connections with our Anishinaabe ancestors, with the land upon which these are based, and with all of creation. Such efforts to settle, colonize, and Christianize the people and lands of Red River and surrounding areas have led Manitoba to be jokingly called the "holy land" by Aboriginal people, because so many places in the province are named after saints.[11] The progression of the Christianization of Métis peoples continued via colonial systems.

Colonial Systems Influencing Métis Spirituality and Identity

The notorious residential school system has radically hindered opportunities for Métis people to follow Anishinaabe spirituality and significantly impacted Métis identity. While increasing attention is being paid to the impacts of residential schools on a national level, there is still much confusion surrounding Métis experiences within this system.

The Récollets and the Jesuits were among the first Europeans to create educational "schools" or "seminaries" within their missions for Native people, and quickly realized that the *young* were more malleable to assimilation, "especially when they were in the custody of the missionaries and removed from their nomadic traditions" (Huel 1996, 73). Grandin created the Catholic Indian residential education policy in the Northwest, basing his model on a reformatory prison for young offenders that he visited in France (120, 124–25). The official residential school period went from 1879 to 1986 (Milloy 1999, xiii, xvii). However, the Truth and Reconciliation Commission lists the final school closure as occurring in 1996 (TRC 2011).

Chrisjohn, Young, and Maraun (1997) describe the colonial rationale for such "education" as attempts to solve the "Indian Problem" and the "Métis Problem"; the federal government thought residential schools would be the most cost-effective way to assimilate Aboriginal peoples (70).[12] The residential school system was one of Canada's "primary methods of accelerating a genocidal agenda against Aboriginal people in Canada," which, along with the churches and Canadian government, "caused the systematic destruction of generations of Aboriginal children" (Logan 2007, 1). York writes that, "In

1920, the pretense of voluntary attendance was dropped and amendments to the Indian Act made school attendance *mandatory* for Indians" (York 1990, 23). Similarly, European-Canadians also had plans to utilize "education" to assimilate Métis people into the larger Euro-Canadian body (Logan 2006a, 2). Before residential schools, Métis children were taught traditionally by "example and experience" (Chartrand 2006, 13).

In the case of the Métis of the Red River area, extensive hunting and travelling left few opportunities for the children to receive a formal education (McCarthy 1990, 25; Chartrand 2006, 13). European authorities did not address formal education for Métis children until Métis nationhood was solidified at the turn of the nineteenth century (13). From 1800 to 1820, mission schools opened for the Métis in an effort to force them away from the bison hunt and toward agricultural settlement. In the Northwest, churches held significant influence over the Métis and would "grow a web of missionary schools set aside for the Metis" (Logan 2007, 12).

Official policy on whether or not the Métis should be forced, or even allowed, to attend residential schools seems to have shifted whenever it suited the government's agenda. In the early twentieth century, Métis who lived on road allowance or in non-Aboriginal communities were often left out of consistent education; on the other hand, many Métis were forced to attend, others (especially Catholic Métis) requested to attend, and still others made up the majority at some schools in the West (Logan 2007, 2, 4). Moreover, the Métis who were turned away from federal-run residential schools for being "too White" were often turned away from provincial schools for being "too Indian" (67).

Indian Affairs developed guidelines in admitting "Halfbreed" students to residential schools (Chartrand, Logan, and Daniels 2006, 15). As during the treaty-making process, a class system was developed to "judge the quality of the Métis that would be allowed entrance into the schools" (Chartrand 2006, 18). A team of school officials from Manitoba, Saskatchewan, and Alberta classified the Métis into three classes, roughly: those who lived "the ordinary settled life of the country"; those who lived "the Indian mode of life"; and those who were "the illegitimate offspring of Indian women" and did not have a White father (Chartrand 2006, 18; Logan 2006b, 72–73). Basically, "the closer the government thought the Métis were to First Nations communities in a geographical or societal sense, the lower class of persons they were deemed to be" (Chartrand 2006, 19). This lower class had priority over other Métis when being considered for admission to residential schools, the rationale being that "such schooling was necessary to ensure these Métis would be 'civilized'" (20). Moreover, further distinguishing between these classes occurred with the evaluation of physical and phenotypical attributes of Métis children, such as skin and hair colour, which also affected their admittance.

Throughout the course of the residential school period, there were a number of other factors that contributed to the likelihood that Métis children would be admitted into the schools. These factors included, but were not limited to, the per-capita attendance system (more attendees equalled more funding), the social class hierarchy, the religious denomination of the school, the location of the school, Métis family history, church influence, and government influence (Logan 2007, 72). The greatest influences were the individual churches and dioceses (75; Milloy 1999, 53), with Catholic schools having the most Métis attendees (Chartrand 2006, 51); still other churches, without federal funding, set up schools specifically for the Métis, such as St. Paul's in Saskatchewan (Logan 2006a, 9).

With the federal government's development of its official policy vis-à-vis Métis rights, official tolerance of Métis attendance at residential schools dissolved. With the explicit directive from Ottawa, in 1911, to severely limit access to residential schools for Métis children, Métis status had to be disguised further in order for school fees to be paid by the department, or else the fees had to be covered by the churches (Daniels 2006, 147). After 1885, most Métis found themselves landless and illegally squatting on Crown land that had been set aside for road allowances (to be used in the construction of future roads or the railroad); they became known as the "road allowance people," and, since they did not pay taxes on the land, they could not send their children to public school (which led to further economic and social marginalization). By the 1930s, most Métis were excluded from formal education due to federal government policy (Chartrand 2006, 20). All this left many Métis in the lower class structure, which was created, in part, by the schools (2).

Determining the actual number of Métis attendees at residential schools is very difficult, especially given the silence both from the government and, until recently, from the Métis themselves. According to the Indian Residential Schools (IRS) Data Project (hereafter Data Project), which based its conclusions on the 1991 *Aboriginal Peoples Survey*, 9.12 percent of Métis people in Canada who self-identified as Métis had attended Indian residential schools (Daniels 2006, 115; Logan 2006a, 9, 12; Logan 2008, 84–85).[13] The majority of these Métis students attended residential schools in the three Prairie provinces, comprising 18.75 percent of Alberta attendees, 15.69 percent in Manitoba, and 8.05 percent in Saskatchewan (Daniels 2006, 115).

The effects of such schooling on Aboriginal people have been devastating and incalculable. Horrendous rates of physical, sexual, cultural, and spiritual abuse, as well as incredible death rates, have left a legacy of pain on all Aboriginal people, even those who are not direct survivors of residential schools. In many schools, a portion of each day was dedicated to manual labour, which has been described by former students as "slavery" and "forced labour" (Logan 2007, 102). To compensate for tuition deficits and lack of space in classrooms, the Métis students specifically would sometimes be assigned more work duties (102–3) since they were viewed as being less in need of colonization than "full blood Indian" students. Severe physical and sexual abuse often occurred in combination with other forms of abuse, such as intellectual, linguistic, emotional, and spiritual abuse. Children from four to sixteen years old were subjected to such abuse in a manner that cut across racial and class distinctions between Métis and First Nations students (98–99). Children often attended funerals of their young friends, and the children who died were often used as examples of punishment for bad behaviour (109).

Spiritual, cultural, and linguistic abuses were also rampant at residential schools. At the same time that Aboriginal children were forced to learn European ways of knowing, they were also forced to "forget" their ancestral ways. Some children tried hard to resist this forced forgetting; for example, by holding secretive puberty rituals (Logan 2007, 102; Grant 2004, 125). Nevertheless, the combination of religious and educational instruction proved potent. One famous example of such racist cultural and spiritual abuse is found in *L'Échelle de Lacombe* (Lacombe's ladder), which depicts two pathways leading to Judgment Day, the left side being the *Voie du Bien* (Way of Good) leading to God and the right being the *Voie du Mal* (Way of Evil) complete with illustrations of devils and evil spirits leading to Hell (J. Miller 2006, 191). Aboriginal children, the students, were taught that the left side was the path of Europeans and the right side was the path of Native peoples who did not convert to Christianity. Former students recall the messages loud and clear: "if you stay Indian you'll end up in hell" (191). Moreover, "The children were told that they should prevent their parents from going to Sun Dances because Sun Dance was forbidden by God" (York 1990, 41). Similar threats were administered against children caught speaking their own Aboriginal language, including Michif (Chartrand 2006, 15), and against left-handed children.[14]

In addition to these forms of abuse, Métis students experienced cultural abuse pertaining to their Métis identity. According to Chartrand (2006), the educational experiences of Métis youth varied and depended more on perceived identity and lifestyle than on any formal legal classifications (18). Often those Métis who were identified as having much in common with their First Nations relatives were viewed more negatively than those who identified more with their European relatives. Métis students were often immediately placed in "the 'Half-Breed' class" and those "who may have previously thought of themselves as family to First Nations families, were taught by Residential School that they were 'Half-Breeds'" (Logan 2007, 98).[15] Despite how the children perceived themselves, the nuns and priests taught the children that Métis and First Nations were differently located from one another socially, thereby arguably creating such distinctions.

As the atrocities of the residential school system became public, it has become apparent that all Aboriginal people are experiencing the intergenerational effects of residential schools whether or not they are direct survivors. Cultural trauma and the "Residential School Syndrome" also affect Métis people today (Logan 2007, 51, 54). Métis survivors are coming to terms with the reality that "much of the loss of traditional culture and language was a direct result of the residential school and its treatment of Métis communities" (Chartrand 2006, 21). Logan explains that "the Métis that later identified themselves as French, Ukrainian or British to gain services or escape racial persecution often picked up these tactics as learned behaviours from Residential School" (Logan 2007, 101).

By 1992, most churches had issued apologies to the Aboriginal people of Canada for their involvement in the residential school system (Milloy 1999, 299). In 1998, the federal government issued a Statement of Reconciliation (Daniels 2006, 100), and the Aboriginal Healing Foundation (AHF) was created to administer a one-time healing grant of $350 million from the federal government to support community initiatives to heal the legacy of physical and sexual abuse resulting from residential schools. Significantly, the Ontario Court of Appeals ruled that descendants of the students who had attended Indian residential schools have the ability to sue the federal government for "intentionally eradicating their culture" (100). On 11 June 2008, Prime Minister Stephen Harper, on behalf of the Canadian government and Canadians, apologized to survivors of residential schools; however, many have denounced this as insincere lip service, especially considering subsequent heavy funding cuts to Aboriginal organizations, continued poor treatment of Aboriginal peoples at the hands of the government, and ongoing refusal of a national inquiry into the nearly 1,200 cases of missing and murdered Aboriginal women in Canada over the past thirty years (Leblanc 2014).

While Métis people technically are included in the common experience payments according to section 14.01 of the Indian Residential Schools Settlement Agreement, there are barriers that deny Métis eligibility for these compensation packages. One barrier is that many schools that were attended by former Métis students are not included in the list of schools that are considered "residential schools." According to the Métis National Council, the vast majority of Métis survivors are being denied financial compensation because boarding schools specifically for Métis and non-status Indians are excluded from the Settlement Agreement (Chartier 2010). As a result, Métis survivors and their families are being denied access to compensation and programs, such as the Non-Insured Health Benefits Program. No provincial or territorial government has yet to offer specific programs for Métis people (Daniels 2006, 23).[16]

On 18 June 2010, Métis National Council President Clément Chartier—himself a residential school survivor—issued a press release coinciding with the TRC's first national event in Winnipeg. Chartier highlights the fact that the schools that Métis attended were nonetheless church-run, government-sanctioned institutions aimed at assimilating the Métis: "Métis Survivors endured the same forced separation from family and community, the same attacks on their culture, and in many instances were victims of the same physical and sexual abuse as those who attended the schools covered by the settlement agreement" (Chartier 2010, A17). Until the exclusion of Métis people from the Apology and compensation is addressed, there can be no closure to the legacy of residential schools and healing will be incomplete (Chartier 2010, A17).

By the time the residential school system began, Métis people had already been exposed to relentless missionary efforts; residential schools were simply the latest form of colonization Métis people were experiencing. In the schools, aggressive efforts were made to convert Métis children to Christianity and induce shame regarding Aboriginal cultural identity and spirituality. That Métis people are being systematically excluded from compensation and healing from the impacts of residential schools reflects ongoing government efforts to divide Métis and First Nations people and make us compete against each other for resources and recognition on our healing journeys.

Métis People and the Child Welfare System

The child welfare system has been yet another tactic used against Aboriginal people and cultures, with the purpose of aggressive assimilation into the dominant Euro-Canadian culture. Once again, Aboriginal children were targeted and stolen from their families, but instead of being placed in residential schools they were usually placed with White families far from their home communities, many never able to return. The consequences of this system are similar to those experienced as a result of the residential school system, including loss of identity, language, culture, and connection to ancestral spirituality.

There are differences and similarities between the experiences of Métis, non-status, and status Indian children across the history of the child welfare system, because they were placed in different categories in the eyes of the government. As described in the final report of the Manitoba Aboriginal Justice Inquiry, "Both Metis and non-status Indians have been considered, for jurisdiction purposes, a part of the *non-Aboriginal* population by the federal and provincial governments" (AJI 1999, emphasis added; Barkwell, Longclaws, and Chartrand 1989, 33). This is consistent with these governments' longstanding goal of assimilation of Aboriginal peoples and their continual denial of Aboriginal status for Métis people. In Manitoba, the child welfare system did not begin to impact status Indian children seriously until the 1950s. However, since the government considered Métis children White, they were subjected to the child welfare system, apprehended and placed in (White) homes for decades longer than status children (ibid.).

In Manitoba, the first Child Protection Act dates from 1889 under the government of Thomas Greenway, who established a child protection system based on the Ontario model; the Act added two new types of organizations to the private orphanages and child-care institutions already in the field: the Children's Aid Societies (CASs) and the Superintendent of Neglected and Dependent Children (SNC) (Hurl 1984, para. 2). The CASs concerned themselves with children in the organized municipalities; private child-care institutions concerned themselves with orphans and dependent children; and the SNC acted as a CAS for the unorganized territories (ibid., para. 3). There were rifts across all three, including fighting over funding and resources, competing for children to fill their beds, and religious denominational fighting. In 1916, the Mothers Allowance scheme was added to the child welfare system in Manitoba, followed by the establishment of the Public Welfare Commission the following year. The latter was tasked with undertaking a study and reporting to the provincial legislature on all phases of charitable welfare in the province, especially child welfare; from this study came the 1922–1924 Child Welfare Act (ibid., para. 10). Following this, the first foster homes were established, and, in the 1950s, the first group homes (AJI 1999). As "non-Indians," Métis children were subjected to all these policies.

In terms of status Indian children and the child welfare system, in 1951, amendments to the Indian Act (section 88) allowed provincial governments to provide child welfare services to First Nations within their reserve communities. According to Pompana (2009), where no mention was made of services—for example, education, child welfare, health, and justice—the provincial governments were to provide services to Indians, usually through cost-shared agreements (34). However, before 1966, status Indians usually received no services due to federal and provincial fighting over who was responsible for them; the provinces provided services only to Indians in life-and-death situations (35). Child welfare services to Indian reserve communities began in earnest with the Children's Aid Society (CAS) in 1966, whereby White social workers would take children from reserves and place them in White middle-class homes (36–38). This came about because of the 1966 Hawthorne Report, a survey of life on reserves for Canada's Aboriginal peoples undertaken by the Department of Indian Affairs and Northern Development (AJI 1999). The same year, the federal government signed an agreement with the provinces to share the costs of extending social services in Aboriginal communities. Aboriginal people were not consulted about these changes, nor were there any commitments to preserve Aboriginal cultures or to provide for local Aboriginal control over child welfare services; these services were delivered by non-Aboriginal agencies and social workers (ibid.).

From the 1960s to the early 1980s, thousands of Aboriginal children were sent to homes of White middle-class couples in Canada and the United States (and sometimes Europe) on the assumption that these couples would make better parents than low-income families on First Nations reserves and in Métis communities (York 1990, 202). There was a strong demand from these families, so it was easy for the child welfare authorities to place the children in White homes. By the early 1980s, approximately 40 to 60 percent of all children removed from their natural families in western Canada were First Nations or Métis (York 1990, 206; Barkwell, Longclaws, and Chartrand 1989, 34). In the province of Manitoba alone, an estimated 3,000 Aboriginal children were removed from their homes and sent by child welfare agencies to couples outside the province (York 1990, 206). Even when agencies did consider placing the children in other Aboriginal homes, their Eurocentric selection process made it difficult for Aboriginal families to adopt Aboriginal children. York (1990) explains that, "agencies often required parents to have a steady income, a good home, and a separate bedroom for each child—clearly an impossible standard for parents on most northern reserves.... 'Whole reserves may be left out of the adoption process because they don't have running water'" (215).

In the late 1970s and early 1980s, Manitoba's Aboriginal leaders, increasingly angry with the province's child welfare policies, "protested the permanent loss of their children—the disappearance of a generation whose cultural identity had been wiped out. They called it 'cultural genocide'" (York 1990, 213–14). Rejecting the Eurocentric child welfare system, the Dakota Ojibway Tribal Council had established an Aboriginal-controlled child welfare agency in southwestern Manitoba by 1981. Then, on 6 March 1982, responding to severe pressure from Aboriginal leaders and the media, the Manitoba government agreed to impose a moratorium on the export of Aboriginal children outside the province (214). Moreover, a provincial inquiry began, headed by family court judge Edwin Kimelman, in order to study the fate of Aboriginal children in the child welfare system.

Surprisingly, Judge Kimelman agreed with Aboriginal leaders not only that Aboriginal children taken from their families by the child welfare system had been victims of cultural genocide, but also that the provincial child welfare policy was remarkably similar to the old policy of sending Aboriginal children to residential schools (214). As part of the inquiry, Kimelman interviewed staff from several child welfare agencies in Manitoba and determined that each one "'seemed abysmally uninformed about native value systems.' They were insensitive to the cultural values of native people and did not understand native attitudes toward child rearing" (216). Aboriginal ways and values that were ignored included the concept of a child as a member of the total community (as opposed to just a nuclear family), the encouragement of young mothers to stay in the homes of their extended families, and giving the child a great deal of independence and freedom. Moreover, First Nations children stolen in this way were never told that they were entitled to certain treaty rights and privileges because of their status as treaty Indians (217).

By the late 1980s, the National Métis Council was arguing that a disproportionate number of Métis children were being taken into care (Barkwell, Longclaws, and Chartrand 1989, 34). After the Kimelman Report, in 1982, the Manitoba Métis Federation (MMF) established a Board Committee responsible for the Métis Child and Family Support Program. In 1984, the MMF signed the first Memorandum of Agreement with the provincial government (Policy Directive 18); another agreement was signed the following year regarding the MMF's role in the placement of Aboriginal children outside of Aboriginal homes (the MMF is only notified when the client self-declares as Métis) (Barkwell, Longclaws, and Chartrand 1989, 46). The Kimelman inquiry also recommended that Manitoba send dozens of letters to the United States to pave the way for the stolen children to return home (York 1990, 219). As a result of this inquiry and resistance by Aboriginal leaders, in 1984, the Manitoba government launched a campaign to help the shocking number of adopted children return to their home communities and established a clear policy to ensure that child welfare agencies make a thorough effort to find Aboriginal homes for Aboriginal children before considering any non-Aboriginal homes (219). In the period between January 1988 and October 1989, 29.2 percent of registered Indian adoptees went into non-Aboriginal homes, while 55.8 percent of Métis adoptees went into non-Aboriginal homes; furthermore, more than 62 percent of all Aboriginal children placed by way of adoption were Métis (49). Despite this, according to Barkwell, Longclaws, and Chartrand (1989), from 1987 to 1989, the MMF had received annual funding of only $140,000 for child welfare activities, while Indian agencies received $8 million annually (46).

On 18 April 1989, the government of Manitoba launched the Aboriginal Justice Inquiry (AJI), a public inquiry into the relationship between Aboriginal peoples and the justice system in Manitoba; Chapter 14 of this inquiry focuses on the child welfare system. In a submission to the AJI, the MMF argued that the single largest cause of the overrepresentation of Métis offenders in the justice system was the treatment of Métis children within the child and family service system (34). The recommendations of the 1991 *Aboriginal Justice Inquiry Report* were ignored for nearly ten years; then, based on the recommendations, negotiations began for the devolution of child welfare services (Bourassa 2010, 4). At the time of the AJI, existing Aboriginal child and family service agencies provided services only to status Indians; the only non-status or Métis children who received services were those living on reserves (4).

The Metis Child, Family and Community Services Agency received a formal mandate from the Province of Manitoba to deliver child and family services province-wide on 13 September 2003; following this, the Child and Family Services Authorities Act was proclaimed on 24 November 2003. By 2006, four new authorities existed in Manitoba: the First Nations of Northern Manitoba Child and Family Services Authority, the First Nations of Southern Manitoba Child and Family Services Authority, the Métis Child and Family Services Authority, and the General Child and Family Services Authority (5). The Aboriginal-controlled child welfare agencies in Manitoba were established under tripartite agreements between the federal government, the Manitoba government, and the tribal councils of each region; they are funded by Ottawa and efforts are made to hire more Aboriginal staff (York 1990, 219–20). The Manitoba Métis Federation is now consulted on child welfare decisions affecting Métis children.

The parallels between the residential school system and the child welfare system, and their consequences, are undeniable. Métis and First Nations families were evaluated by the Eurocentric government child welfare system and children were taken from homes considered "unfit" by Euro-Canadian standards. Measures taken by child welfare and social services included using the residential school system, from the 1930s to the 1950s, to take away children, as well as taking away family allowance cheques for residential school "tuition" (95). In 1982, the Kimelman inquiry determined that the seizure of "Indian" (and Métis) children escalated just as the residential schools were winding down in the 1960s (York 1990, 214–15). Logan (2008) argues that the child welfare system was "ideologically an extension of the residential school model" whereby the White social worker, following hard on the heels of the missionary, the priest, and the Indian agent, was convinced that the only hope for the salvation of the Indian people lay in the removal of their children (81). Apprehension of Indian children by CAS paralleled the compulsory attendance of Indian children at residential schools; this system exacerbated the problems caused by the schools in First Nations (and Métis) communities, and had largely the same effects (Pompana 2009, 37). It is estimated that there are "three times more Aboriginal children in the care of child welfare authorities now than were placed in residential schools at the height of those operations in the 1940s" (Blackstock 2003). According to the 2011 National Household Survey, "of the roughly 30,000 children aged 14 and under in Canada who were in foster care, nearly half (48.1 percent) were Aboriginal children. In 2011, 14,225 or 3.6 percent of Aboriginal children were foster children, compared with 0.3 percent of non-Aboriginal children" (Statistics Canada 2013b).[17]

The intergenerational effects of the child welfare system are similar to the effects of the residential school system for Aboriginal children who survived these systems, but also for their families, their communities, and Aboriginal peoples in general. York (1990) describes these effects as a form of post-traumatic stress disorder (PTSD) and "symptoms of cultural confusion," because the stolen Aboriginal children had no one to teach them how to be proud to be Aboriginal (220). Instead, as was the case in the residential school system, they were taught to be ashamed of being Aboriginal, and some children experienced various forms of abuse as well as daily efforts to convert them to Christianity (226). Since the extended family had traditionally been the primary social unit in Aboriginal communities, the child welfare system also damaged a distinct way of life, resulting in a "serious weakening of

Indian and Métis society" (219). Combined with these assaults on Aboriginal cultures, Aboriginal children were never taught how to speak the languages that their relatives spoke. Those who were eventually able to return to their biological families suffered the effects of estrangement and alienation, among others. They sometimes felt "like a white person in a native community" (209), or their families saw them in that way and now feared them; some attempted suicide (226–27).

As a result of extensive numbers of First Nations and Métis children being submerged into a foreign culture, "their native identity soon disappeared. They became a lost generation" (206). Again, similar to the effects of the residential school system, those of the child welfare system have spilled over into the rest of Aboriginal communities. For example, the disproportionate rate of Aboriginal people in jails is not an unrelated coincidence, and Aboriginal children are still over-represented in the child welfare system today (219).

In summary, colonial policies and legislation (such as the Indian Act and its amendments) have taken away Aboriginal peoples' right to name and define themselves, have externalized Métis people, and have purposely created divisions between Métis and First Nations people. Indeed, for Métis people to explore spirituality otherwise associated with "Indianness," breaking down these colonial categories is essential.[18] The history of Christianization among Métis people has had similar effects, and has been very effective at inhibiting Métis people from developing meaningful relationships with Anishinaabe spirituality over time. Moreover, colonial systems (such as the residential school and child welfare systems) have continued to usurp Aboriginal peoples' rights to define ourselves, have continued to create false divisions between us, and have nearly severed our relationships with Anishinaabe spirituality. In addition, the colonial and historical context discussed in this chapter illustrates the existence of diverse and common experiences among different Aboriginal groups. This colonial history has created devastating intergenerational consequences for all Aboriginal peoples that continue to directly affect contemporary realities of Métis identities and the relationships of Métis with First Nations peoples, as well as with traditional Anishinaabe spirituality.

CHAPTER 4

A Métis Anishinaabe Study

It took me a long time to realize ... that other aspect of willingness to include that spirituality in life. See, that's that part we don't always talk about in academia because people think you're nuts. We don't talk about it.

—Laara, participant

Indigenous voices have also been suppressed in the creation of knowledge in academia; our world views, ways of learning, and knowledge have not been welcome in universities. Until recently, only Western paradigms and methodologies were considered legitimate (Guba and Lincoln 1998, 217).[1] This has prevented the creation of new knowledge from Indigenous perspectives and ensured that academia remained a colonial institution. Being forced to work within Western standards in these ways leads to *cognitive assimilation* (colonization of Aboriginal minds);[2] the lack of space in academia for Indigenous methodologies has also been called "methodological discrimination" (Kovach 2009, 13). Despite this, Indigenous scholars are working "to articulate their own research paradigms, their own approaches to research, and their own data collection methods in order to honor an Indigenous paradigm" (S. Wilson 2003, 166; Gaywish 2008, 70, 74).

According to Cree scholar Shawn Wilson (2001), Indigenous ontologies (world views/what we believe about reality), epistemologies (how we come to know), axiologies (system of ethics and values), and methodologies (guidelines for arriving at new knowledge) are fundamentally different from European paradigms (176). Indigenous research involves lifelong learning and relationship-building (S. Wilson 2003, 168), centring Indigenous voices (Rigney 1999, 141), and the belief that "research is a ceremony" (S. Wilson 2008, 11). An Anishinaabe world view teaches us that spirit is everywhere and that to live a good life we must be balanced physically, mentally, emotionally, and spiritually. In Maracle's words, "Spirituality is re-connecting with the self and with our ancestry. It is doing the right thing for our family and our community" (Maracle 1996, 134). These beliefs inform our work as

Indigenous scholars, including developing Indigenous methodologies and doing Indigenous research.[3] This resonates with the Seven Fires Prophecy; Simpson (2008b) suggests that one of the tasks of the Oshkibimaadiziig is "recovering and maintaining Indigenous world views and applying those teachings in a contemporary context" (15).

I have taken up this challenge and designed a Métis Anishinaabe study centred upon Anishinaabe knowledge learned through ceremony (especially Three Fires Midewiwin). Key Anishinaabe principles guide my world view, my relationship with knowledge, my personal ethics and values system, and the way I approached this research. I also incorporated select Euro-Canadian research tools.

Métis Anishinaabe World View

For the Anishinaabeg, everything begins with and leads back to Creation; everything is accounted for in our Creation Stories and *aatsokaanag* (sacred stories, legends). I have often heard Elders say we must know who we are and where we come from if we hope to learn why we are here and where we are going. Creation Stories help us come to these understandings and pursue *mino-bimaadiziwin* (good life, good relations). Since time immemorial, these teachings have been transmitted through the generations orally and through writing systems, which include *wiigwas* (birchbark) scrolls, petroglyphs and petroforms, wampum belts, and "Medicine Wheels" made of stones and boulders.

In the Seventh Fire of Creation, Gichi Manidoo (Creator) was ready to bring forth humankind, so s/he took four parts from the first woman (Mother Earth) to create Original Man and lowered him to the Earth; from this one came the Anishinaabeg (Benton-Banai 1988, 2–3; Simpson 2011, 39). Gichi Manidoo created four Original Peoples: Yellow, Red, Black, and White.[4] Each corresponds with a cardinal direction and was given distinct gifts, responsibilities, and Original Instructions for *mino-bimaadiziwin*. Today, all people can trace their lineage back to these Original Peoples. Anishinaabeg are descendants of the Red People, and Caucasians are descendants of the White People.

I believe that, as Métis people, we trace our lineage back to the Original Red People *and* the Original White People. In the Midewiwin Lodge, I have heard that "you cannot walk both (or two) paths." I believe this has to do with the Original Instructions; in other words, Métis people are welcome to honour both lineages but we are encouraged to walk one path. I have come to this understanding partly as a result of two other teachings from Grand Chief Benton-Banai: *We should never be ashamed of who we are*, and *It only takes one drop of Anishinaabe blood to be Anishinaabe* (and thus enjoy the birthright to an Anishinaabe identity, teachings, ceremonies, and ways of life).[5] I myself identify as Métis Anishinaabe-Kwe and try my best to walk the path of my Anishinaabe ancestors who descend from the original Red people because it resonates more within my spirit; part of my path in life includes learning how to live this way while also honouring my father and our ancestors who descend from the original White people.

In other words, Anishinaabe Creation Stories inform my identity and enable me to understand my place in Creation as Métis Anishinaabe-Kwe and to live my life accordingly on a daily basis. *Endaso-giizhigad Métis Anishinaabe-Kwe ndaaw miinawa abiding Mide-Kwe ndaaw*: I am Métis Anishinaabe-Kwe and First Degree Midewiwin every day. My identity informs every decision I make. My decision to undertake this topic of study is deeply tied to my identity, but is also informed by my understanding of the Seven Fires Prophecy.

According to an Anishinaabe world view, we understand the world from our own experience and it is from there that we can speak. This belief was echoed when a friend encouraged Métis researcher Jannine Carriere to choose a research topic that reflected her own experiences (in her case adoption): "You should be doing this research on adoption. This is who you are, this is your story and this is what you should be contributing" (quoted in Kovach 2009, 105). In a spiritual (and literal) sense, the Seven Fires Prophecy is the story of all Indigenous peoples, including all Métis peoples; it is also my own personal and family history. Therefore, it makes sense that I have arrived at the topic of Métis relationships with Anishinaabe spirituality and identity.

Just as our creation stories help me understand who I am as Métis Anishinaabe-Kwe, the Seven Fires Prophecy provides additional guidance for understanding our role as Métis people in creation. This prophecy has so deeply influenced my world view that it has become part of my life's work: encouraging Métis (and other Aboriginal) people to relearn our place in creation from an Anishinaabe perspective; with this book, I contribute to this work. These understandings influence my relationships in creation, including my research relationships.

In *Treaty Elders of Saskatchewan: Our Dream Is that Our Peoples Will One Day Be Clearly Recognized As Nations*, Cardinal and Hildebrandt (2000) define the Nêhiyáw concept of *miskâsowin* as "Finding one's sense of origin and belonging, finding 'one's self,' or finding 'one's centre'" (21). They employ this concept to discuss the importance of remembering the spirit of the treaties and creation stories in order to heal from colonization and relearn how to live in a balanced way (21–24). Similarly, Kovach (2009) explains "*Miskâsowin* is a Nêhiyáw term that means going to the centre of yourself to find your own belonging" (179). Fluent Anishinaabemowin speaker Charlie Nelson generously shared with me a similar concept in that language: *mikwayndaasowin*. According to Nelson, *mikwayndaasowin* means "recalling, or remembering, that which was there before," and this "can include the knowledge of our past, and our beginnings" (pers. comm.).

My growing awareness of the concepts of *mikwayndaasowin* and *miskâsowin* encourages me to keep learning about our collective past as Anishinaabeg (indeed, as all Original Peoples), and my own personal sense of belonging in creation and within my own self. As a part of creation, my relationships are endless and include human beings, spirit beings, sky beings, water beings, flying beings, and so on. This again brings me back to *mino-bimaadiziwin*: given that I am related to everything in creation, I have responsibilities toward all beings to live in a good way that promotes health and balance. Spending time with Elders and participating in ceremony helps me learn how to accomplish this.

The concepts of *mikwayndaasowin* and *mino-bimaadiziwin* also remind me of the importance of doing research in a good way. As an Indigenous researcher, I always want to nurture and honour relationships in the research context and promote *mino-bimaadiziwin*. If I am paying close attention and doing research from my heart, I will also come to know more about who I am in creation. In a research context, this deepening self-awareness and understanding can occur in relation to research concepts, participants, goals, and findings.

Métis Anishinaabe Relationship to Knowledge

My relationship to knowledge is also informed by my Métis Anishinaabe-Kwe perspective. For me, "thinking Anishinaabe" essentially means understanding the world from an Anishinaabe perspective; it is a call to live life according to Anishinaabe beliefs (like our Original Instructions), values (like *mino-bimaadiziwin*), and ways of being (like Midewiwin). Thinking Anishinaabe has been a steep learning curve for me because I did not grow up with traditional teachings or Anishinaabemowin. Some may wonder if it is possible to learn to "think Anishinaabe" without being a fluent speaker. While certainly some things are lost in translation, we still have connections to spirit, ancestors, cultural heritage, and ceremony, which I believe make it possible to learn how to "think Anishinaabe" *over a lifetime*.

It is a result of colonization that so many Aboriginal people no longer know our languages. Three Fires Midewiwin Grand Chief Benton-Banai has received direction from spirit not to leave anyone behind just because, through no fault of their own, they do not know the language. The Three Fires Midewiwin lodge translates most things into English so everyone can understand. This helps me learn how to "think Anishinaabe." Taking Anishinaabemowin courses and using the language whenever possible also helps. Janice Acoose (2008) does this by "substituting English with Nêhiyaw and Nahkawè in strategic textual places" (221). She points out that Nêhiyaw scholar Neal McLeod (2007) does this in his book *Cree Narrative Memory*. According to Acoose (2008), McLeod "bundles medicine Nehiyâwiwin words into the fabric of written English. As the medicine-powered words transfuse the text, organisms within the cultural body become revitalized. McLeod's ritualizing critical performance adheres to important cultural protocol that honors Nehiyâwiwin being, both spiritual and physical" (223). Likewise, I have tried my best to include "medicine words" and concepts throughout this book.

For me, "thinking Anishinaabe" is also a reminder that colonization has deeply affected us all. We must make efforts to decolonize our minds of the destructive values, beliefs, and ways of being that come from a colonial mentality and divorce us from our own Anishinaabe systems of thought and being. Daily, I try to "think Anishinaabe" or "think Midewiwin" with every decision I make. The more I participate in ceremony and learn the teachings, the more naturally this comes. I have tried my best to "think Anishinaabe" throughout this journey, from my choice of topic, to the ways I relate to the participants, to the goals of this book.

Knowing where to look for answers is directly linked to thinking Anishinaabe. Anishinaabeg recognize that sources of knowledge include dreams, ceremonies, prayer, and personal experience, and that important teachings may be given by all living beings (Ermine 1995; Dumont 1979, 1990; Gaywish 2008; and Benton-Banai 1988). Teachings can come from any being, at any time, anywhere.

Marlene Brant Castellano (1998) speaks of two primary types of knowledge that are especially valued in Aboriginal cultures: "empirical knowledge gained through careful observation ... by many persons over extended time periods," and "revealed knowledge ... acquired through dreams, visions, and intuitions that are understood to be spiritual in origin" (23–24). Kovach (2009) explains that, "from a Nêhiýaw epistemology, attention to inward knowing is not optional. From a traditional Cree perspective, seeking out Elders, attending to holistic epistemologies, and participating in cultural catalyst activities (dream, ceremony, prayer) are all means for accessing inward knowledge" (49–50).

In addition to learning from books and professors, it has also been important for me to stay close to the teachings, practise daily prayer, work with traditional medicines regularly, and consult my spiritual advisors throughout this research journey. Early in this process, I participated in a traditional fasting camp for guidance from spirit on what topic to choose for this study. On the third night without food and water, spirit communicated with me through a dream. When the fast was over, I approached one of the ceremony-makers with *asemaa* (tobacco) for help to understand the dream. I now believe spirit was helping me understand the generations of disconnection of Métis people from our ancestral Anishinaabe spiritual ways and the importance of reconnecting and remembering our place in creation.

This brings to mind a conversation I once had with a Métis friend in which she emotionally referred to us—Métis people—as *the lost children*, but at the time was not able to articulate why. Pitawanakwat (2008), a scholar with mixed Aboriginal ancestry, echoes this sentiment when he states, "The trouble with being (almost) assimilated is that I know something is missing but I am not sure what" (161). I have come to understand that many Aboriginal people feel this inexplicable sense of loss because colonization has forced us to forget the Original Instructions given to us by creator; this can lead to living life feeling lost, unbalanced, and spiritually unfulfilled. In this way, fasting and a message from spirit helped shape my research topic (and my life's work).

When knowledge (especially spiritual knowledge) is shared with you, you have a responsibility to incorporate it into your daily life for the greater good. Cora Weber-Pillwax (2001) states, "I had a vision about something I was to do, a vision that has not been completely fulfilled, but it is still unfolding.... Now I ha[ve] the responsibility to do something about it" (166–67). Often the responsibility to act upon the knowledge we receive is understood to be lifelong. When we gain access to other levels of reality through dreams and ceremony, we take on the responsibility of maintaining a lifelong relationship with creation in this way (Dumont 1979, 38). Moreover, we must also give ourselves time to integrate the knowledge so we can be of use to our community (Kovach 2009, 50). Kovach shares that such responsibility resulting from "guidance from dreams and spirit became a part of [her own] research," and names this "spiritual methodology" (ibid. 58–59).

In this way, it becomes easy to understand that, according to Indigenous researcher Shawn Wilson, "Indigenous research is a life-changing ceremony" (2003, 169). Wilson (2008) argues, "If research doesn't change you as a person, then you aren't doing it right" (83). In other words, I have a personal responsibility to make use of knowledge I receive through spirit, as well as that shared by the participants. Through my dream, I have a responsibility to help other Métis people return to *mino-bimaadiziwin*; this book is one way that I can work toward fulfilling this responsibility.

Métis Anishinaabe Values and Ethics

My personal ethics and values are also based on my Métis Anishinaabe-Kwe perspective and have influenced this project. By this point, it should already be obvious that *relationships* are central to the way I understand reality and knowledge, and the way I approach research. Shawn Wilson (2008) highlights the importance of relationships and relational accountability in Indigenous research; they "can be put into practice through choice of research topic, methods of data collection, form of analysis and presentation of information" (7). He goes on to state, "reality is in the relationship that one has with the truth. Thus an object or thing is not as important as one's relationship to it" (73). Here, Wilson begins to lay out the importance of relationships in Indigenous research paradigms from the beginning to the end of the research process. He also touches upon another principle that guides my own values when conducting research: relational accountability.

There is a fundamental value among the Anishinaabeg of being accountable to all of your relations in creation; this is one way to strive towards *mino-bimaadiziwin*. It can also be a guiding value for conducting ethical research. The system of ethics and values in Indigenous research is built upon *relational accountability*; it is about, according to Wilson, "fulfilling a role and obligations in the research relationship—that is, being accountable to your relations.... Respect, reciprocity and responsibility are key features of any healthy relationship and must be included" in Indigenous research (2008, 77).

The *ethic of reciprocity* stems from the Anishinaabe understanding of reality as essentially spiritual and interdependent, and the importance of balance. According to Nêhiyaw scholar Herman Michell (1999), "When you take something from nature, balance is disrupted. And when balance is disrupted, there is a need for the restoration of harmony" (6). He continues, "when you take a story from a person, you are taking something from that person. You are taking something from nature that leads to the disruption of balance" (9). Likewise, Nêhiyaw Elder Pauline Shirt's grandmother would "finish telling a story with 'now you owe me'" (quoted in Anderson 2011, 23). When such knowledge is shared with you, you can offer the knowledge holder a gift, such as *asemaa* (tobacco), to restore the balance.

Similarly, balance may be disrupted when participants share their stories in an interview, and balance must be restored. With this in mind, I offered *asemaa* to each participant when asking if they would participate in an interview. I also had occasion to practise accountability when I accidentally divulged the identity (to another participant) of one of the people who wanted to remain anonymous in this study. I approached Mide-Kwe Gaywish for advice; she suggested I approach both participants with *asemaa* to explain what I had done and to apologize. First, I offered a tobacco tie to the one to whom I had divulged the information; the person smiled, accepted my *asemaa*, and said, "Of course, my girl, I haven't told anyone—not even my partner—and I will not. We all make mistakes; don't beat yourself up over it," and chuckled. Next, I offered *asemaa* to the person whose identity I had revealed; I apologized and asked if they wanted to withdraw from the study. This participant also chuckled and replied, "Oh, that's okay. I'm not even sure why I wanted to remain anonymous in the first place. Don't lose sleep over it or anything, Chantal. I still want to stay in the study." I felt really good about being able to remain accountable to the participants in that way. As Indigenous researchers, we must continue to respect the participants, their stories, and the research after it is done.

My spiritual advisors helped me remain accountable throughout this study; whenever I did not know how to proceed *in a good way*, I asked them for advice. Importantly, I put together a list of excerpts of my text where I talk about knowledge I have received from the Midewiwin lodge and Grand Chief Benton-Banai, and sent these with Mide-Kwe Gaywish when she travelled to visit him. After reviewing them, Benton-Banai gave full permission to include this knowledge in my book (24 September 2011). I did something similar with the section I wrote on the Spruce Woods Sundance and documentary; I showed the section to the Sundance Chiefs David and Sherryl Blacksmith to ensure accuracy and to invite feedback. They were pleased with the write-up, thanked me, and offered other important things for me to consider (21 August 2013).[6] I believe that, as Indigenous researchers, we must balance our use of sacred knowledge by ensuring we are also protecting it. Prayer, community input, and advice from spiritual advisors can help us do so.

Another Anishinaabe value I kept in my heart throughout this journey is *benefiting the greater good*. Wilson suggests that our communities are encouraging us, as Indigenous researchers, to focus on the positive. He writes:

> What I've learned from Elders while I've been doing this thinking
> is that focusing on the positive in Indigenous research focuses on
> harmony. It forms a relationship that pulls things together—they
> are linked. Making a connection in this way allows for growth and

positive change to take place. Researching the negative is focusing on and giving more power to disharmony. Its focus is alienation or lack of relationship and does nothing to form relations but rather can tear them apart. So we have an obligation as researchers to help others to see this. And I think this is what our communities are demanding. (S. Wilson 2008, 109)

He continues, "The strength of your bonds or relationships with the community is an equally valued component of your work" (81). Wilson suggests that building and strengthening relationships through research is another example of research as ceremony. He explains that relationships and space between people and their environment is sacred and can be strengthened when the space between them is lessened.

I have taken this demand by our communities to heart by choosing to focus on a topic that benefits our peoples by focusing on a positive aspect of our lives—Métis Anishinaabe healing journeys—which has the potential to build and strengthen Métis and Anishinaabe relationships and communities. I hope my research draws people together, lessens the space between us, and strengthens our collective healing.

Métis Anishinaabe Approach to Research

My world view, relationship to knowledge, and values and ethics are the foundation of my Métis Anishinaabe approach to research. *Methodology* means a set of rules and practices that the researcher follows in order to study a particular topic. In an Indigenous research paradigm, methodology is about relationships. If you want to understand someone or something better, you can increase your understanding of it by developing more relationships with it; this also presents opportunities to create new knowledge and theories about these relationships.

As a Métis Anishinaabe-Kwe researcher, I felt it made sense to incorporate both Indigenous and Western research tools in this study. Anishinaabe and Métis cultures are *alive* and have a history of incorporating useful knowledge and tools from other cultures if it contributes to a better life. Grand Chief Benton-Banai encourages us to *use the tools you have at hand*, including some Western technologies, to further the healing journey of our peoples. Nêhiyaw Métis author Maria Campbell (2011a) recalls a similar teaching from her Elder, the late Peter O'Chiese, encouraging her not to discount anthropological and ethnographic texts as a way to uncover more of our own stories (xviii). While I made use of select Western research tools to gather stories and to begin to make sense of them, the heart and spirit of this research is

Métis Anishinaabe. I believe that my use of both Western and Indigenous tools contributes to the strength of my research overall.

Since Métis people are not a homogeneous group, I chose to use *quota sampling* for this study; a type of non-probability sampling where participants are chosen by the researcher herself (rather than being selected randomly).[7] Initially, I wanted equal representation across gender, age, French and English Métis ancestry, and Bill C-31 registered Indian status. The five original criteria for participation in this study were: (1) Métis ancestry;[8] (2) born and raised in Manitoba; (3) grew up off reserve; (4) born without registered Indian status; and (5) following traditional Aboriginal spirituality (as defined by the participant).[9]

I chose these parameters because I wanted to listen to people often ignored in discussions on "Native topics" and accused of not being "*real* Natives," in order to learn what draws these people to a life of ceremony despite such exclusion. I am referring to the belief that certain characteristics (such as Indian status, living on reserve, and fluency in a Native language) are measures of authenticity and anyone who does not have these characteristics is "less Native" or not a "real Native." I call this phenomenon the *hierarchy of Nativeness*. This hierarchy is socially constructed and is a consequence of colonization and colonial policies like the Indian Act.

Steve Julian (2011) of Sagkeeng First Nation wrote a blog post called "Are you Indian enough? The Hierarchy of Aboriginal people," in which he discusses this phenomenon. He writes:

> You ever hear the terms, redbone, apple, nosebleed, wannabe, Mooneyash, wemittigozhi, waabishkizi, baakwaayish, and wiisaakodewinini? Probably not. If you are an Indian you may not appreciate other Natives saying those things to you. There is a real battle going on in Indian country and it is the *battle of identity*. We are battling among ourselves as to who is an Indian. Can't really blame us for being in that predicament. The governments of both countries, the United States and Canada, tried to eliminate the Indian. They attempted to get rid of the Indian by many different means; genocide, persecution, prosecution, sterilization, and assimilation. Governmental Policy has always been a tool to get rid of the Indian. The latest policies have Indians being killed off by categories.

Julian outlines a "hierarchy of Aboriginal people" and compares it to Maslow's hierarchy of needs, but calls it a "tipi." In decreasing order, the hierarchy includes "Full-Blooded Indians" (FBIs), who have not gone to residential school, speak their language, have ties to the land, know their traditional teachings, and have not been indoctrinated by Christianity; "Indians," who are not fluent but not Christian; "mixed blood Indians," who are fluent but not Christian; "Full-Bloods" adopted into White families; "Born-Agains," who were "originally ignorant of their own Indian-ness"; "Born on the Rez Indians"; "Born in the Hood/Inner-city Indians"; and "Wannabe Indians" without Indian blood (Julian 2011). Julian references a radio broadcast by Jeff Howrich illustrating a similar battle of Aboriginal identity in an American context: "The U.S. government decided more than 100 years ago that blood quantum was what made an Indian.... [But] when you're not Indian enough, many tangible benefits stop. Generations within families can be divided by tribal enrollment. And Indian communities are torn between losing members through intermarriage, and the real or perceived role of blood quantum in keeping the remaining cultures pure and strong" (Howrich 2011; Chapter 3). Indeed, the effects of legislated suppression of Aboriginal cultures in North America has meant that, "as the suppressed culture becomes increasingly inaccessible to subsequent generations and phenotypic markers of Indianness are lost, many Indigenous people feel that they are 'not really Indian' or 'not Indian enough'" (Lawrence 2012, 201).

I caution against getting caught up in the details of the hierarchy categories, because we risk losing sight of the fact that it is a harmful colonial construction fuelled by assimilationist policies designed to divide and conquer us. As Aboriginal people, when we police each other's identity, we are doing the colonizers' work for them. My book seeks to render such hierarchies meaningless by exposing the effects of colonial policies and systems upon Aboriginal identity and the subsequent divisions between Aboriginal peoples, and by encouraging our families and communities to mend these divisions and return to our original Métis Anishinaabe identities.

When I started doing interviews, I realized that my criteria for participation were too specific. I had to allow for flexibility regarding equal English and French ancestry, age, status, and residence. Reasons that I have struggled to find such people may include my own lack of contacts, and the general disconnection of Aboriginal people from ceremony resulting from ongoing assimilation by the government and Church (Chapters 2–3).

Participants' ancestries are so complex, it rendered my original criterion almost meaningless. Given the Métis history of Manitoba, I assumed French and English would be the main Euro-Canadian ancestries. However, while these ancestries are common among Métis people, they are not mutually exclusive and often exist in combination with other Euro-Canadian ancestries within a single participant (Chapter 5).

Likewise, while I interviewed an equal number of female and male participants, I was unable to fill the age categories equally. At the time of interview, participants ranged in age from twenty-five to seventy-six.[10] It was easiest to fill the forty-five–plus age category, despite the fact that this generation was most likely to have personally experienced residential school and/or the Sixties Scoop. One reason might be the effects of colonization and the "fast life" among our young people. According to the Anishinaabeg, there are seven stages of life through which humans progress.[11] Due to colonization, our young people are getting stuck in the "fast life," straying from the path of *mino-bimaadiziwin*, distracted by drugs, alcohol, promiscuity, and other risky behaviours. Ideally, a person moves from this stage to the next in their early to mid-twenties. I have often noticed a lack of teenagers and people in their twenties at ceremonies, whether I am participating in Manitoba, Ontario, or Wisconsin, and whether the ceremonies are Anishinaabe, Nêhiyaw, or intertribal in nature.[12]

With the criterion of being "born without registered Indian status," I had in mind people who obtained Bill C-31 status later in life, as I wondered if this influenced their relationship with spirituality. Since the Indian Act purposely excluded Métis, most Métis people do not have registered Indian status. Indeed, there exists a stereotype that Métis people *cannot* have Indian status. This is false (especially after Bill C-31). I also included three participants with non-Bill C-31 status (i.e., 6(1) and 6(2) status), because they highlight the complexity of the issues of status and spirituality among people with a connection to Métis ancestry. There are an equal number of participants in this study with and without status (Chapter 5).[13]

I wanted to speak with participants born and raised off reserve in Manitoba to learn more about the experiences of Manitoba Métis. In the end, no participant in this study grew up solely on a reserve, and each one was either born in Manitoba or moved here at a young age and was raised here (Chapter 5).[14] My overall sample remains logical and useful; the more flexible criteria enable a picture to emerge of the complex realities of some people with Métis ancestry who live according to Anishinaabe spiritual values.

Selecting participants that are already known to the researcher is an encouraged practice in Indigenous research because it promotes accountability (Kovach 2009, 51; S. Wilson 2008, 129). Researchers are responsible to the circle of relations and the use of an intermediary (in my case, Mide-Kwe Gaywish) gives the participant "an opportunity to ask candid questions about the nature of the research and the motives behind it" (S. Wilson 2008, 129–30). When searching for participants, I began with my own contacts, then moved outward to increasingly larger circles of community.

I approached each participant with a handmade tobacco tie and asked if they would participate in an interview; each one accepted my *asemaa*. As the first medicine, *asemaa* is a messenger given to us to communicate with the creator (Gaywish 2008, 4, 50). Truth is bound in a sacred commitment (Kovach 2009, 102); therefore, when one accepts tobacco from someone seeking knowledge, "they are saying that they will tell the truth as they know it. They are bound in the presence of the Creator as witness to speak from the heart, to speak their truth" (Stevenson 2000, 249). The protocol of offering *asemaa* directs the petitioner to be clear about what is being asked and sets the context for a petition to be made (Gaywish 2008, 50). Michell (1999) explains that offering tobacco "reinforces the ethic of reciprocity in a cosmological understanding of interdependence, balance, and harmony" and "allows [participants] to become involved in the research process as equal and respected members" (5, 10). With my *asemaa*, I acknowledge and honour the participants' knowledge, correct imbalances that may result from asking for their stories, and promise to respect these.

By using qualitative semi-structured interviews, I recognize the participants as *experts* of their own experience, knowledge, and stories.[15] I asked the participants about demographics, family history, personal experiences and self-identification, and relationship to spirituality.[16] I brought a snack and water to each interview to show my appreciation to the participants. Shawn Wilson (2008) reminds us of the importance of sharing food and water in ceremony: "This again is how things should be, starting and finishing with a prayer and sharing food" (83).

Before we began the interview, each participant was given the option of smudging with *mushkodaywushk* (women's sage), which I had handpicked; the smudge could also be relit during the interview if the need arose. Smudging is a purifying ceremony that helps to cleanse one's spirit, centre one's attention on the task at hand, prevent the influence of negative energy, and enable one to proceed in a good way with a good heart (Bailey 2005, 39).[17] The use of *asemaa*, *mushkodaywushk*, food and prayer, and a medicine bundle (handpicked sage in a cloth drawstring bag also made by me) as a parting gift of gratitude helped me follow appropriate Anishinaabe protocol to ensure relational accountability, promote *mino-bimaadiziwin*, and restore balance with the participants.

I also followed appropriate Western research protocol to protect the participants.[18] Before the interview, each participant was asked to read and sign an informed consent form and was given a copy.[19] This encourages participants to give feedback and ensures relational accountability through transparency. "Transparency" refers to being explicit about the research process, including how participants are chosen and how data is analyzed (Bryman and Teevan 2005, 158–59). After the study, a five-page mini-report of the key findings, written in plain English, was also given to each participant.

In an Indigenous research paradigm, the use of real names allows for relational accountability, which is found in oral cultures (Kovach 2009, 48–49). According to Wilson, this "goes against the rules of most university ethical research policies. However, how can I be held accountable to the relationships I have with these people if I don't name them? How can they be held accountable to their own teachers if their words and relationships are deprived of names?" (S. Wilson 2008, 63). The use of real names encourages accountability between the researcher and the participant because the motives and consequences of actions are not cloaked in anonymity. This also gives participants an opportunity to demonstrate where they obtained their teachings and to honour those teachings; most participants chose to use their real name.[20]

In order to make sense of the stories shared by the participants in their interviews, I used Western and Anishinaabe approaches: thematic coding and prayerfully intuitive analysis. Thematic coding is a qualitative approach to data analysis involving a "search for themes in transcripts or field notes" (Bryman and Teevan 2005, 318).[21]

I also used prayer and intuition to understand the participants' stories. My intuition is guided by prayer in the form of petitions to spirit with sacred medicines and through participation in ceremony. I began each day by offering *asemaa* to give thanks for the help I was receiving—human and non—in conducting the analysis of my research. I regularly smudged before an analysis session to clear my being, centre myself, and open myself to seeing the patterns that I was meant to see. I smudged myself and my work space anytime I became frustrated during the analysis. I was also able to approach my spiritual advisors for help. Finally, I participated in ceremonies throughout this research journey, including the analysis stage. In this way, I combined spirit-direction with my own agency to uncover patterns in the stories.

Meeting the Participants[22]

There is this division now that was created by the government be-
tween Métis people and First Nations people.... that division that
was created by government policy.

—Benny, participant

Running Elk[23]

Running Elk is a twenty-five-year-old male. Running Elk grew up in
Winnipeg, Manitoba, and continues to reside there as an adult. He is currently pursuing a BA at the University of Manitoba as a full-time student.
During Running Elk's upbringing, his father self-identified as Métis. Also, as
a child, Running Elk's paternal grandmother would take him with her when
she attended a Cree-speaking Catholic church in Winnipeg. He has section
6(2) Indian status. His father is Métis (with Cree and Irish ancestry) and his
mother is Ojibwe.

Today, Running Elk acknowledges his Métis side, but self-identifies more
with having registered Indian status. Moreover, he is increasingly interested
in traditional Cree/Ojibwe spirituality, especially with regard to traditional
drumming and singing. He works with traditional, sacred medicines, mostly
through smudging; he also participates in cultural and spiritual events
whenever possible. The barriers that continue to impede his commitment to
traditional spirituality include colonization, in the form of Christianization
on his mother's reserve, and his ongoing, occasional use of drugs and alcohol.
He shared that when he is able to maintain permanent sobriety, he will be
ready to commit to a life of traditional spirituality full-time. On the other
hand, key factors that have contributed to his interest in and desire for such
spirituality include the traditional drum group he joined while still in high
school and stayed with for several years beyond high school, as well as post-
secondary education and subsequent access to cultural teachings and Elders.
Also influential in his journey to spirituality has been the fact that relatives
on his dad's side are Midewiwin and have taken him to ceremonies, including
sweat lodge, and organized his naming ceremony.

Kyle McClintock

Like Running Elk, Kyle is also a twenty-five-year-old male. His father is of
Irish and Welsh ancestry, and his mother is Métis with French and Cree
ancestry. Kyle's childhood residence was Swan River, Manitoba, which he
describes as "very racially segregated," with Aboriginal residents living on one
side and non-Aboriginal residents on the other. As an adult, Kyle now lives in

Winnipeg. He is pursuing an undergraduate degree in social work as a full-time student. While he was growing up, Kyle's father self-identified as Irish, and his mother let him know he was Métis, but getting her to self-identify as such was (is) like "pulling teeth"; his family preferred to think of themselves as "average White Canadians." Kyle and his sister were raised according to the faith of the United Church—his father's faith—and made to attend church. His mother is Roman Catholic. He does not have registered Indian status.

Now, Kyle self-identifies as Canadian, Aboriginal, and Native. While still a teenager, Kyle decided that traditional Ojibwe/Cree spirituality was the spiritual path for him. He participates in cultural and spiritual gatherings as often as possible, and enjoys working with Elders. He also works with traditional medicines in his home and includes his children whenever possible. As a youth, Kyle struggled with racism, loss (of a girlfriend, child, and grandmother), addictions, and even attempted suicide as a teenager. Thankfully, a couple of key family members helped him get back on his feet; these family members also happened to be interested in traditional knowledge and spirituality to varying degrees. Kyle also found solace, self-esteem, and pride through post-secondary education, which gave him access to Elders and cultural workshops. In addition, Kyle's desire to be a good role model to his children is a constant motivator for him to participate in traditional ceremonies and teach his children as much as he can in this respect.

Michael Brant[24]

Mike is twenty-six years old. Mike's ancestry reflects his father's Ukrainian/ Austrian and English roots, and his mother's Ojibwe ancestry; there are stories on his maternal grandmother's side of taking Métis Scrip and being kicked off reserve. As a child, Mike lived in Gypsumville, Manitoba, a rural non-Aboriginal community surrounded by at least four First Nation reserves. Mike describes Aboriginal and non-Aboriginal relations in Gypsumville as stable and mostly amicable because everyone has regular interactions with one another (i.e., gas station, grocery store, and the like). Mike now lives in Winnipeg, and is a full-time student working toward an undergraduate degree in social work. During Mike's childhood, his father self-identified as Ukrainian Caucasian and his mother self-identified as Indian. Also, while growing up, his father did not follow any spirituality, but Mike was raised in the Pentecostal faith. He attended a Native-run Pentecostal church with his maternal grandparents, and occasionally with his mother. He has Bill C-31 registered Indian status.

Today, Mike self-identifies variously as First Nations, Aboriginal, Native,

Indian, as well as with his Bill C-31 status. He is most interested in traditional Ojibwe spirituality and explains that, while he is not quite ready yet, he is preparing to commit fully to this spirituality sometime in the future. In the meantime, he participates in traditional sharing circles and other cultural and spiritual events. He has been near sweat lodge ceremonies, but has not yet personally entered the sweat lodge. Mike's journey to traditional spirituality has likely been slowed down due to internalized colonization within his family and community (and some of the surrounding reserves) at the hands of the church. Ceremonies like pow wow and sweat lodge have been suppressed, and many in his community still fear being associated with these. Luckily, he has found encouragement in post-secondary education, cultural gatherings, and his own artwork. He has also been influenced by the legacy of the residential school system; he recognizes that a return to traditional spirituality is helpful in the healing journey.

Benny Michaud

Benny is a twenty-seven-year-old female. Her biological father is Scottish from Newfoundland, while her adoptive dad (by whom she was raised) is French from Quebec. Her mother is Michif (with Cree and some Saulteaux and French ancestry). Benny spent a portion of her childhood living in the Annapolis Valley of Nova Scotia, a rural non-Aboriginal community; however, her family moved often because her father was in the military.[25] At the time of the interview, she was living in Ottawa, pursuing a Master of Arts degree full-time; she also has a BA from Carleton University and a BEd from Queen's University. During her childhood, her maternal grandparents and mother self-identified as Michif until the family moved east. Also, while there is Roman Catholic influence in her family history, Benny and her sister were not raised as church-goers. She is a card-carrying member of the Métis Nation of Ontario (MNO). She does not have registered Indian status.

As an adult, Benny passionately self-identifies as Michif/Métis and is pursuing traditional Aboriginal spirituality. She is involved with a women's traditional hand drum group, goes to ceremonies such as sweats when she can, and works with medicines, especially in the form of smudging. Barriers she has faced in her spiritual journey include divisions between Métis and First Nations people, especially the belief that only the latter participate in traditional ceremonies. She has also faced discrimination at ceremonies due to her fair complexion. Factors that have greatly influenced her spirituality have been the women's drum group, receiving her spirit name, and a personally meaningful conversation with a specific Métis Elder leading up to her naming ceremony.

Dawnis Kennedy

Dawnis is a thirty-three-year-old female. Her father's ancestry is Irish and English from Newfoundland, and her late mother's was Anishinaabe Ojibwe from the Roseau River First Nation in the Treaty 1 area.[26] Dawnis spent the first part of her childhood living in Brandon, Manitoba, and then moved back and forth from there to her mother's reserve (Roseau River) after age fourteen. She has been living in Sault Ste. Marie, Ontario, for the past few years pursuing a doctorate in law through the University of Toronto. She also has a BA and a Master of Law. At the time of her interview, she was soon to begin a job as a Professor of Law and Justice in the Department of Law and Politics at Algoma University. While growing up, her family self-identified variously as Ojibwe, Anishinaabe, Indian, First Nation, and Treaty 1, and her grandmother referred to Dawnis as a Halfbreed (not derogatorily). Moreover, Dawnis's family has been influenced by the legacy of residential school and its accompanying Catholicism, especially among her grandparents' generation. However, her family was of the Midewiwin faith before the residential school era; her mother's generation has marked a return to the Midewiwin within her family. She has Bill C-31 registered Indian status.

Dawnis herself self-identifies as Ojibwe Anishinaabe-Kwe and recognizes her father's lineage through her clan, Waabizhayshii. She also understands herself to be of duality, both physical and spiritual, according to the Anishinaabe Creation Story. She is first-degree Midewiwin in the Three Fires Midewiwin lodge and attends ceremonies regularly. She is a pipe carrier and participates in a traditional women's drumming group, among many other spiritual pursuits. She has been committed to this way of life for more than ten years. Barriers that she has faced along the way include the legacy of residential schools and internalized spiritual colonization within her family; her family is healing from this. Factors that have influenced her commitment to the Midewiwin way of life include her family's return to the Midewiwin during her childhood, as well as their involvement with the American Indian Movement (AIM).

Shirley Delorme Russell

Shirley is a thirty-four-year-old female. Her adoptive dad (who raised her) is of Ojibwe ancestry, and her mom is Métis (with Cree and French ancestry).[27] Shirley was born and raised, and still lives, in Winnipeg, Manitoba. She has a BA, a BEd, and a Diploma in Aboriginal Languages. She is employed as the Education and Cultural Resource Coordinator at the Louis Riel Institute (LRI). During her upbringing, her family self-identified mainly as Indians and worked hard not to be perceived as "dirty Indians." She was raised in the Catholic faith—although sporadically, at times. She is a card-carrying member of the Manitoba Métis Federation (MMF). She does not have registered Indian status.

Over the years, she has come to self-identify proudly as Métis and Ojibwe, and has developed an increasing interest in traditional Aboriginal spirituality, but still also follows some Christian practices. In terms of Aboriginal spirituality, she works with medicines, smudges, attends cultural teachings, and has participated in some ceremonies over the years. Ongoing barriers she faces in terms of her spiritual journey include a lack of connection to ceremonies (not knowing where they are held, or who to go to), people who are judgmental of the fact that she respects both Aboriginal spirituality and Christianity, and hostility at ceremonies when she is "just there to learn." She has also, at times, experienced an unwelcoming environment at ceremonies which she believes is due to her fair complexion and perceptions about her identity. On the other hand, her spiritual journey has been positively encouraged by post-secondary education and subsequent access to Elders, teachings, and work with medicine. She has also been influenced by her cultural mentor, Lawrence Barkwell at LRI, with whom she attends ceremonies.

Joseph Ouellette

Joe is a thirty-five-year-old male. His father is Métis (with Plains Cree, French, Scottish, and Irish ancestry), and his mother is Cree with some Scottish ancestry. Joe began his childhood in Coal Lake, Alberta, but moved to Fisher River First Nation in Manitoba (his mother's reserve) at age six. He moved to Winnipeg around age eight, and then moved back and forth between Fisher River and Winnipeg until age fifteen, at which time he moved to Calgary. He now lives in Winnipeg. He has a BA degree and works as a youth care worker, as well as a third-level carpenter's apprentice. Throughout his childhood, his grandparents and mother self-identified variously as Indian, Native, Aboriginal, and First Nation, and explained to Joe that he is half Indian or half Native (not derogatorily). His grandparents brought him to the United Church, but they began increasingly following traditional Cree/Ojibwe spirituality while he was still a youth. Also, one of his maternal uncles was a medicine man and taught him traditional spiritual ways while growing up. He has Bill C-31 registered Indian status.

Joe self-identifies as a "First Nations person with White ancestry," as well as Native, Indian, and mixed. He decided to pursue a more traditional spiritual life while he was still a teenager. Today, he practises traditional

Ojibwe/Cree spirituality, works with medicines, smudges, participates in sweats and Sundances, is a pipe carrier, and has worked as a *shkaabewis* (helper) at various times over the years. His spiritual journey has, at times, been hindered by his experiences with racism at the hands of non-Aboriginal people, as well as his own spiritual fundamentalism as a youth. On the other hand, he has been encouraged by his experiences with traditional spirituality during his upbringing at the hands of his uncle and, increasingly, his mother and her parents (his grandparents). Also influential have been his *shkaabewis* work with Elders, his stay with a Midewiwin family in Wisconsin during early adulthood, and his desire to teach these ways to his children.

Tim Johnstone

Tim is a thirty-five year old male. His ancestry reflects that his late father was Anishinaabe and Scottish, and his mother is Métis (with Anishinaabe and French ancestry). He grew up in the Métis community of Seymourville, Manitoba; he eventually moved to the nearby Hollow Water First Nation as a youth, and has lived there ever since. Tim is a high school graduate and was unemployed at the time of the interview; however, his last job was as a labourer working in the mines for five years. While he was growing up, his family mostly avoided self-identifying, but if asked, responded with Indian. During Tim's childhood, his father was a practising Protestant and his mother was a practising Catholic, so Tim was made to attend one church, then the other, on alternating Sundays. He has section 6(1) registered Indian status.

Today, Tim self-identifies without hesitation as Anishinaabe. He practises a blend of traditional Anishinaabe spirituality and some Christian traditions, such as reading the Bible and going to church occasionally. In terms of Anishinaabe spirituality, he participates in sweat lodges, fasts, traditional drumming and singing, among other practices. He also works as a *shkaabewis* for his brother-in-law and other traditional knowledge holders in his community. Over the years, barriers to his spiritual development have included ongoing struggles with addictions and the party life, as well as the effects of colonization at the hands of organized Western religion within his community and the suppression of traditional ceremony. Among the key factors that have solidified his commitment to Anishinaabe spirituality are powerful dreams/visions, spiritual guidance from his brother-in-law and other community members, and his desire to be a good role model for his children. He has also been profoundly influenced by his first experience as firekeeper for a sweat lodge ceremony and his participation in Midewiwin ceremonies that took place for four days near his community some years ago.

KaKaKew Esquew[28]

KaKaKew is forty-seven and female. Her father is Métis (with French and unknown Native ancestry), and her mother is French Italian. She grew up in Winnipeg, Manitoba, and moved to a rural community of mixed Aboriginal and non-Aboriginal population when she was nine years old. She has lived most of her adulthood in Winnipeg, which is where she currently resides. KaKaKew has a diploma in the field of child care from Red River College. She was unemployed at the time the interview was conducted; previously she was employed in the social work field. While growing up, her family self-identified adamantly as French-Canadian and vehemently denied any Aboriginal ancestry. She was raised Roman Catholic. She has obtained her Métis card through the MMF. She does not have registered Indian status.

KaKaKew now self-identifies proudly as Métis, or Métis French, and has chosen to live a life of traditional Aboriginal spirituality. She is a Sundancer (Cree lodge), a pipe carrier, and works with medicines. Along with Sundance, she participates in sweat lodges, dark room ceremonies, and other ceremonies whenever she can. She has faced several barriers in coming to follow these traditional ways, including a severe battle with addictions and the loss of her then husband's life to addiction. She has also had a painful experience at a sweat lodge ceremony, and has felt unwelcome at some ceremonies due to her fair complexion and people questioning her identity. Moreover, she has felt divisions between Métis and First Nations people, including with regard to ceremony, and has struggled with significant internalized racism within her family. Thankfully, her spiritual development has been encouraged and influenced by her Sundance family, her long-term sobriety, and her desire to be a good role model to her son. She was also significantly influenced by her first sweat lodge ceremony.

Diane[29]

Diane is a fifty-one-year-old female. Her father was Métis (with Saulteaux and French ancestry), and her mother was Saulteaux. Diane grew up in a Métis community with a First Nation reserve nearby. As an adult, she moved to her then husband's community, a Manitoba First Nation reserve. She has been living in Winnipeg for a number of years now. Diane obtained an undergraduate degree from a university in Manitoba and has been working within the child welfare system ever since. When she was a child, her family did not self-identify; according to Diane, "we knew we were different" because they could not self-identify either with the non-Aboriginal people in the community or with the status Indians on the nearby reserve. Diane was raised in the Roman Catholic faith and was made to do her first communion and confirmation within the church at a young age. She gained treaty status through marriage.[30]

Today, Diane self-identifies unwaveringly as Anishinaabe. She was initiated as Midewiwin some years ago and remains steadfastly committed to this way of life. She participates very actively and regularly in a range of different ceremonies. Some of the barriers she has faced along her spiritual journey include colonization and suppression of traditional spirituality at the hands of church and government. Such colonization became internalized within her own family and community, with people believing traditional spirituality was *silly* at best and *evil* at worst. She was encouraged not to give up her traditional spiritual pursuits by her involvement in the American Indian Movement, as well as within the Midewiwin lodge. Additional key influences upon her spiritual path are sobriety, her traditional husband (at the time), and her ongoing desire to raise her kids according to traditional Anishinaabe values and ways.

Sandra DeLaronde

Sandra is a fifty-two-year-old female. She has a rich diversity within her ancestry; her father's ancestry is Mohawk, Ojibwe, and French, and her mother's is Cree, Dakota, and Scottish, from Cross Lake First Nation in Manitoba. Sandra spent her childhood in The Pas, Manitoba, a rural community with Aboriginal and non-Aboriginal residents. Her adult residence has been, and continues to be, Winnipeg. Sandra's extensive education includes an MA from Royal Roads University in British Columbia; plus she is currently pursuing a PhD through Santa Barbara's Fielding Graduate University. She is the executive director of Community and Aboriginal Justice Issues for the Department of Manitoba Justice. She also manages the Helen Betty Osborne Foundation for the government. Her family self-identified as "products of the Red River," Métis, and Indigenous while growing up. In terms of childhood spirituality, she and her siblings were raised going to Catholic mass in the morning, and then a Protestant service at night; her father was Catholic and her mother was Protestant. She has Bill C-31 registered Indian status.

Today, Sandra continues to acknowledge her Métis identity, but prefers to self-identify simply as a human being, or a person; she also goes by her legal identity as First Nations with Cross Lake (Cree Nation). Sandra felt drawn to traditional Aboriginal spirituality as a youth, and has pursued this path ever since. She became a Sundancer years ago, and continues to participate in Sundance regularly. She has also been a pipe carrier for many years. Sandra points out that she does not feel that she *follows* Aboriginal spirituality, but rather that it is a *way of life*. She did not mention many barriers that have inhibited her spiritual growth; however, she did touch upon the effects of colonization through the church, which her mother may have internalized, causing her to worry about *bad medicine* and what the church would think when Sandra began pursuing traditional spirituality. Factors that have positively influenced her spiritual path include her involvement with the local pow wow group and the American Indian Movement as a youth, and a profound experience with an eagle.

Lance Wood

Lance is a fifty-five-year-old male. Both his parents' ancestry is Ojibwe, Irish, and English. Lance grew up in Manigotagan, Manitoba, a rural Métis community near Hollow Water First Nation. As a youth, he moved to Hollow Water and has lived there ever since. In terms of education, Lance has completed grade ten. He has been employed as a counsellor for the Community Holistic Circle Healing Centre in Hollow Water for a number of years. When he was little, Lance's family self-identified as Métis. Lance and his siblings were raised Catholic and were avid church-goers; his mother is Catholic and his father is Protestant. He does not have registered Indian status.

Today, Lance self-identifies as Anishinaabe, and practises a blend of traditional Ojibwe spirituality and Christianity. He continues to feel the importance of Christian prayer and going to church. In addition, he also participates in sweat lodge and fast ceremonies, among other ceremonies, and often works as *shkaabewis* for these ceremonies. Barriers that have challenged his spirituality over the years have included those who say that you cannot be both Christian *and* traditional at the same time, as well as internalized spiritual colonization within himself and his mother, who worried at first that ceremonies were *bad*. Key factors that positively influenced his spirituality include a Native Elder at a spiritual conference years ago, who told him it was indeed okay to follow both Christianity and traditional Aboriginal spirituality. He has also been influenced by open-minded priests who participate in sweat lodge and fast ceremonies in Hollow Water. Finally, his work as *shkaabewis* for different ceremonies inspires him to continue his spiritual work for the community.

Rainey Gaywish

Rainey Gaywish is a fifty-six-year-old female. Her father's ancestry was Icelandic, and her mother's was Cree with some French ancestry. Rainey grew up in Riverton, Manitoba, a rural community with Aboriginal and non-Aboriginal residents (mostly Icelandic). Rainey has lived most of her adult life in Winnipeg. She has an MA in Canadian Studies from Carleton University, and a few years ago she obtained a PhD in Indigenous Studies from Trent University. She is the program director for Aboriginal Focus Programs of the Extended Education Department at the University of Manitoba. During her upbringing, her family proudly self-identified as Halfbreed. Also, while her father was Lutheran and her mother was Anglican (Anglican Church of Canada), they were not church-goers. However, as a child, Rainey chose to attend the Mennonite church that moved into their town because they had programming like summer camp for children. She is a member of the MMF, but lost her membership card some time ago and has not felt the desire to obtain a replacement. She does not have registered Indian status.

Today, Rainey self-identifies as Cree Anishinaabe-Kwe and understands herself to be "spirit in human form," according to the Anishinaabe Creation Story. Rainey has been very active within the Three Fires Midewiwin lodge since its inception in the 1970s; she is third-degree Midewiwin and one of the lodge historians. She participates in Midewiwin ceremonies regularly as a *way of life*. She is also a Sundancer and works with a women's hand drum. Occasionally, she also conducts full moon ceremony in her backyard for any women who wish to attend. Over the years, challenges to her spiritual path have come in the form of internalized racism within her family and a lack of connection to ceremonies in her early life. Positive influences for her spiritual development have included her involvement with the New Nation Chanters and Dancers Powwow Group, the Morley Ecumenical Conference/Youth Elder workshops, and the American Indian Movement, as well as with the early development of the Three Fires Society. Also particularly influential for her was the first time she heard the Little Boy Water Drum. In addition, she has been encouraged by various Elders and traditional teachers, and is motivated by her desire to be a good role model and raise her children in a good way.

Ron Richard

Ron is a fifty-eight-year-old male. Both of his parents were Métis. His paternal grandfather was Métis and his paternal grandmother was Saulteaux (with some Cree and French ancestry) from Roseau River First Nation. His mother's ancestry was Cree, Ojibwe, and French. Ron was raised in Camperville, Manitoba, a rural Métis community. Ron has lived in Winnipeg for more than ten years now, but he also maintains a residence in Camperville, which he refers to as "home." He attended the Parkland Campus in Dauphin, studying business administration, but soon began working instead for Manitoba Hydro, where he continues to work as the Aboriginal Employment Relations Specialist. During his upbringing, Ron's grandfather adamantly self-identified the family as Anishinaabe and Halfbreed, and then, beginning in the 1960s, as Anishinaabe and Métis. Ron was raised a staunch Roman Catholic, being an altar boy for many years and even considering becoming a priest. He has Bill C-31 registered Indian status.

Today, Ron continues to self-identify fixedly as Anishinaabe and Métis. In addition, after becoming disillusioned with the church—due to the sexual abuse scandal within the residential school system—Ron left the church and began exploring traditional Aboriginal spirituality. He became involved with the Sundance several years ago as a *shkaabewis*, and finally became a dancer in his own right a few years ago. He was a Midewiwin Initiate for many years and recently initiated as first degree. He participates in various ceremonies regularly, especially Sundance. Barriers to his Anishinaabe spiritual path have included colonization and suppression of traditional Aboriginal ceremonies, and the subsequent silence within his family, especially regarding the fact that one of his uncles was Midewiwin. Ron does not consider his indoctrination within Roman Catholicism as a youth to be a barrier to his spiritual develop-ment; rather, he credits it with the strong commitment to faith and prayer that remains within him today (albeit now directed toward Anishinaabe spirituality). He was also influenced by his participation in sweat lodge and receiving his spirit name, among other key influences.

Laara Fitznor

Laara is a sixty-year-old female. Her father's ancestry was Cree, German, and French from The Pas/Opaskwayak First Nation, and her mother's is Cree from Nelson House/Nisichawayasihk First Nation with Oji-Cree and Scottish ancestry. Her maternal grandfather was from Big Trout Lake, Ontario. Laara's childhood residence was Wabowden, Manitoba, a rural community with high Aboriginal and non-Aboriginal populations. As an adult, Laara's home has been in Winnipeg. She has a doctorate in education from the Ontario Institute for Studies in Education at the University of Toronto. While growing up, her father self-identified as Halfbreed and Native, and encouraged the family to self-identify as "Cree with German Scots ancestry." In terms of spirituality during childhood, half her extended family was Catholic and the other half was Anglican. She herself was raised with a syncretic blend of Anglicanism and traditional Cree spirituality, especially by her grandfather, who preached at a Cree-speaking Anglican/Cree church. She has Bill C-31 status.

Today, Laara continues to honour all her ancestry by self-identifying as "Cree First Nation (or Nisichawayasihk Cree Nation) with German Scots ancestry." She participates in ceremonies whenever possible. She has been attending Sundance ceremonies for several years—not as a dancer, but she helps however she can and is sometimes asked to be an inspirational speaker there. Challenges she has faced during her spiritual development include suppression of ceremonies within her community by church and government, as well as silence within her own family about traditional ways in an effort to protect the family, given the suppression of the times. Key factors that have influenced her commitment to traditional spirituality include her grandfather's syncretic spiritual teachings, being taught to work with medicines during her upbringing, and what she calls being "embedded" within the Cree language.

Stan LaPierre

Stan is a sixty-three-year-old male. Both of his parents were Métis; his dad had Cree and French ancestry and his mom had Cree, Ojibwe, and unknown European ancestry. He grew up in Lestock, Saskatchewan—a rural community with a high Aboriginal population at the time—and then moved to McAuley, Manitoba, which he describes as an all-White Protestant community, at age ten. He has lived in Winnipeg his entire adult life. Stan obtained his grade twelve accreditation, as well as a welder's certificate, through Red River Community College. He is employed as the Coordinator in Justice of the Aboriginal Spiritual Care Department at the Manitoba Youth Centre. During his youth, Stan's family self-identified as Métis. As a child, Stan was raised Roman Catholic, especially by his mother and maternal grandparents, who were avid church-goers. He does not have registered Indian status.

Today, Stan proudly self-identifies as Anishinaabe; he is second-degree Midewiwin of the Three Fires Midewiwin lodge, and participates in ceremony regularly. He has been *shkaabewis* to various Elders and traditional teachers over the years, and he helped run sweat lodges for youth at Camp Manitou for several years. Barriers that have challenged his spiritual development over the years include his experiences with racism within the dominant society, and his own subsequent anger as a youth. He has also struggled with the silence about ceremonies within his own family; again, this was done as an effort to protect the family, given the hostile Canadian environment toward Aboriginal people and spirituality. Key factors that have helped his spiritual development include a trip to the United States as a young adult and his participation in his first dark room ceremony. On that same trip, he also assisted as firekeeper for the first time at a sweat lodge ceremony. He has also been greatly influenced by the Midewiwin lodge and the first time he heard the sound of the Little Boy Water Drum.

Jules Lavallée

Jules is a sixty-eight-year-old male. His father was Michif/Métis (with Cree, Saulteaux, and French ancestry), and his mother's ancestry was Saulteaux. Most of Jules's ancestors are from St. Laurent, Manitoba (a rural Métis community), which is also where he himself spent the first ten years of his life. At that point, he and his family moved to Rivers, Manitoba—a rural, non-Aboriginal community. Jules has spent his adult life living in Winnipeg. In terms of education, he has completed grade eleven, but has also obtained university certification courses that enable him to deliver life skills training, as well as to develop and evaluate university courses. He is one of two Elders-in-Residence at Red River College in Winnipeg. Jules also developed the Miskobiik Training Centre and the Red Willow Lodge, both of which were incorporated in Winnipeg. His family self-identified as Métis, and to a lesser extent French, during his upbringing. Jules was raised Roman Catholic. He does not have registered Indian status.

Today, Jules wholeheartedly self-identifies with his spirit name, Binesii-gaa-gii-gwetung ndizhinikaaz, and as Métis and Anishinaabe.[31] He is a Sundancer and a Sundance Chief, conducting his own Sundance ceremonies; he also conducts other ceremonies, including sweat lodge. He is also a *gwiimeh* (namer) recognized as being able to petition Spirit to find people's spirit name. Through the Red Willow Lodge, he offers traditional teachings, such as medicine walks, and conducts ceremonies; he has brought groups of university and college students there as part of a course he developed called *Gagii-maajiiyaang* ("a way of life"). Over the years, challenges he has faced in his spiritual path include the strict Catholic indoctrination within his community and a lack of connection to ceremonies as a youth due to their suppression by the church and government. Factors that have helped him commit to traditional Anishinaabe spirituality include being taught his grandfather's medicine bundle (by his grandmother), beginning at age five, as well as a powerful experience during his first sweat, which was for his own naming ceremony.

Mae Louise Campbell

Mae Louise is a seventy-six-year-old female. Both of her parents were Métis; her father was of Scottish and Saulteaux ancestry, and her mother was of

Saulteaux and French ancestry. She grew up in Kississing Lake (also known as Cold Lake), Manitoba—a rural Métis community. As an adult, Mae Louise has been living in Winnipeg. She has completed grade nine. Mae Louise is one of two Elders-in-Residence at Red River College in Winnipeg. While growing up, her family self-identified as Halfbreed and Métis. She and her siblings were raised Roman Catholic; however, she was not made to attend church regularly, especially after her mother separated from her father. She does not have registered Indian status.

Today, Mae Louise proudly self-identifies with her spirit name, Ishkiday-Kiday-Kwe, and as Métis Ojibwe.[32] She lives by traditional Aboriginal spiritual values and has done so for many years. Mae Louise began and ran the Grandmother Moon Lodge—a traditional healing lodge especially for women— in the rural Métis community of St. Laurent, Manitoba, for sixteen years. She works with medicines and specializes in women's medicines and teachings. Barriers that have threatened to hinder her spiritual development over the years include societal racism, internalized racism within her family, and a general lack of connection to ceremonies due to government and church suppression of traditional Aboriginal spirituality. Other challenges she has faced include an abusive and alcoholic father and ex-husband. Key factors that have positively influenced her commitment to Aboriginal spirituality include a powerful first sweat lodge experience, and hearing the sound of the drum (in that sweat) for the first time. She has been influenced by Elders and spiritual teachers, her work with medicines, and her own artwork.

CHAPTER 5

Residence, Education, Employment, Ancestry, and Status

The Métis community is the fastest growing one in Manitoba. Fifty-eight percent increase in people identifying themselves as Métis over the past ten years is linked not only to birthrate but to a cultural awakening.
—quoted in *Mémère Métisse/My Métis Grandmother*
(dir. Janelle Wookey, 2008)

The Canadian government sought to divide and conquer Aboriginal peoples by differentiating between First Nations and Métis people, generally forcing First Nations to live on reserves and Métis to live in settlements or towns. The scrip system created a legacy of landlessness among Métis people and distance from our First Nation relatives, both of which can potentially influence relationship to spirituality.

In this study, participants' places of birth, childhood communities, and adult residences generally correspond with the following categories: Métis community, rural mixed community, rural non-Aboriginal community, urban community, or reserve. To identify whether communities were "Métis" (i.e., having more self-identified Métis residents than any other group), or "mixed" (i.e., having significant Aboriginal and non-Aboriginal populations, but not identified as an "Aboriginal community"), I consulted the Aboriginal Canada Portal (a Government of Canada website), Statistics Canada on-line, and the City-Data website, which has as its source Statistics Canada's community profiles. According to Statistics Canada, a community is identified as "Métis" when the population of self-identified residents is 25 percent or greater.

Most participants were either born in an urban community, or (slightly fewer) in a rural mixed community. Benny, KaKaKew, Shirley, and Mike were born in Winnipeg. Running Elk, Joseph, and Dawnis were born in Toronto, Vancouver, and St. John's, respectively. Those born in rural mixed communities are Mae Louise (The Pas, Manitoba), Rainey (Riverton, Manitoba), Diane

(Ste. Rose du Lac, Manitoba), and Stan (Lestock, Saskatchewan).[1] Jules, Lance, and Ron were born in St. Laurent, Manigotagan, and Camperville, respectively—all Manitoba Métis communities. Only Kyle and Tim were born in rural non-Aboriginal communities: Beausejour, Manitoba, and Devon, Alberta, respectively.

No participant was born on a reserve. Laara's mother wanted her to be born on Laara's paternal grandparents' reserve (Opaskwayak Cree Nation) but due to complications during birth and increasing government control over midwifery, she ended up being born in The Pas. As Laara told me, "She wanted the midwives to deliver me and they started off and everything was going fine. But I guess there were complications and I was taking forever to come out, that they started to get scared and worried. This story comes from my mom, so it's part of the oral traditions. They started to get worried and they said that if they don't take my mom to the hospital, which is like ten minutes across the bridge in The Pas, that they'll get in trouble by the law. Because that's when they started to insist that the children will be born in hospitals, right. Because they kind of banned midwifery in the fifties—'cause I was born in '49." Stories of government control like this one were a key theme in the participants' lives.

The following participants spent their childhoods in a Manitoba Métis community: Mae Louise (Kississing Lake/Cold Lake), Ron (Camperville), Diane (Eddystone), Lance (Manigotagan), Tim (Seymourville), and Laara (Wabowden). Jules lived in the Métis community of St. Laurent, Manitoba, until age eleven, and then moved to Rivers, Manitoba (a rural non-Aboriginal community). KaKaKew, Dawnis, and Joe spent a significant portion of their childhoods in both an urban community and a reserve or a rural community. Dawnis moved back and forth between Brandon, Manitoba, and Roseau River First Nation, Manitoba, after the age of fourteen. Joe moved from Coal Lake, Alberta, to Fisher River First Nation, Manitoba, to Winnipeg, then back and forth between Winnipeg and Fisher River, then to Calgary, and eventually back to Winnipeg. KaKaKew grew up in the French quarter of Winnipeg (St. Boniface), then moved to Ste. Agathe, Manitoba (a rural non-Aboriginal community), at age nine. Sandra, Rainey, and Stan grew up mainly in rural mixed communities: The Pas and Riverton, Manitoba, and Lestock, Saskatchewan, respectively. Kyle, Mike, and Benny grew up mainly in non-Aboriginal rural communities: Swan River and Gypsumville, Manitoba, and Annapolis Valley, Nova Scotia, respectively. Finally, Running Elk and Shirley grew up in the urban city of Winnipeg.

All except Diane, Lance, and Tim have been living in an urban setting for most of their adult lives (some also during their youth). Most live in Winnipeg, but Benny lives in Ottawa and Dawnis lives in Sault Ste. Marie, Ontario. Only Ron still has a house he considers "home base" in the Métis community of his birth/childhood (Camperville), where he stays during long weekends and holidays; he has been living and working in Winnipeg for eleven years. The remaining three participants have been living on a reserve since the ages of sixteen (Lance), eighteen (Diane), and nineteen (Tim). Lance and Diane moved onto a reserve as a result of a romantic relationship; Tim moved onto one when his family did. Overall, participants have more direct relationships to Métis communities, in terms of having lived there themselves, than they do to reserves. As adults, Lance, Diane, and Tim are now living on reserves. No participants are living solely in a Métis community or in a rural non-Aboriginal community; the majority have made cities their home.

In fact, the number of participants now living in an urban setting is more than double the number who were born in an urban setting; the difference is even greater when compared to childhood residence. This pattern is consistent with larger residence patterns for Aboriginal people across Canada. In 2006, 54 percent of all Aboriginal people in Canada lived in urban areas, up from 50 percent in 1996; and Winnipeg was home to the largest urban Aboriginal population (68,380) (Statistics Canada 2010). For Métis people specifically, 69 percent lived in urban areas, up from 67 percent in 1996, with Winnipeg recording the largest Métis population (40,980) (ibid.).[2] An urban existence is increasingly an Aboriginal experience; Aboriginal people are changing the urban landscape.

Participants were also asked if anyone in their family ever lived in an Aboriginal community, such as a reserve or Métis community. Slightly more participants spoke of their families' connections to Métis communities than to reserves; however, the reverse appears to be true among their families' eldest generations. All except Rainey's, Kyle's, Joe's, and Dawnis's families have direct relationships with Métis communities.[3]

Just over half the participants have knowledge of Métis scrip (for land or money) within their family. Most have this knowledge because they, or more often someone in their family, have conducted family history research. Ron, Mike, and Joe are aware of Métis scrip in their family because this knowledge was passed down through oral family history. Only Benny, Jules, Sandra, and Ron know what became of their family scrip. In Benny's and Jules's families, the scrip holder sold their scrip for $250. Sandra's family received neither land nor money, due to the corruption of the scrip system. Ron's family redeemed their scrip for land in Camperville and put it into trust with the church in the 1920s, after which the church gave it to the federal government. The remaining participants do not know what became of their family's scrip; they do not know if the scrip holder(s) in their family chose to redeem their scrip for land or money, or if they were swindled like most other Métis. None of the participants' families still have their scrip land today; this is reflective of the history of the scrip system (Chapter 3).

All but Benny, KaKaKew, Sandra, Rainey, and Mae Louise indicated that their families have relationships with one or more reserves.[4] It is often grandparents who hold connections to these reserves; for others, it is one or both sides of the family, or a sibling who moved to the reserve in adulthood. In Laara's case, her maternal grandmother's father was a hereditary (pre-Indian Act) chief in Nisichawayasihk First Nation (Nelson House, Manitoba) and her paternal grandmother's father was the first Indian Act chief of Opaskwayak First Nation (near The Pas).

A few participants knew oral history about their family's relationship to a reserve; some of these relationships reflected Canadian governmental control and hardship. Lance did not know the details, but he knew that his grandmother's reserve, St. Peter's reserve, had "got moved."[5] Kyle's grandmother used to live on the Pine Bluff reserve (part of Chemawawin First Nation), which in 1963 had to be relocated due to extensive flooding caused by the Grand Rapids hydro station; families were relocated to Easterville and Grand Rapids, Manitoba, and experienced numerous hardships as a result (Chemewawin Cree Nation 2011). A far greater number of participants' families have a direct relationship with at least one reserve than do the participants themselves; younger generations' personal relationships with reserve life are increasingly distant.

Whether or not participants in my study had ever lived on a reserve or in a Métis community, many spoke of strong, ongoing connections to their traditional territories and communities. In addition to Ron's attachment to a Métis community, despite living in the city for over a decade, Dawnis expressed a similar attachment to her mother's reserve: "All my family live on the reserve; I lived, we lived in Brandon. And I always heard that that was just for work. Like, I never grew up thinking that we weren't welcome on the reserve.... But even in the cities, we still had a lot of linkages to our communities and there was a lot of flow back and forth; people would visit back and forth." In another example, Benny shared, "My great uncle has this tradition where he goes and bottles some of the dirt [on land where our family was given scrip] and he gives it to people in the family to remind people that, you know, this is where you come from; this is who you are." Mae Louise's brother Bob, who is in his late eighties, was devastated when he had to move to a town, away from their northern ancestral land, for medical reasons. As Mae Louise said, "Part of him kind of died, you know, his spirit kind of died, I think, because he loved being out there. He loved being by the lake and being bushed, being able to go hunting and that kind of stuff."

According to the 2010 Urban Aboriginal Peoples Study (UAPS), "[urban Aboriginal people's] links to their communities of origin are integral to strong family and social ties, and to both traditional and contemporary Aboriginal cultures" (29). Furthermore, the report said, "UAPS participants stay connected to their communities of origin, though only a minority has ever returned. Majorities of Aboriginal peoples (first and second generation) in Canadian cities today retain a sense of connection to their home communities and places of origin, either their own, or that of their parents and grandparents. This is particularly true for those who strongly identify as Aboriginal (i.e., those who feel they belong to a mostly Aboriginal community and know their family tree very well). Nonetheless, only two in ten have ever moved back to their community of origin or plan to return permanently" (28).

In these ways, the residence patterns of the participants in my study are consistent with larger patterns across Canada. Intergenerational consequences of the scrip and reserve systems include separation from land and divisions between Métis and First Nations people. For example, as Mike describes, in his family there are stories of coming from Saskatchewan to Manitoba because of scrip and conflict, "like kicking them off reserve and stuff like that." Such separation and division also create distance from Anishinaabe spirituality, which is predicated upon our relationship with land, as well as distance between Métis people and the spiritual ways of our Anishinaabe relatives.

Relationships with Education and Employment

The majority of the participants in this study are highly educated. Laara and Rainey each hold doctoral degrees, and Sandra and Dawnis are currently pursuing them. Benny has a master's degree, and Shirley has two bachelor degrees and a college diploma. Joe and Diane each have an undergraduate degree, and, at the time of interview, Running Elk, Mike, and Kyle were each pursuing one. KaKaKew has a college diploma, and Jules and Stan have university/college certificates. Ron's education and work experience were assessed by the Prior Learning Assessment and Recognition (PLAR) system as equivalent to university level. Finally, Tim graduated high school, and Lance and Mae Louise completed grades ten and nine, respectively. In other words, eight participants have at least one university degree; six have two degrees;

and two have three degrees. The high level of educational attainment reported by the participants in my study is somewhat consistent with the larger pattern of increasing educational success among urban Aboriginal people in Canada.[6]

Since many participants were chosen from my own and Dr. Gaywish's contacts, as is consistent in Indigenous methodologies (Chapter 4), it makes sense that participants in this study are highly educated and that some have a connection to the Midewiwin (Chapter 8). She and I are both Midewiwin and have a doctoral degree; over the years, we have made many contacts in academia and developed many relationships in the Midewiwin lodge. Many Three Fires Midewiwin people have pursued post-secondary education, with doctors, professors, teachers, and judges among us. The relationship between higher education and Anishinaabe spirituality would be an interesting topic for future research.

Likewise, the participants' employment reflects their high degree of post-secondary education. At the time of interview, five participants worked in the field of education: Rainey is a program director for an Aboriginal educational program; Laara is an assistant professor; Shirley is an education and cultural resource coordinator; and Jules and Mae Louise are Elders-in-Residence at educational institutions. Running Elk, Mike, Kyle, Benny, and Dawnis were full-time students. Sandra and Stan worked in the field of justice as the executive director of Community and Aboriginal Justice Issues for Manitoba Justice, and the Coordinator in Justice of the Aboriginal Spiritual Care department at the Manitoba Youth Centre, respectively. Diane, Lance, and Joe worked in the field of social work for Child and Family Services, as a counsellor at the Community Holistic Circle Healing Centre in Hollow Water First Nation, and as a youth care worker (and a carpenter's apprentice), respectively. KaKaKew and Tim were unemployed at the time of interview; KaKaKew previously worked in the field of social work, and Tim worked as a miner. Ron works in human resources for Manitoba Hydro as an Aboriginal employment relations specialist.

The majority of participants in this study are employed in the tertiary sector; namely in education, justice, human resources, and social work.[7] A number of participants feel their employment has been an enabling factor in their connection to Anishinaabe spirituality; the number is even greater for those who identify higher education as a key factor (Chapter 8).

Relationships with Aboriginal and Euro-Canadian Ancestry

Ancestry within the Métis Nation is a complex and controversial topic with many scholars and activists passionately defending boundaries of belonging, which include some and inevitably exclude others. They are quick to point out, as stated earlier, that being Métis is more than simply a combination of Aboriginal and European ancestry; it comprises a distinct nation, culture, history, language, and geographic region, among other factors (Andersen 2014). Asking participants about the details of their ancestry exposes their older parent cultures (e.g., Saulteaux, Cree, French, and English), which, some might argue, risks obscuring Métis nationhood. Nonetheless, the ways participants discuss their ancestry is telling, and exploring these details engenders insights; for example, highlighting aspects (such as traditional territory), they feel, brings them closer to Métis (or First Nations) identity. This section on ancestry must be considered in relation to the sections that precede and follow it to gain a more holistic understanding of these families and their relationships to the Métis Nation, whether others, or indeed they themselves, judge them to be included or excluded.

Participant responses to the question "what is your ancestry?" illustrated eight combinations of Aboriginal ancestry; in decreasing order these were: Métis/Cree/Ojibwe; Ojibwe; Cree; and Métis/Saulteaux.[8] Benny, Jules, Ron, Running Elk, Shirley, and Stan identified Métis/Cree/Ojibwe ancestry. Dawnis, Mike, Lance, and Tim have Ojibwe ancestry. Kyle and Rainey have Cree ancestry, and Mae Louise and Diane have Métis/Saulteaux ancestry. Joe, Laara, and Sandra have Cree/Métis, Cree/Oji-Cree, and Métis/Dakota/Cree/ Mohawk/Ojibwe ancestry, respectively. KaKaKew shared that, while she is of Métis ancestry through her father, she is unsure of their exact ancestral lineage.

All but one participant indicated their Aboriginal ancestry is Ojibwe or Cree or some combination of the two.[9] This is not surprising given that the study was conducted in and around Winnipeg. South-central Manitoba is part of the traditional territory of Ojibwe people, while north-central Manitoba is part of the traditional territory of Cree people; and southern Manitoba is the traditional territory of the Métis. Eleven participants said Métis (or Michif) while discussing their ancestry; seven used the term "Métis," and Jules, Mae Louise, Benny, and Ron used the term "Michif" interchangeably with "Métis." Regarding the participants' parents, seven fathers and six mothers were identified as Métis; and Ron and Stan identified both their parents as Métis.

Illustrating the complexity of the issue of Aboriginal ancestry among participants, Sandra explained: "We like to say that we're products of the Red River. To be mindful of all of our ancestry, we just say we're Indigenous. But I'm registered to Cross Lake First Nation, which is where my mother's home was. But so in our ancestry, in our mother's side, of course there's the Dakota and Scottish and Cree. On my father's side is Mohawk and Ojibwe and French. So, all of that, of course, is being Métis, right. But—not but—it has all those components, but not really identifying with one particular group." The issue of ancestry becomes even more complex when Euro-Canadian ancestry is included in the discussion.

The diversity of Euro-Canadian ancestry among the participants is greater than the diversity of Aboriginal ancestry. Thirteen participants included French in their ancestry, seven included Scottish, five included English, and another five included Irish. German, Icelandic, Welsh, Ukrainian, and Italian were each recorded once. Benny, Mae Louise, Ron, Sandra, and Tim identified Scottish/French ancestry; Diane, Jules, and Stan have French ancestry; and Dawnis and Lance recorded Irish/English ancestry. The remaining participants identified unique Euro-Canadian ancestries: French/Scottish/Irish (Joseph); French/Italian (KaKaKew); Ukrainian/English (Mike); Irish/Welsh/French (Kyle); German/Scottish/French (Laara); Icelandic/English (Rainey); Irish (Running Elk); and French/English (Shirley).

Dawnis, Stan, KaKaKew, and Shirley were unsure of some part of their ancestry. Dawnis and Stan were unfamiliar with the Euro-Canadian ancestry in their maternal line. As mentioned earlier, KaKaKew knows her father is Métis, but is unsure of his precise ancestry. She explained that her family suffers from internalized racism against Aboriginal people and tries to deny their Aboriginal heritage, choosing instead to self-identify simply as "French Canadian." Several participants also spoke of difficulties when trying to trace their genealogy, expressing frustration over the fact that often Aboriginal ancestors in their family genealogy are described only as "Indian," "North American Indian," "sauvage," or even "squaw." In KaKaKew's genealogy, one of her female ancestors "was not named. In fact, what they put her as is 'unknown squaw.'" When discussing her genealogy, Shirley stated, "It's pretty clear that it's French, French, French. But in terms of the Aboriginal ancestry it sometimes says 'Cree,' it sometimes just says 'Indian,' it sometimes says sauvage. It's not clear what nation the Aboriginal ancestry comes from on my mom's Métis side." This lack of specificity does not just occur in historic records; the oldest participant, Elder Mae Louise Campbell, explains: "Halfbreed: that's what's written on my birth certificate. It says, 'Father: Scotch Halfbreed. Mother: French Halfbreed. Child: Mixed Halfbreed.'"

Interestingly, when asked about their ancestry, many participants responded in terms of where their family's traditional territory is located, their relationship to treaty/status, and/or in terms of the Aboriginal language(s) their family speaks, which indicates that these issues are important to consider in a discussion about ancestry. Benny shared, "My mom's ancestry is Michif. I mean our family, our traditional territory, is in and around the city of Winnipeg. Before that, it would have been the Qu'Appelle Valley in Saskatchewan. And before that, it was back at the Red River Settlement." Jules answered, "Most of my ancestors lived in St. Laurent.... My grandfather on my mother's ... side was from Sandy Bay First Nation. But he wasn't—he was registered as a Treaty Indian in Sandy Bay, but he didn't really come from Sandy Bay originally; he came from Sweetgrass, Montana, and he settled in Sandy Bay back in the 1800s, and he just happened to be counted in treaty and so he became treaty." In another example, Laara explained, "I grew up in a family where both of my parents were of mixed heritage. In terms of blood quantum, we have more Cree in our blood quantum line. But sometimes that doesn't mean anything; it's what you get raised with. So our first language was definitely Cree, Swampy Cree."

Relationships to Registered Indian Status

Like their relationships with ancestry, Métis people have complex and controversial relationships with registered Indian status. As discussed at length in Chapter 3, the colonial government agenda of assimilating Aboriginal people into Euro-Canadian cultures was based on a racist Eurocentric belief in the superiority of Euro-Canadian cultures that looked down on Aboriginal cultures (and still does). According to these beliefs, Métis people were not as uncivilized as "Indians" but still were in need of a degree of assimilation if they hoped to raise themselves to the level of Euro-Canadians. The closer Métis people were to "Indians," the more aggressive Euro-Canadian attempts to assimilate them were; the closer they were to Euro-Canadians, the more they were left to fend for themselves. Due to these beliefs, Métis people were at times allowed to take treaty (instead of scrip), which heightened their chances of being enrolled as registered status Indians. As time went on, the federal government sought to lower the number of status Indians (and therefore their fiduciary responsibilities and need to honour treaty and Aboriginal rights) through forced enfranchisement[10] which continues to this day. Targeting "Halfbreeds" and Métis for exclusion from registered Indian status was a favoured strategy among assimilationist efforts. As a result, the relationship between Métis people and registered Indian status is notoriously complicated to the point where the misinformed stereotype that Métis people can't have status persists today.

This relationship to registered Indian status has influenced the participants' identities and experiences, and indirectly influences their relationships to spirituality. The participants' and their families' relationships to status reflects the government's creation of a hierarchy of types of status and enfranchisement. One-third of the participants shared unsolicited stories of enfranchisement; most identified gender discrimination as the reason for enfranchisement within their family. In each case, a female family member with registered Indian status married a non-status male, thereby rescinding her status through enfranchisement laws. Both Laara's maternal and paternal grandmothers lost their status when they married non-status men. She shares, "When my grandfather, who would have been considered non-status, married my grandmother, the moment they said 'I do,' she was no longer Indian. So, legally, she could not live on the reserve." This occurred despite the fact that Laara's grandfather was Aboriginal and her grandmother's father was the hereditary chief of Nisichawayasihk First Nation. The same thing happened on her father's side, so her father was born without status. Had her father been born with status, he would have lost it anyway when he purchased private property in Wabowden, because purchasing private property was another cause for enfranchisement.

Participants shared stories of yet other ways in which the government revoked Indian status in Aboriginal families. Tim's grandmother lost status for leaving the reservation in search of employment. He explained, "When a woman or a man left the reserve, they had to give up their status in order to get employment, and in this case that's what happened with my grandmother." Jules's maternal grandfather lost his status because he refused to give his produce to the Indian Agent (a representative of the government created through the Indian Act). Jules shares: "[My grandfather said] 'why should I give the agent what I'm gaining from my farming initiative? ... I'm not going to give you anything.' And so, he was what was called a disenfranchised [sic] Indian because he didn't follow the rules." In these overlapping ways, families were at risk of having their status stripped from them at the hands of the Canadian government's unrelenting goal of assimilation.

Only Tim and Running Elk have a parent with 6(1) status, which the government considers to be the most "pure" form of status. Running Elk and five of his seven half-siblings have 6(2) status, which the government considers one step below 6(1) status. Just below this form of status, seven participants have immediate family with Bill C-31 status, including Shirley's adoptive father and forty-five siblings divided among the other six participants. In total, sixteen participants spoke of a cumulative sixty-nine family members having registered Indian status at some point in their lives, but many did not specify, or were unsure of, the type of status. Mae Louise and Lance were the only participants whose families never had a status family member; or at least they had no knowledge of one.

Dawnis, Joe, Mike, Laara, Ron, and Sandra have Bill C-31 status. Running Elk has 6(2) status, Tim has 6(1) status, and Diane gained treaty status through marriage.[11] Had Diane not gained treaty status through marriage, she would be eligible for Bill C-31 status. She clarifies, "I was born Métis and got my treaty status when I married.... All my siblings, though, have gotten their status through Bill C-31, so I would have gone that way, too, if I didn't marry.... [It's] clear as mud [laughs]." Some participants were unsure of the type of status they hold, and asked their parents, grandparents, or AANDC for clarification. Tim believed he and his family would obtain Bill C-31 status only to discover they were eligible for 6(1) status. Registered Indian status is complicated, with cardholders themselves often confused about the details of their status.

All but one participant with Bill C-31 status shared stories of how they came to obtain their status. Many spoke of a process of questions, (family history) research, paperwork, and a family member initiating this process. Others spoke of how strange it is to receive a letter in the mail telling you that you are "Indian." Sandra received one such letter in 1995: "The letter says, 'You are now an Indian.' It was like, 'oh, okay.' [We both laugh]. That's the line in the letter: 'You are now an Indian registered to Cross Lake First Nation.'" Dawnis was about nine years old when her mother received their letter in the mail: "We're all jumping up and down, and she's like, 'We're Indians! We're Indians!' and then all of us were, 'We're Indians! We're Indians!' [chuckles]. And my cousin was living with us at the time ... his parents both have Indian status and are Ojibwe, so he never lost it. And he was looking and he said, 'Aren't I an Indian?' He was wondering why we were so excited. I didn't really know either, I didn't have a full comprehension, but I knew my mom was really excited about it. So that was kind of an odd little thing [chuckles]."

Some participants spoke of the consequences of receiving Bill C-31 status, especially with regard to identity and relationship with non-status Métis people. After years of being deeply active in Métis politics, Sandra's Métis colleagues initially shunned her when she received Bill C-31 status; she is no longer active in Métis politics.[12] As Sandra related, "I felt like Jonathan Livingston Seagull after I got my status, because the Métis people that I grew up with in that movement kind of turned their back [on me].... Because that whole issue of Bill C-31, you know, there was this expectation that you're different or ... some people may have thought that, you know, you're an interloper; well, you weren't really Métis to begin with if you can get status...."

But once you get status, you don't have a vote. So you don't have a vote in the [Métis] political process, but it doesn't change your blood, you know, or how you were raised or the people you were raised with or grew up with." She continued, "I think that a lot of people just kind of didn't understand that their Aboriginal title stemmed from the fact that they had [sic] Indigenous roots. It was almost like being Métis was different than being First Nations."

Sandra was not the only participant to suggest that First Nations and Métis have more similarities than differences, and that status does not change your biology and identity. Ron, who continues to be very active in Métis politics and has obtained Bill C-31 status, asserts, "I'm Métis first—I'm Anishinaabe or Métis first—and then everything else after that is government" and "I identify as Anishinaabe. And if people want details, well, I tell them I'm a Métis with treaty rights." He continued, "I say I'm a Métis with status. Because as a Métis person, I applied for a government program and I qualified for some of it, but I didn't qualify for all of it. So, I have some treaty rights. Because when I was on the [Manitoba] Métis Federation before, I was always fighting for Métis rights, Aboriginal Métis rights. And I always said, 'they're the same, we have the same rights ... as treaty people do, to a certain extent.' And I was always thinking that we should have done something like the North-Angle Métis did in the Fort Frances area over there, where the Métis actually did an adhesion to the treaty [Treaty 3]. So, they maintained their Métis identity, but they were recognized as having treaty." Ron insists "the Manitoba Act was a Métis treaty," and "Bill C-31, that's the virus that's going to kill the treaties." I quote our conversation at length below, because his words illustrate the effects of Bill C-31 status, including the government's forced division between First Nations and Métis familial relations:

R.R.: [Bill C-31], it's going to pick away at that third generation. It's just like they talked about, this thief that stole millions of dollars from the banks, because he had this program that went around and it stole just a little bit from each bank.

C.F.: So they wouldn't notice.

R.R.: Yeah! But over time, all of a sudden, wow, it's quite a bit! And that's what this Bill C-31 virus does. To me, that's what it is; it's a virus within our status process, and it's going to start eliminating people. And the next thing you know, there will be no status people left. And if there's no status people left, then the government has no need for these treaties, because these treaties are with "status" people. And Bill C-31 is slowly eroding that status to the point where there will be no more status. I was just listening to the women at Peguis [First Nation] a couple springs ago. That spring there were sixty-one children born on that reserve with no status. So, who is going to look after them, then? The government has already said, "well they're fourth-generation kids now, you know, we don't have to worry about them." Or their parents were Métis, so it's blood quantum; it's just like what they're doing in the States. It's all on blood quantum. And to me, that's wrong, because if a Métis marries a Métis, well, the blood stays the same. But they're saying, "No, that's another generation away from your First Nation." But Métis and Indians keep marrying all the time, and that's an ongoing thing. To me, that just refreshes the blood, that doesn't take you away from your original source of treaty status; you renew it every time. But [the Canadian and American governments] don't recognize [that].

Participants like Sandra and Ron highlight some of the consequences of Bill C-31 status and the effects it can have on Métis/First Nation identities and relationships. It is important to make note of these forced divisions, especially if there exists an assumption that only "Indians" (not Métis) have the right to participate in ceremony (see Chapter 8). In this way, if Bill C-31 is indeed the virus that will kill status and treaties, it could also contribute to further widespread loss of relationship to Anishinaabe spirituality among Métis people; indeed, among all Aboriginal people.

CHAPTER 6

Family History

Maybe today you're proud, but in our time we were not proud to be Métis.
—quoted in *Mémère Métisse/My Métis Grandmother*
(dir. Janelle Wookey, 2008)

While I asked each participant specifically to consider their family history with both parent cultures, their stories illustrate complex relationships with Aboriginal and Euro-Canadian cultures blended in unique and syncretic fashions. It is useful to discuss these relationships separately to gain insight into where influences on identity and spirituality are coming from; however, these influences and relationships exist simultaneously, often without clear cultural boundaries. There are also instances where distinction between cultures is apparent. This is perhaps most apparent in participant stories and experiences that touch upon pressures to assimilate to Euro-Canadian cultures, identities, and spiritualities.

As discussed in Chapters 2 and 3, colonial attempts to assimilate the Métis into Euro-Canadian cultures have been numerous and effective including by means of Christian conversion, legislation, and the residential school system. Assimilation attempts increased after the failed Northwest Resistance of 1885 when many Métis distanced themselves from their Aboriginal culture and identity, going so far as to change their last names to avoid any identification with Métisness. The consequences of the resulting silence around all things Aboriginal has meant intergenerational separation from Aboriginal cultures, identities, and certainly, spiritualities. The stories of family history shared below speak to this ongoing intergenerational separation and loss in more recent history and contemporary times.

Thankfully, there are also many family history stories of resistance to such assimilative pressures. Themes of passing on Aboriginal cultural beliefs, values, and customs through the generations also arise; although, these were often unnamed in family history as a matter of survival. In other words, while a love of traditional Métis foods and a place of honour for our Elders, to name two examples, were often taught in the participants' families, they were rarely explicitly identified as Métis-specific cultural attributes. The themes identified below illustrate an intriguing push and pull of assimilation and resistance to various aspects of Métis culture existing within participant family histories as influential to identity and spirituality.

Relationships with Aboriginal Languages

Indigenous languages are sacred to Indigenous peoples. I agree with Métis scholar Sherry Farrell Racette, who said that "Michif is made up of French nouns and Cree or Saulteaux verbs (depending on the region); it is a verb-based language which means the heart and soul of Michif is Indigenous. So it is with Metis culture; the heart and soul of Metis culture is Indigenous" (12 February 2013). In the Three Fires Midewiwin lodge, Anishinaabemowin is referred to as the language of spirit. In a course lecture delivered on 11 November 2011 at Shingwauk University, Benton-Banai shared that "'Anishinaabemowin' describes all the original languages.... The whole language family is known as an Algonquin language family.... It was really … *Algokowin* meaning 'entirely'.… All of the people that are now known as Métis/Michif, their basic language pattern comes from [that] same language family." These languages were given to us by Creator; our spiritual teachings are found within the languages. When we lose our languages, we risk also losing our teachings. Assimilation and forced use of European languages contribute to the "forgetting" of our teachings.[1] Many of us are now relearning our languages and teachings; learning the language helps our understanding of ceremonies, and participating in ceremony strengthens our grasp of the language.

The experiences related by interviewees in my study reflect the important links between language and identity. Only KaKaKew and Rainey do not have at least one family member who can speak an Aboriginal language. Kyle, Laara, Benny, Joe, Jules, Ron, Running Elk, and Sandra indicated at least one family member who could speak Cree. Ron, Benny, Mae Louise, and Shirley said the same about Michif; and Laara's father could speak Oji-Cree. Shirley and Ron used the term "French Michif," Mae Louise said "Michif with an Ojibwe/French foundation," and Benny simply stated "Michif." Eleven participants identified at least one family member who could speak Anishinaabemowin.[2] Some participants explained that people in their family could speak multiple Aboriginal languages, and others noted that some family members could speak one Aboriginal language and multiple European languages.[3] Ron's and Sandra's parents could speak Saulteaux/Ojibwe and Cree

(Ron's could also speak Michif); Sandra's siblings "speak a degree of Cree and Dakota"; Jules's parents were fluent in Saulteaux and Cree; and Laara's father could speak Oji-Cree and Cree.

In comparison, most participants themselves cannot speak an Aboriginal language. While Laara's first language was (Swampy) Cree, Joe, Sandra, and Ron can speak some Cree. Sandra and Jules can speak Ojibwe/Saulteaux; and Sandra can also speak a bit of Dakota. Laara explains how she and the other, older siblings in her family were able to maintain Cree in the face of pressures to assimilate to English: "I could go home everyday and get re-immersed back in our Cree language and hearing it and living it and listening to my dad's words ... we would counter what we were learning [at school], or supplement what we were learning."

Just over half of the participants who cannot speak an Aboriginal language are making efforts to learn their language through summer immersion programs, classes, traditional drumming and singing, ceremony, and learning from older family members and from their partner's family. Benny spent the previous summer in a language immersion program learning Michif in a Manitoba Métis community. She spoke of the challenges of learning Michif: "You have to have those people that speak the language around. And because the majority of the people who speak the language are Elders, it's very difficult to find the appropriate way of being around them. Especially ... for a person like me who is living outside of Manitoba, it's very difficult. For me to continue my language learning process, I would have to stay with somebody in a community. Over the long term, I think that is something that I will do. And long term, I think that it's an achievable goal." Laara echoes these challenges and desires for her own family: "They can understand bits and pieces, but it's getting lost. It's getting misplaced. Not lost, but misplaced—because you can always learn it."

Eleven participants discussed the lack of transmission of Aboriginal languages within their family with statements such as: "[My parents] both identified themselves as being Saulteaux and were fluent, too ... but never taught us young'uns" (Diane), and "My brothers and sisters were quite fluent in Saulteaux, and I missed [being taught] the language because I was the youngest.... In those years, there was a lot of discrimination, so my mother, I guess, decided it wasn't a good thing for me to be able to speak the language.... Your parents thought you would be safer not knowing the language" (Mae Louise).

Many identified factors for why their family did not pass on their language(s): Euro-Canadian education (especially residential and boarding school); influence of the church; the change from nomadism to settlement; forced incarceration in sanatoriums; moving away from home communities; and racism at the hands of non-Aboriginal family members. Dawnis and Tim shared stories of themselves or family members being beaten in school for speaking Anishinaabemowin. Tim explains, "I used to get a strap in the school for saying *boozhoo* or *aniin* [hello]. It was very confusing during that time; not having a positive image of who we were as a people." Kyle's grand-mother "didn't really teach her kids the language because she was married to a pure French man and she was Cree.... The story she told us was her mom kind of pressured her [to] 'find a White guy and you'll have a better life....' It's just kind of like that whole idea that White was the right way and just kind of disown your Aboriginal ancestry." These participants illustrate the intergenerational phenomenon of not passing on Aboriginal language(s) and contemporary efforts to relearn them.

Relationships with Aboriginal Cultures[4]

Participants' family relationships with Aboriginal cultures emerged over the following areas: cultural values, cultural subsistence practices, cultural activities, ways of relating to Aboriginal cultures, and change over time. Most participants spoke of Aboriginal values, including the importance of family (and kinship); the importance of intergenerational cultural transmission; and respect, especially for Elders, but also for oneself and in general.

A third of the participants identified the importance of family and kin-ship while growing up, even when a family had very few connections to Anishinaabe spirituality. Rainey explained, "We had no teachings or spiritual practices that I can see coming from my grandfather but an absolutely solid sense of family values." Growing up in the 1950s, Stan also shared, "We had a lot of cousins there in Lestock from my dad's side of the family, and we got along with the family like a family should. And we shared food, we shared everything back then in the fifties, I remember that." He illustrates the sense of duty and responsibility that accompanies this sense of family: "When I first left home, it was probably grade seven. I left home because, back in those days, it was not uncommon for the men—for the boys of the family—[to leave] home because it would mean more food for my sisters. You sort of sacrificed yourself; you had to make your own living back then, so your sisters and your mothers could have more food on the table." This importance of fam-ily extended to very distant relatives. Laara shared a story about travelling with her mother and daughter to attend a family gathering of Cree-speaking distant relatives they had never met and being warmly welcomed and looked after: "The people were so good to us. As soon as they knew we were a Tait connection, especially the old people, they would come up to us and tap us, 'Tait, Tait.' And just like lovingly [tap us].... By four o'clock we had eaten four meals [laughing]. [We were] accepted even though they don't know you, just because you share in that cultural link, that linguistic link, that ancestry." In another story, she tells of discovering that an older female student in one of the courses she was teaching was likely a distant relative, and arranging for her mother to meet this woman: "It's just like old people that knew each other, like there was no stranger. Those stories ... are very much embedded in that Cree way of knowing, in that Cree understanding, the kinship. It's that knowing ... that person is a descendant to the people that you know; that relation is there."

The same number of participants highlighted the value of transmitting cultural heritage across generations, especially in relation to language, child-drearing, traditional knowledge, and even teachings on how to be a good man and provide for family. Benny talked about oral stories within her family about her ancestor, Big Joe, and his desire to pass on the cultural heritage even if he did not pass on the language: "The way he lived his life was representative of his knowledge of the language.... The way that he raised his children and spoke to his children and the things that he got them to do as far as medicines ... that's what he passed on. He passed on the culture, but not the language." Kyle also recognizes that despite overwhelming pressure to assimilate to Euro-Canadian culture within his family, his mother and grandmother passed on Aboriginal values to him through childrearing. As Kyle said, "I guess I grew up kind of 'White.' But coming to university, I noticed that ... my mom—whether she likes it or knows it or not—she has a lot of the Aboriginal values instilled in her through being raised by her mom who did all the childrearing, who is Aboriginal. So, she kind of instilled a lot of those in me and my sister." Other examples come from Jules and Laara about their grandparents teaching them to work with medicines and now passing on those teachings to their own children. Said Laara, "That's that teaching from one generation to the next." This value also comes across as Laara describes a patchwork wall hanging with pieces representing work by her grandmother, mother, herself, and her daughter: "There's four generations of women; the Cree heritage that's speaking through."

Mike, Stan, Rainey, Dawnis, and Kyle spoke of the importance of respect within their family, especially for Elders. Mike recalled, "I always had that respect for Elders ... that's just how my mother raised me. I always have that deep respect for people who are older than me, especially in Aboriginal community." Similarly, Dawnis shared, "[my family] welcomed people, like when we were younger we used to make tea for the Elders, when people would come over. We'd make tea, or go get water, or go do this." She identified one instance where her family received an important teaching about respect: "One of my family's teachers, Eddie Benton-Banai, he often talks about his grandfather and the teachings from the lodge. They would always say 'every Creation Story is true....' That's a recognition of other people's spirituality and a respect for that." Stan's grandfather taught him about self-respect in the face of racism by confronting Stan's first boss for shortchanging him: "'My grandson, he worked hard for you. He come home dirty. He come home tired, worked long hours in your fields. And you only paid him ten dollars; that's not enough.... You paid that White man thirty dollars for driving a tractor. How come you paid my grandson only ten dollars?'" The farmer ended up handing over more money. In these ways, participants identified the value of respect as important in their families.[5]

Living off the Land

Two-thirds of the participants highlighted ways their families sought to provide food and other necessities for their survival; these cultural subsistence practices have been passed down for countless generations and include relationship with land; holistic education/modelling; hunting; traditional foods; fishing; trapping; and harvesting.[6] The most frequently reported cultural subsistence practice was relationship with land, and it sheds light on the other subsistence practices. While growing up, the participants' families maintained an intergenerational, conscious relationship with the land as a living, familial entity that influenced subsistence efforts and life in general. For example, Ron's family has been identifying the land in kinship terms for generations: "We were very close in terms of the way we looked at nature. We were hunters and fisherman and gatherers, and we harvested from Mother Earth. And that's how my parents and grandparents made their living; either harvesting logs or berries or medicines or fish, or trapping. My uncle is still probably the last trapper in Camperville right now." Jules, the second-oldest participant, remembers a time when many Métis families' relationship with land was characterized by a life in tune with the cycle of the seasons and hunting the bison: "I think we had a very beautiful way of life as Métis people; we followed the rules of the buffalo hunt. And I can remember that. I can remember going out, when I was probably about seven or eight years old, in the bush and living out there for days and days and days and it was just a beautiful experience."

This relationship with land also arose in discussions of "living off the land" and "growing up in the bush." In her late seventies, the eldest participant, Mae Louise, explained that as the youngest among her siblings she was the only one who was not born on the land and had not worked the land. Said Mae Louise, "They lived off that land; all my siblings, even most of my sisters, even their husbands ... they lived off the land ... and they were born right there on the land." She pointed out that this relationship forms identity: "[My sister] was also very knowledgeable when it came to living in the bush; survival. She had a lot of knowledge there because they had to ... that was who we were" and that "the culture, the traditions, you know, living off the land, the trapping, the fishing and all of that kind of stuff was very much a part of our family." Likewise, Sandra explained, "We weren't that far removed from the land," especially "when we would go up to Cross Lake in the summer—that's where my mom's family lived—we really got to live off of the land." She recounted spending time in her grandfather's ice house, hauling water, picking berries, and that "my father still hunted and still fished ... and we learned how to do those things like smoke fish and cut meat and pound it—you know, the pemmican, that kind of stuff.... It was part of our living." She recognized the importance of this relationship from a young age: "All those things we got to do, and just sort of like that sense of connection to the land, even as a child, was very important."

Just over a third of the participants told stories of holistic education, whereby grandparents and parents used teaching methods emphasizing multiple senses and environments, repetition, modelling, and encouragement. When Jules's grandmother began teaching him his grandfather's medicine bundle in 1946, she told him, "'I want you to smell all of these medicines because once you smell and once you taste something you'll never forget....' Today, I'll be walking in the bush or in a field and I'll smell a medicine and I'll know that it came from the time I was sitting with my grandmother at the age of five." Such a holistic education, especially involving modelling, can also be heard in a story by Joe: "My grandfather would always go trapping and fishing and hunting and would teach us certain aspects of each of his jobs. And we would oftentimes go out to my uncle's, who was a medicine man, and we would be taught about our culture in that regard—the spiritual aspect of it. So, my grandparents provided the physical 'this is how you do things in the bush, and this is how a Native person is,' and they modelled the behaviour for us. And my uncle modelled the spiritual aspect of it for us."

Other cultural subsistence practices that arose include hunting, fishing, and trapping. These subsistence practices often occur in combination, as can be heard in the stories above. Stan lovingly recalls his grandfather teaching him about life on the land: "He taught me about life: he taught me how to hunt; he taught me how to trap; he taught me about the animals, about the seasons. There wasn't an animal that could fly across the sky [that] I wouldn't know the name of just by their flight pattern [or] … when I heard a sound in the bush [and could] identify that … animal by the sound it made or … by how he walked." Like Ron's uncle, the last trapper in Camperville, Mae Louise's brother Bob "chose to live [in the bush] and even raise some of his grandchildren out there, and still went hunting every fall to get meat for the winter and still fish to have fish all winter." Subsistence living has become rare in modern society, and older generations are especially sad about this; with the exception of Tim and Joe, the oldest participants were the ones to discuss these activities.

Several participants also spoke of harvesting traditional foods, and their preparation. Families harvested things like wood, vegetables, berries, and medicines. Many families harvested multiple goods, as we heard from Ron, whose "parents and grandparents made their living either harvesting logs or berries or medicines or fish." Laara's family harvested roots and other medi- cines: "We always went out to the bushes and we tapped juice from the trees." Mae Louise, Ron, Sandra, and Tim spoke of their families picking berries. Seven participants said traditional foods were part of their diet while growing up, including berries, roots, wild meat, fish, and pemmican made from fish and bison. Shirley identified traditional Métis foods from her childhood: "We ate bannock and stew and tortières (meat pies) and boulettes (meatballs)." In addition, Mae Louise, Laara, and Sandra discussed food preparation, includ- ing pounding, drying, and smoking fish and wild game (especially to preserve it as pemmican and/or for consumption during winter months), and canning. Mae Louise's mother would "can moose meat and she would can fish." Laara commented that "people don't talk enough about how food was preserved…. You know pemmican? Well they used to do that to fish, too. I saw that being done, it was really pretty neat, the way they … dry up the fish, cook it, and use fish and oil till it's really dry and flaky. And it's really nice; you eat it with the berries…. That's growing up very much embedded in [Cree world view]."

Several participants talked about taking part in cultural activities as part of their family's relationship to Aboriginal cultures while growing up, such as jigging and fiddling, pow wows, drumming, and singing. Fiddling and jigging are part of traditional Métis culture, even though their roots can be found in Europe. Mae Louise explained, "my father … played the fiddle and my mother would jig and she played the mouth organ. Those kinds of things

... [were] actually incorporated from the French and from the Scottish ancestry." Benny shared, "My grandparents grew up in a very specific culture with very specific traditions: jigging, fiddling, the sash, dancing ... the whole kind of Michif deal. They grew up in that culture. So, my mother was exposed to old-school fiddling, step dancing, and jigging." Sandra was the only one to mention that her family participated in fiddling, jigging, and pow wows: "We always had family jigging contests [laughs hard] and we attended pow wows." Running Elk's family continues to follow the pow wow trail (going from one pow wow to the next during pow wow season, and participating in various ways, including being a spectator, dancing, drumming, singing, and selling arts, crafts and food).

While growing up, participants' family relationships with Aboriginal cultures were often troubled due to the ongoing effects of colonization and assimilation. Three major patterns arose regarding the ways families related to Aboriginal cultures while growing up: disassociation (a conscious distancing from all things Aboriginal), *kiimoochly* (secretively), and lived/embedded (a part of life without naming/identifying it or consciously discussing it as such). Half of the participants reported disassociation: relationships marked by denial, disconnection, shame, marginalization, distrust, and silence. Internalized racism can be heard in many of these stories; for example, in response to the question "while growing up, what was your family's relationship with Aboriginal culture?," KaKaKew replied, "It was nothing. It was hidden. There was no such thing; we were not as Métis people. My dad was not willing to accept that. My grandmother was not willing to accept that. Her mother perhaps, I don't know how she was raised. But back in the day ... to identify yourself as a Métis person would bring upon a lot of hardship." Kyle's non-Aboriginal grandfather was a significant factor contributing to their internalized racism. Benny shares the consequences of her grandparents moving east, away from traditional Métis territory: "There's a bit of a tradition of hiding that [Michif] heritage, beginning with my grandparents.... My grandparents did not carry on those traditions on purpose—those Michif traditions." Mike identified Christianization as contributing to his family's disassociation: "Back in that area, and pretty much the surrounding reserves, pow wows are something that's looked down at. [It's] very colonized [with a] high concentration of ... Pentecostal and some United ... Christian Churches. Even today, pow wows are something that you have to travel two hours, maybe to Peguis, to see." Shirley also hints at widespread assimilation in her family and in the city of Winnipeg: "I was a kid in the eighties, right, in the early nineties. We didn't pow wow or square dance or jig or go to events or hang out at the friendship centre, or anything like this. I don't know that if my parents even wanted to, that they would have even known where to go. And I can't think of any school that I went to ... where I was ever aware that there was a whole bunch of other Native kids, [or] that from the school Native culture was supported or encouraged."

Several participants also shared stories about their family having to do things *kiimoochly* (secretively) because of government laws banning traditional practices and the difficulty of being Métis after the Northwest Resistance of 1885. Laara spoke of the Cree concept *kiimooch* while discussing laws designed to suppress Aboriginal people, including Indian Act laws that made it illegal for more than three "Indians" to gather in public (except in church) without an Indian Agent present (for fear of another resistance), or to participate in ceremony. Nevertheless, said Laara, "they continued the practicing in spite of the bans." She continues:

> My word *kiimooch* is very important, because they still continued to do it in secrecy. They did it behind [closed doors]; they shifted things around so that they could still pray. A good example of *kiimooch* is [in Shawn] Atleo's book, [*Tswalk: A Nuu-chah-nulth Worldview*].... He said, "sometimes our people, we used to have these big drawing on logs and boards, but Christianity started to come and priests were becoming strong and powerful. As soon as you [saw] a priest coming, they transferred their pictures, symbols onto blankets. Because you can take the blankets down and roll them up and hide them. It's hard to take your logs down and roll them up and hide them." ... They continued the practicing in spite of the bans.

Jules recalls being told by his mother as a small boy to hide a sack of wild fish and game in the bushes whenever government authorities came to search houses for anything "illegal," and that his grandmother secretly taught him medicines. He comments on the price of being caught doing something "illegal":

> Always remember that it was against the law to do these things....
> I would see the RCMP [Royal Canadian Mounted Police] coming into the village [of St. Laurent] and taking, it was usually a man.... I later found out that they were either taken to Ninette Sanatorium, or they were taken to Stony Mountain. Stony Mountain is the big penitentiary here, and Ninette was the place

where people went who were diagnosed with TB (tuberculosis). I went to Stony Mountain later on, a few years later, and to my surprise, most of those men that disappeared from our village were in Stony Mountain penitentiary. All my relatives! But why did they go there? It must have been they did something that was considered to be illegal—maybe they were fishing out of season, maybe they were hunting out of season ... because Métis hunted year round and fished year round; that was our way of life. That was our subsistence. (Jules)

Mae Louise's mother boiled traditional medicines on the kitchen stove to help her deliver babies in their community, but she did not talk about it (recall Laara's reminder that the Canadian government banned midwifery in 1950). Two of the youngest participants, Mike and Tim, noticed that people still did not want to be associated with ceremonies, but some did them secretly, while they were growing up, even though many of these laws had officially been repealed by then: "The adults who were children around the time it was outlawed, they didn't understand what their parents were doing because they had to wait in the bush during the night. And they would hear these rattles, drums, singing, and they didn't know what was going on and their parents didn't want to tell them because of the law at the time. They didn't want them to get their parents in trouble.... That got passed down. And a lot of them today still feel that it's taboo. My parents didn't really talk about it" (Tim). These examples demonstrate the overwhelming control that the Canadian government exerted over Aboriginal people in every aspect of life, literally from birth to death.

Despite this control, Dawnis's, Sandra's, Jules's, Laara's, and Mae Louise's families managed to maintain closer connections to ancestral ways, explaining their experience of Aboriginal cultures as "lived/embedded." Sandra stated, "The presence of culture though wasn't, that was never an issue in our family because we lived it. And we experienced it.... It was part of our living." Likewise, Laara said, "Our upbringing was very Cree, because it was embedded in the language." Dawnis explained that while her family may not have had the "details of the cultural knowledge," due to assimilation and colonization, "they had a way about them that was very rooted in our culture.... The more that I learn [about our culture], I can see it in the way that they carried themselves, in the stories that they have about their families.... There was a lot there, and yet there was also a lot missing that was our inheritance; that was taken." Families had to hide practices that had previously sustained their well-being for generations. This certainly impacted relationships with spirituality; more and more family members had no personal experience of these cultural and spiritual practices. Families resisted these pressures and maintained connections to spirituality and culture when they could.

Half the participants indicated that their family's relationship with Aboriginal cultures has improved since their childhood, as reflected in increased acceptance, understanding, effort, and participation. Diane explained that her parents did not want their children playing with the children from the nearby reserve; however, they eventually came to develop good relationships with these neighbours. She continued, "Over the years, I see that a lot of my family have a lot of good friendships with people that live on the res[erve].... I have cousins that have married into [the reserve]; like, their spouses come from there. I think it's improved. And there's probably a better understanding of what reserve life is." While discussing his family's and community's relationship with ceremony, Mike shared that his mother has been reaching out to learn more about Aboriginal culture and ceremony, and that "It's becoming a little more acceptable. But it'll still be a long time [before] that is welcomed in the community."

Families are demonstrating an improved relationship with Aboriginal cultures, in part as a result of the participants themselves. Rainey shared, "Over the years, I think, things have changed, where they're not involved in any kind of traditional spiritual activity, but they respect me. And they respect what I've done." In response to the question, "has your family's relationship with Aboriginal culture changed over time?" Jules had this to say: "Tremendously! I did everything possible to have my sons take pride in their Métis ancestry. And I do the same thing with my grandchildren, to feel good, to feel proud … to know that we contributed immensely to society as it exists today. There's a lot of Métis influence. Many of our ancestors could be role models today as we continue to go forward in life."

Family Relationships with Euro-Canadian Cultures

The most often cited aspects of participant families' relationship with Euro-Canadian cultures are, in decreasing order, Euro-Canadian education and employment; Euro-Canadian control; desire to fit in/blend in; positive relationships; Euro-Canadian languages; Indigenous rights and resistance; and whether or not this relationship has changed over time.[7]

When discussing their family's relationship with Euro-Canadian cultures during childhood, half the participants mentioned Euro-Canadian education, and almost as many highlighted employment. Many participants spoke of Eurocentric education, especially in relation to residential, boarding, and day schools. Ron explained that he, "and the generation before me—like my parents ... we went to a day school, but it was almost that [we] were treated, and the intent was the same, as the residential school next door.... The nuns and the priests that ran the residential school also ran our [day] school in Camperville." Jules shared that the day school in St. Laurent run by the Catholic Church coerced children to say they would commit to life as clergy, and in exchange they would be treated more favourably by staff: "The Europeans had a big influence to turn us into Catholics. Many of us subscribed to that, even to this day.... I can tell you stories that would turn your stomach of what I experienced and what I saw. We have nightmares about those days, but many Métis didn't declare abuse ... because they were afraid about the repercussions from the community." Eurocentric attitudes were often internalized by those who attended the schools. Similarly, Mike's mother never wanted him to go to a reserve school because she felt he would receive an "inadequate education."

Many participants spoke of employment, especially the type of job that their grandparents and/or parents worked. These jobs included generations of railroad workers (Benny's family); the Department of National Defence (Jules's father); and "fisherman, trapper, mining, building, labour, carpentry and ... railway [labour]" (Laara's father). Mike and Ron specifically noted that their family had good economic relations with Aboriginal and non-Aboriginal community members during their childhood. On the other hand, Mae Louise and Stan spoke of challenges their family members faced regarding employment in a racist society. Mae Louise's family internalized Eurocentric beliefs; she explained that they aspired to be like "White people," but "you could never be like [them] no matter how much you tried." Her mother could only get jobs cleaning White people's homes, hotels, and restaurants. Said Mae Louise, "You would have that interaction with White people, but they would treat you as a servant. My mother was treated that way when she worked for them as a servant. And so she didn't speak of them too much, she just did her work and was happy to receive the little bit of pay that she got." Similarly, Stan explained that only certain jobs, such as farmhand, were open to Aboriginal men while he was growing up: "It was not unusual to have an Aboriginal person as a farm hand ... back in those days.... You can get jobs with farmers and they'd be glad to put you up for the winter for feeding their cows and their pigs and their chickens.... That's the only jobs we got is farm labour jobs. That's the only, *only* jobs we got is labour jobs." Participants' stories of Eurocentrism in education and employment do not appear to leave much room for meaningful relationships with Anishinaabe spirituality; it seems more likely that these aspects of Euro-Canadian culture have contributed to a further disconnection between Métis (and First Nation) families and Anishinaabe spirituality.

About half the participants' stories of family relationships with Euro-Canadian cultures were marked by subtle or overt control. Such control spanned the areas of hunting and fishing laws; laws against midwifery; laws against Native people gathering together in one place; the power to name a people; control over resources; the power of the Indian agent to control and restrict movement; and the control that social workers have over Aboriginal children.[8] Jules commented, "I think the resourcefulness and the strong, fierce self-determination and need to be independent—to do as we please—was seriously damaged by laws that included the Métis." The Métis were made to feel like criminals for living a life they had always known; for instance, providing for one's family became illegal when Euro-Canadian authorities made up laws illegalizing hunting and fishing, thereby outlawing Métis ways of life. Laara explained that Euro-Canadian control over Aboriginal people also existed in their disregard for our original names—for example, calling the Nêhiyawak by the name "Cree." Discussing Nêhiyawe author Phyllis Cardinal's book, *The Cree People of Canada*, Laara shared that, "When the priests and missionaries were coming into our northern communities in Ontario, they observed Cree people as being very prayerful and sacred.... They spoke in very sacred ways in the language. So they called us Christino, almost like the image of Christ, because we act the way Christ would have acted in kind ways.... Over time, that [be]came Anglicized [in]to 'Cree.'" She also believes that, because the Indian Act forbade "Indians" from gathering, Aboriginal people agreed to participate in churches because it was one place where our people could gather in numbers without being overtly persecuted. Commenting on the power of the Indian agent, Ron explained how they would "force [us] to stay on reserves. Because if you've got to get a pass to get off the reserve, well, you better treat your Indian agent good. If you ever piss him off, you're going to be stuck on that reserve for the rest of your life. And that happened to a lot of families, they weren't even allowed to go to the next reserve to go and see your kin folk out there." He argues that instead of Indian agents, "now they're using corporations to go in there and keep doing that with the land now ... they're going after the resources." In other examples, Stan and Shirley pointed out the power of social workers over Aboriginal families. In adulthood, Stan bumped into the social worker he had as a child, who told him: "'I had a lot of pressure from the mayor and council members in McAuley to apprehend you and put you in boarding school.'" (Stan continued, "There was a lot of pressure put on him because mom was a single parent and the community, the White community, thought she didn't have the skills to bring us up.... If it wasn't for him, we would have wound up in boarding school someplace totally without an [Anishinaabe] identity." Shirley's social worker prevented her from attending the Children of the Earth (COTE) High School, because it had a focus on Aboriginal culture (which Shirley longed for), saying, "'No. You should probably stay here. You're really smart. You should stay where the smart kids are. You'll have lots of time to learn about culture when you're older.'" In these ways, Eurocentrism and Eurocentric control inhibited relationships with Aboriginal cultures.

The same number of participants discussed their family's desire to fit or blend into White, Euro-Canadian cultures; many of these families viewed White, Euro-Canadian cultures as superior to Aboriginal cultures because of internalized racism and colonization. Recall, for example, the intergenerational encouragement in Kyle's family for the women to marry White men—or the preferential treatment lighter-skinned family members received from his grandfather. Mae Louise's and Shirley's families also tried hard to adopt Euro-Canadian cultural practices and values, desperately trying to "be like them" (Mae Louise). Similarly, KaKaKew's family "blended. We fit into the norm.... We just kind of fit in." Thanks to their lighter complexion, they were more successful in living solely as "French Canadian" and denying their Aboriginal ancestry. Other participants explained that their family's desire to blend into Euro-Canadian culture can be understood as a survival tactic. Diane's parents were aware of "the stigma from reserve life"; she explained that instead they "wanted to see us fit in more [with Euro-Canadian society] so that we wouldn't get caught up in that lifestyle.... My mom and dad, we were on welfare almost all our lives, and I think they wanted us out of that and to be more financially stable and have those benefits ... because they could see what [White people] had around us; we didn't have running water the whole time we grew up." For some participants' families, assimilation represented the path to a life where their children might suffer less discrimination.

On the other hand, just under half the participants explicitly mentioned that their family had some positive relationships with Euro-Canadian cultures while they were growing up; these were often community-specific stories of positive relations with Euro-Canadians. According to Mike, in his community of Gypsumville, the non-Aboriginal community members got along well with the Métis people in town, as well as with the First Nation people in the surrounding four reserves. Ron spoke of "White merchants" being on friendly terms with the Aboriginal residents of his community in

Camperville, because "they adopted a lot of our ways and we became friendly with them very quickly." Diane shared that "White ranchers" in her town got along well with her parents—perhaps, she explains, because her parents tried so hard to "fit into" Euro-Canadian society. Also, Jules and his brother were well-accepted when they moved to the non-Aboriginal town of Rivers, Manitoba, because, he believes, they both excelled in athleticism. In Laara's opinion, Wabowden, Manitoba, is "a good model of mixed-heritage people … the first White people that lived in Wabowden learned to speak the language…. I remember seeing these Icelandic people speaking Cree. It wasn't unusual. So it can be done." Stan recalled a time when he was foreman at a York Tire outlet, and a racist customer demanded that a manager call the owner, Lou Libold, a Jewish man. Libold replied, "'Tell that man to go take all his tires … we don't want his business. We don't need his business.' So I was supported; I felt good." These community-specific stories and stories of Euro-Canadian individuals making efforts to learn Aboriginal languages and cultures and confronting racism against Aboriginal people suggests the potential for Euro-Canadians to encourage meaningful relationships with Aboriginal cultures; this potential is significant, and must not be forgotten amidst stories of Euro-Canadian control.

Joe, Dawnis, Jules, Ron, Tim, and Laara briefly mentioned their family's relationship with Euro-Canadian languages. Joe and Laara shared that their families were forced to learn English in school; Joe mentioned that this was the case after the Indian agent finally caught up with his family and placed them in school. Several stories were about participants' family and/or community speaking both English and French while they were growing up. This was the case for Jules, Ron and his mother, Tim and his maternal grandmother, and Laara. Dawnis mentioned that her family refused to learn French in school because the school would not also teach Anishinaabemowin. Many of these stories involved coercion and being forced to learn Euro-Canadian languages; the flipside of this is being forced to abandon or "forget" Aboriginal languages. While Dawnis's family tried hard to resist this coercion, more families did indeed adopt Euro-Canadian languages, often at the expense of loss of Aboriginal languages within their families. Importantly, participant families found other ways to resist assimilation.

When asked about their family's relationship with Euro-Canadian cultures while growing up, Running Elk, Dawnis, Ron, Sandra, and Jules explicitly discussed Indigenous rights and resistance. Running Elk, Dawnis, and Ron spoke of activism regarding treaty rights as significant in their family's relationship with Euro-Canadian cultures during their upbringing. Dawnis and Running Elk also spoke of their families refusing to claim "Canadian citizenship" (choosing instead to honour First Nation citizenship) and activism at the Canadian/American border. Running Elk's mother taught him about "sticking up for our rights and protecting treaty rights. I was taken to a number of marches and protests when I was very young.... One of them I remember was Sault Ste. Marie, where we did a border-crossing, and there was like hundreds of Aboriginal people ... crossing back and forth from Canada and U.S. border." Dawnis's family, who were very involved with the American Indian Movement, refused to sing "God Save the Queen" or recite the Lord's Prayer in school. She shared, "I was always raised to say 'I'm not Canadian.' And for a long time, my family didn't even vote in the elections; we were really strict." In her own words, "I support that there'd be more than one language in Canada and there's a recognition of Francophone culture within Canada and I support that—but I support also Indigenous languages—all of our languages. I'm not going to learn another colonial language before I learn my own." Sandra and Jules spoke of Indigenous resistance during their upbringing on a more general level. Sandra was involved in the American Indian Movement along with other teenagers in her community, and Jules talked about Métis people as a whole and our efforts to resist shame at the hands of colonization. The tradition of resistance to Euro-Canadian control as illustrated in these families is part of a larger pattern of resistance among Indigenous people.

Diane, KaKaKew, Joe, Mike, Kyle, Lance, Running Elk, Sandra, and Tim reported "no change" in their family's relationship with Euro-Canadian cultures since their upbringing; whether they indicated poor or positive relationships, they remain largely unchanged. Dawnis and Running Elk do mention a slight improvement. Running Elk explained that on his reserve some of his band and council are getting along better with Euro-Canadian governments and implementing new agreements such as "the Land Code Management ... which is also known as the Land Management Act, [as well as] new framework agreements to the treaties." However, he was quick to share his opinion that these agreements are "ultimately going to deteriorate this community, my community's entitlement to the land." Dawnis's uncle has been trying to better their relationship with Euro-Canadian cultures by "establish[ing] political allegiances with politicians and look[ing] at participating in Canadian society, Canadian elections, those kinds of things," but "not at the sacrifice of who we are as Anishinaabe." She explained that, "because there's a total denial of Nishinaabe existence, continuing existence of Anishinaabe people as peoples within our own territory ... there's a lot of conflict there because of that." Running Elk and Dawnis both indicated an improvement in their family's relationship with Euro-Canadian cultures, but that much work is still needed before this relationship can be considered healthy.

Joe and Shirley both reported that their family's relationship with Euro-Canadian cultures has worsened; in both cases, it appears that as the participants' families became more educated regarding Eurocentrism, their relationships with Euro-Canadian cultures deteriorated. The more she learned about Canadian history, the more Shirley's mother became disillusioned with "Canadian culture." In Shirley's words, "[Now] she understands why she was poor and had to deal with racism as a kid, right. Not just because they didn't like her particularly but because it was a broader systemic thing. So, I think because my mom understands a little bit more background, that she can look at Canadian culture generally more objectively, and that it's not so glorious and needs to be strived for." According to Joe, his family's relationship "actually worsened a little bit. They were really horrified with Oka—I know that. It really bothered my grandfather quite a bit."[9]

Mae Louise described changes in her family's relationship with Euro-Canadian cultures as a result of modernization, including running water, television, and no longer living off the land but in towns and cities instead. Integration into Canadian society has been easier for the younger generations in her family, and painful and confusing for older generations who feel they have no choice in the changes: "All kinds of emotions that you feel when you're trying to—how you say—integrate yourself into this [Euro-Canadian] world, eh. But once you're there, and of course you have your own children then, you get married and you know that they have to learn to live in the world, so we have to change, we have to change."

Family Relationships with Spirituality

Christian influence is the most prevalent pattern that arose regarding participant families' relationships with spirituality while growing up; every participant indicated significant Christian influence of one or more denominations. The following Christian denominations were identified: Roman Catholic (15), Anglican (4), United Church (3), Protestant (2), Pentecostal (2), Evangelical (1), Lutheran (1), and Mennonite (1).[10]

All but Rainey, Joe, Benny, and Running Elk indicated they were raised primarily within one or more spiritual faiths. Twelve participants were primarily raised in the Christian faith.[11] Laara was the only participant to say that her family was primarily raised within an integrated Anglican and

Cree spirituality; and Dawnis was the only one to assert that, while her family had Catholic influences while growing up, their primary spirituality was Anishinaabe. Joe, Benny, and Running Elk indicated that, while both Christian and Aboriginal spiritual traditions were present during their upbringings, neither held a primary position. Rainey's family held multiple Christian influences while growing up, but again, none was primary.

The significant influence of Christianity in the lives of participants and their families was apparent in the many shared stories. Mae Louise explained, "I had to go to Sunday school, and I had to learn catechism, and I had to do all those things because you know that's what they believed already, now, probably two or three generations." Stan recalled going to Catholic mass with his family every Sunday, every second day during Lent, and even travelling many miles by rented car after the family moved just to get to a Catholic church. Sandra's family went to Catholic mass in the mornings, then Protestant services in the evenings: "We were raised as Catholic in the morning [chuckles] ... my dad was Catholic and my mother was Protestant. So in the evening, we'd go to a Protestant service." Similarly, Tim's father was Protestant and his mother is Catholic; Tim and his siblings would alternate between Protestant services and Catholic masses on Sundays.

Tim and Ron both wanted to enter the priesthood at one time in their lives. Tim changed his mind at age twelve, when he learned that Catholic priests do not marry and must remain celibate; later in life, he learned that Protestant pastors could marry, but by then that path was no longer for him. Ron was raised in a strong Catholic family in a Catholic community; his grandparents hooked up their horses and caboose and travelled ten miles to attend church. Ron served mass as an altar boy at the convent every morning before attending day school, and he attended catechism every day. By age ten, he was an altar boy, could recite the entire mass and all the prayers in Latin, and was being seriously groomed to attend the seminary at Fort Alexander to become a priest. Around that time, however, rumours about sexual abuse of children by clergy at seminaries and residential schools began to emerge, so Ron and his family decided against the priesthood for Ron.

Laara, Dawnis, and Joe were the only ones to mention that Anishinaabe spirituality was a significant influence upon their family while they were growing up. Laara's immediate family integrated Anglicanism and Nêhiyaw (Cree) spirituality. The community of Wabowden had an Anglican Church and a Catholic Church, so half of Laara's family was Roman Catholic. As Laara reported, "We always had these little, probably ideological discussions about what is hell and heaven and earth. Roman Catholicism was very clearly defined, and my Roman Catholic cousins were always so scared they were … going to hell!… But yet, at the same time, we'd all be in the bush doing our Cree things … just living it. You don't articulate it, you just live it." Her grandfather was an Anglican lay minister who also taught the family about traditional medicines, Nêhiyaw values, Nêhiyaw language, and how to live off the land. She explained that her family "read the Bible and [went] to church, but then never ever turned their nose up at the tobacco." Laara's mother told her she had once asked Laara's grandfather why he had become an Anglican minister, and his response was, "this way our language will survive."[12] She continued: "We used to go to church with him, and because I was his favourite I'd go with him every Sunday. But what was interesting was everything was in the Cree language. It was never in English, because he didn't speak English. So it felt comfortable; it felt okay. It didn't feel like this Christian influence. And because he was a trapper and he was very much [an] on-the-land person, it didn't feel like the Christian influence. It felt like we had our own brand of that." Joe shared that while his grandparents would occasionally bring them to church, their medicine man uncle also sometimes taught him and his siblings about Nêhiyaw and Anishinaabe practices, such as sweat lodge, while they were growing up. While Joe's family was exposed to both Christian and Aboriginal spirituality, they adhered neither to Christianity nor to Aboriginal spirituality in any primary or consistent way. For Dawnis's family, both Christian and Anishinaabe spiritual influences were present, but Anishinaabe spirituality—specifically Midewiwin—was their primary (and ever-increasing) spiritual influence. It is not surprising that most participants indicated significant Christian influence, as opposed to Anishinaabe influence, while growing up, given the relentless pursuit of the Métis and First Nations by Christian assimilationists; as adults, however, most of the participants themselves primarily follow Anishinaabe spirituality.

While most participants reported not having consistent, significant Anishinaabe spiritual influences while growing up, a majority did report the presence—to varying degrees—of individual Anishinaabe spiritual practices, ceremonies, and people. Many stories were shared about traditional medicines; one or more immediate or extended family members (or community members) worked with these medicines for purposes that included healing sickness, cleansing the spirit, and maintaining good health.[13] Dawnis, Joe, Benny, and Laara also made mention of a family member (ancestor or living) who was/is a medicine person. Sandra was the only participant to mention "bad medicine"; her mother was fearful of such medicine being used in their community.

The other participants all spoke positively about the stories and use of traditional medicines within their family and community. Jules fondly recalled his grandmother secretively teaching him about his grandfather's medicine bundle when he was a child. In another story, Benny explained, "[My ancestor Big Joe] used medicines. He knew how to heal himself. He healed other people. You know ... my great-great-uncle still uses medicines. My great-great-auntie still makes medicine.... Those stories have always been there [in my family]." Similarly, Laara stated, "We grew up on the land and I grew up picking medicines from the land, so, you know, that's always been a part of me, and we used that traditional way of offering or placing tobacco on the land." She is quick to recognize that her family's experience and knowledge of traditional medicines is not common among Aboriginal people as a result of colonization. She came to this realization after wondering why others were so excited to learn about medicines: "I realized people are ... disconnected from it [because of] the banning, and [therefore, not] many generations of people still have experience of doing that. And, because of where I was raised—we were raised in the bushes and kind of away—we can do [those] things." Despite a general disconnection from ceremonies in participants' families, some families maintain use of traditional medicines, especially among older generations.

Ten participants indicated that their family's relationship with Anishinaabe spirituality while growing up was marked by conflict. They shared stories about Anishinaabe spirituality and secrecy; internalization of the effects of suppression of ceremony; and negative views of Anishinaabe spirituality held by family members. Secrecy regarding Anishinaabe spirituality while growing up is part of the broader issue of secrecy regarding Aboriginal cultures discussed earlier. Stan recalled learning from his mother in her hospital bed that his parents participated in ceremony; according to Stan, she said: "'Your dad and I used to [go to ceremony] in Lestock....' I said to her, 'that was in the fifties, Mom. How come you sent me to church all the time, yet my dad and you went to ceremonies?' She said, 'it was hidden, back in those days. It was outlawed.... We didn't want you to learn these ways, back in those days....'" In adulthood, Ron discovered that one of his uncles was Midewiwin: "When you study the history of the Midewiwin, they've been around a long time, they just went underground too. Like my uncle, that was a well-kept secret [in my family]—that he was Midewiwin, and that he was that high of degree of Midewiwin." Older generations purposely did not teach their children Anishinaabe ways to spare them persecution from church and government; thankfully, ceremonies were sometimes continued *kiimoochly*.

Participants hinted at internalized colonization in their family resulting from the church. A story from Mae Louise illustrated the powerful influence the community priest held over Métis families: "We have to remember what happened. I mean we were Christianized, very much so…. What I remember as a child, anyway, all I can remember is being Catholic. The priest came to visit you all the time, and if you weren't behaving you were disciplined. All of that kind of stuff already was affect[ing] us already. So because of that, you just followed these people who were, who you felt were much wiser than you were. [Who] knew about worldly things and made us feel as though we were 'savages' and ignorant people, and they had to tell us how to live and how to be and how to believe. And so a lot of our people went in that direction." She went on to say: "The Métis community, it was almost compulsory for them to go to church every Sunday, because if they didn't the priest was there to meet them immediately. He'd be knocking at the door and saying, 'I missed you at church. You should be coming to church.' So, they felt as though it was something they had to do. And it was really forced upon you." Mae Louise's sister Florence had many children and often could not get to church. After mass, the priest would go to Florence's house and scold her for not being at church: "He didn't care about her having no food for the kids sometimes, it just didn't seem to matter. But you had to be at church every Sunday."

Suppression by the church and governmental laws against ceremonies worked in tandem, and became internalized beliefs among many Aboriginal people over the generations. Jules explained, "It was against the law to do a sweat…. There was a threat of excommunication … if anybody participated in those types of activities like ceremonies…. I think it was around 1962 that law was lifted, where now you could participate in Sundances and Potlatches…. That law was enforced back in my time—in the forties and in the fifties—it was enforced.[14] And when someone got excommunicated from the church, it was a disgrace. Once the church decided that you weren't going to be buried in the Catholic cemetery … that was ultimately a disgrace to the family. I had an uncle that wasn't allowed to be buried in the cemetery and that was a big disgrace to the Desjarlais family." Laara also commented on the effects of such suppression: "Christianity was already coming into our communities, too, because with the Indian Act and with the colonization, they were plunking these churches [into our communities]. And they used the church as a way to control people to not sing and dance the Cree singing or the Nishinaabe singing." She recalled hearing her grandfather chanting when he thought he was alone, because he could no longer do those things openly. She continued, "[My grandfather] was doing it privately in his own private space; and I'd hear the chanting ... because those are the things that were starting to be pushed away in favour of Christianity."

The church demonized Anishinaabe spirituality, and this was internalized among many families. This can be heard in stories shared by Mike, Sandra, and Running Elk about family members believing that Anishinaabe spirituality is "wrong," "bad," or "evil." Running Elk shared, "Some people on the reserve actually think that ... smudging and praying and Ojibwe spirituality and sweats are witchcraft ... but I think they might have had some influence from the church." Sandra stated, "Where [my mother] grew up, there was good medicine and bad medicine, but mostly bad medicine.... A lot of what we consider our daily practice now was ... frowned upon because there's that sense of the internalization of the church's teaching that it was wrong." In Mike's community, "people don't really want to be associated with [Anishinaabe spirituality] because they don't really know [about] it, they just know that it's bad."

Relationships with spirituality have been consistent for at least three or more generations within more than half the participant families. Catholicism has been the primary faith for three or more generations within Diane's, Jules's, KaKaKew's, Lance's, Ron's, Tim's, and Sandra's families. The same is true of integrated Cree and Anglican faith in Laara's family. Dawnis's family has had significant Catholic influence for three or more generations, but their primary faith is increasingly Anishinaabe spirituality. Several participants' grandparents were active church-goers, but their parents were not. For Stan, Shirley, Mae Louise, and Rainey, their parents often made them go to church even though they themselves did not attend regularly. Mike's and Running Elk's grandparents were highly influential in their spiritual lives. Finally, for Benny and Joe, only their grandparents attended church regularly; they themselves and their parents did not.

Among two-thirds of the participants, unlike during their upbringing, one or more family members now participate to some degree in Anishinaabe spirituality. Stan's youngest sister received her Anishinaabe name; Sandra's siblings (especially her sisters) support at Sundance; Running Elk's siblings, mother, and grandmother smudge and learn traditional songs. Ron's family members have "all been involved in a sweat. They've all gone to the ceremony. They're all aware of what the ceremony is all about. Some of us follow it stronger, and some of us they don't go to the Sundance any more than they'll go to Sunday mass." A movement away from Christianity towards Anishinaabe spirituality seems to be taking place.

Anishinaabe spirituality is now the family's primary faith in the families of Dawnis, Joe, Jules, and Laara (with the exception of one sister), and Ron's sister. According to Jules, "We were primarily Catholic … [but] my family is not primarily Catholic … anymore. My family is primarily [adhering to] Aboriginal spirituality; we follow the culture of our Aboriginal side. And it's by choice. That doesn't go for all members of my family, but some members of my family." When asked if his immediate family participates in traditional ceremonies, Joe replied, "Yes, all of them. We're all named, clan-ed, have danced, some of us have danced…. All of us have gone to sweats and some of us have Sundanced as participants, others as *skahbeh*s [helpers]. And all have had certain other ceremonies. We've all pursued our own ways and such, but all of us do [follow Anishinaabe spirituality]."[15]

CHAPTER 7

Self-identification and Personal Experiences

There are many people who could claim and learn from their Indian ancestry, but because of the fear their parents and grandparents knew, because of past and present prejudice against Indian people, that part of their heritage is clouded or denied.

Joseph Bruchac, "Elders Mediation of the Day,"
15 August 2010

"I'm a paradox to a lot of people and I don't think that's such a bad thing anymore.... There were moments where I would feel ashamed of the fact that I seem to not fit the expectations other people had for me as a Métis person, and now I feel very secure in my skin. I'm still aware of my skin, but I feel very secure in it."

—Benny, participant

As with family stories that reflect on the relationship to Aboriginal and Euro-Canadian cultures and spirituality, this chapter illustrates the existence of subtle, nuanced, and sometimes conflicting pressures to self-identify in one way or another as influenced by simultaneous pressures to assimilate and desires to resist such pressures. Consequences of colonial oppression of Métis people are apparent in the participants' family histories regarding self-identifying names and labels. Some family members vehemently denied Aboriginal identity, while others held onto Aboriginal self-identification with fervour, often within a single family.

Moreover, participants' stories of personal experiences with racism and discrimination highlight ways in which such experiences influence choices in self-identification both consciously and subconsciously. A single racist encounter can produce strong physiological effects (fight-or-flight reactions including racing heart, sweaty palms, and shortness of breath accompanied by a fear for one's personal safety) as well as long-lasting psychological and emotional wounds. Imagine what sustained and ongoing experiences with racism and discrimination can do to a person. It's hard to be proud of Aboriginal identity, and name ourselves as such, if this identity is repeatedly singled out for discrimination.

On the other hand, participants also shared stories of resilience and refusal to be silenced by racial and gendered discrimination. Despite negative experiences with such discrimination and oppression, participants are choosing to maintain an Aboriginal self-identity. In fact, these experiences sometimes fuel the determination and will of the participants to live authentic lives and self-identify in a way that proudly highlights their Aboriginal identity.

Family Self-Identification

More than a third of the participants indicated that their families self-identified as Métis or Michif while they were growing up. Rainey, Ron, Laara, Dawnis, and Mae Louise reported use of the term Halfbreed.[1] For example, Rainey shared, "We actually identified very clearly, very proudly, as Halfbreeds. [I] never heard the word 'Métis' until I was an adult and had moved to Winnipeg. Actually, I never heard the word Ojibwe [chuckles] until I was an adult and moved to Winnipeg, either because the Native people—like, our background was Cree, and the other name was 'Saulteaux.' So, the Ojibwe people we knew, we knew as Saulteaux, and then, Cree ... I was born and raised as knowing myself as a Cree and Icelandic Halfbreed." Although her family self-identified as Ojibwe and/or Anishinaabe, Dawnis highlighted that "it was common to be called a 'Halfbreed' or 'half Indian....' My grandmother used it once when she was writing [about me]: 'my Halfbreed grandchild.' But it wasn't derogatory; it was just the language they had.... She always said, 'You can't be a half-Anishinaabe.... You either are or you aren't. You can be more than one thing, but nobody is a half-Nishinaabe." Dawnis, Joe, Mike, Shirley, and Tim also said their family self-identified as Indian. Mike explained, "When I grew up, we used the term Indian and it was fine.... We'd say 'us Indian people have to stick together....' That's still how people in that group refer to each other."

KaKaKew, Mike, and Kyle reported that their families (or a family member) self-identified with a Euro-Canadian identity category while they were growing up: French-Canadian in KaKaKew's family; Ukrainian and/or Caucasian for Mike's father; and Irish-Canadian for Kyle's father. Rainey's, Sandra's, Jules's, and Laara's families acknowledged their Euro-Canadian ancestries, but maintained a primarily Aboriginal identity. According to

Laara, "Our first identification was always Cree, but [with] the memory and the remind[er] that we shouldn't diss [sic] our White ancestors. My dad said 'No, you're Cree; you have to fight for that because that's the part that people will try to put down. But you never dismiss your ... German Scots [ancestry]' ... even though they dissed us [laughs]!"[2]

Several participants' families used multiple names for themselves. Jules's family self-identified as Métis and French; Ron's family as Anishinaabe and Halfbreed; Laara's family as "Cree with German and Scottish ancestry"; and Mae Louise's family as Métis and Halfbreed. Shirley's family self-identified as Métis, Ojibwe, and Indian; Sandra and her siblings identified as Dakota, Scottish, Cree, Mohawk, Ojibwe, French, and Métis; and Dawnis's family as Ojibwe, Anishinaabe, Indian, and First Nation, and her grandmother once referred to her as Halfbreed. According to Shirley (who has brown hair, blue eyes, and fair skin), she and her siblings "run every gamut for Aboriginal identity.... The five of us are a good example of how we all grew up in the same environment, but we are all ... different in terms of how we perceive our Aboriginality." She continued, "I look like I look, and I strongly identify as a Métis and Ojibwe woman. My next sister and brother are obviously ... Ojibwe ... but they'll tell you they're just 'Indians'.... My next brother is a fair-skinned kid who is obviously Native.... Then my youngest brother is extremely fair-skinned, very blond, very blue-eyed; you'd have no idea [that he is Aboriginal]. And he just says, 'I'm Casper the Indian ghost.'"

Half the participants shared stories about family members preferring to leave themselves unnamed, not discussing their identity, or even trying to pass as White; the effects of racism and internalized racism can be heard in many of these stories. Diane recalled, "We didn't really talk about it.... We just knew we were darker than everybody else [laughs]." Joe stated, "My father didn't ever really speak of his Frenchness or the fact that he was of any ethnicity. My mother never really spoke about her ethnicity, either. I was told that their marriage was a 'mixed marriage'; that's an old term, somewhat derogatory." Mae Louise's family tried to separate themselves from other Aboriginal people by using us-and-them terminology: she explained, "[My family] knew but never spoke [of the fact] that part of 'them' were part of 'us'.... They always tried to create that separation." In a story from her childhood, Shirley recounted a time her family was setting up a card table outside, when someone left the door open and her aunt yelled, "Close the door, we're going to look like a bunch of dirty Indians!" When Shirley replied, "Auntie, we are Indians," her aunt said, "No—dirty Indians! It's bad enough we're Indians already." According to Kyle, "It's like pulling teeth to talk about identity with my mom; even to this day, she doesn't like to really identify"; rather, his family identified as "average White Canadians."

Benny's family also wanted to be perceived as a "typical Euro-Canadian family"; her mother did not view being Aboriginal as a positive thing, and "if she could pass as something else, she was more than happy to do that." Benny's mother learned to be scared of self-identifying as Aboriginal from watching her parents (Benny's grandparents) not correct people who would mistake them for Mexican or Spanish: "They went out of their way to not identify as such." This is also the case for Benny's fair-skinned cousins; Benny explained that they do not "feel like they could claim any Native identity without being the subject of ridicule. I think for them it was ... more like a survival technique.... But even those that could pass as a First Nations person ... have predominantly identified as non-Native ... because there's this history of not having a voice," which Benny believes comes from "being so removed from our land base ... the place of our cultural origin." Similarly, Diane shared, "we tried to blend in as much as we could," and "my mom and dad tried their best to make us fit into it and tried to make us be more like White people rather than Métis people or Halfbreeds." Likewise, her siblings "didn't really identify with being Métis, they just tried to fit into society and raise their families.... They just tried to survive" (Diane). On her (Métis) father's side, KaKaKew's grandmother and great-grandmother married French men and raised their children to hide their Aboriginal ancestry and self-identify solely as French-Canadian. She explained, "Back in those days it wasn't a good idea—for the protection of the children—to be named as Métis ... due to the fact that Métis people had no identity; they had no status in Canada, due to the fact that Halfbreeds were not accepted into communities. Another factor is a lot of Métis children were taken into residential school systems." KaKaKew's comments highlight reasons why Métis families may have chosen to hide, deny, or downplay their Métis identity and instead pass as White.

Another common pattern that emerged was identity being defined by others, including government, organizations, and Aboriginal and non-Aboriginal people. Mae Louise remembered, "We were so used to being called Halfbreeds—it was like a shameful thing.... It came from the stories that you heard from non-Aboriginal people, mainly." Stan highlighted other derogatory names given to Aboriginal people: "We were identified as spear-chuckers, wagon-burners by the White community.... My nickname was nigger." When Dawnis's mother lost status for marrying a non-Aboriginal man, she attended an MMF meeting because they were discussing that issue, but left after learning they wanted people to enroll as non-status or Métis.

According to Dawnis, her mother said, "'I'm not Métis. I'm still Ojibwe. I'm still Anishinaabe. I still belong to Roseau River Anishinaabe First Nation....' She said she's just 'not recognized.'" Similarly, Ron pointed out that even the term Métis was sometimes forced: "there's been different terms used to identify us and I guess Métis was just some other term" (Ron). Tim reminds us that being named and labelled has led to stereotypes that are sometimes internalized: "there's still a lot of stereotypes out there, and not just by [non-Aboriginal] people in Canada, but also [by] our own people."

Participants were also asked to recall their family's feelings toward the way they self-identified. Despite the fact that half the participants mentioned having one or more family members who remained silent about their Aboriginal identity or tried to pass as White, a third of the participants reported that their family felt pride in their identity. This can be heard in Running Elk's comments: "My dad was a proud Métis" and "He told me about Louis Riel and how [he] is someone ... who we should be proud to be a part of that culture [with]: Métis culture. And that Métis are a strong people, and they have the best of both worlds." Sandra explained that in her family, "there was always a sense of pride in that because we had such a ... variety of family traditions ... like Indigenous tradition, or Scottish, or French." Laara shared, "my dad pushed for us to have pride in our heritage. 'Be proud to be Cree. Be proud of that; you come from good family, good people.'" Also, recall that Rainey's family identified very proudly as Halfbreeds. Dawnis also asserted, "Oh my family was really proud! Yeah, they were really proud." In another example, Mike said, "My mom ... was always proud to be Indian."[3]

Participants were not asked if their family's self-identification had changed over time, but some changes were mentioned. Dawnis, Mae Louise, KaKaKew, and Stan reported residential school as impacting their family's identities. Dawnis's grandparents came out of residential school newly identifying as "Indians." Dawnis explained, "The fact that we identified as 'Indian' was a huge change that came out of residential school. Actually, it came from our grandparents ... [who] came back saying that they're 'Indian' ... because they treated them like 'Indians,' not as Ojibwe, not as Dakota. They didn't want them to know their languages." Diane and Ron mentioned that their family began self-identifying as Métis (not necessarily consistently) as a result of the Métis political movement that arose in Manitoba and elsewhere in the sixties and seventies. While Benny's family stopped openly identifying as Michif when they moved to the East Coast, Joe's immediate family began self-identifying more as Native when they moved to their mother's reserve. Benny explained, "There's been a bit of a turn towards more of an acceptance," and that "it was a reciprocal thing that was happening: I was giving them a new sense of pride because of my interest [in their stories], and they were helping me to develop my own positive Michif identity by gifting me those stories."

Participant Self-identification

Today, many participants self-identify as Anishinaabe; Tim, Stan, Diane, and Lance self-identify unequivocally as Anishinaabe. Ron and Jules self-identify as Anishinaabe and/or Métis. In Ron's words, "I identify as Anishinaabe. And if people want details I tell them I'm a Métis with treaty rights." He added, "I'm Métis first and—I'm Anishinaabe or Métis first—and then everything else after that is government." Jules stated, "I identify as Métis—no ifs, ands, or buts: Métis." He added, "I'm Métis or Anishinaabe," and explained that "a simple translation of Anishinaabe means 'human being....' But human being is Anishinaabe." Dawnis self-identifies as "Ojibwe Anishinaabe-Kwe" and Rainey identifies as "Cree Anishinaabe-Kwe."

Slightly fewer participants self-identify as Métis today. In addition to Ron and Jules, KaKaKew asserted, "I'm a Métis person: Métis heritage, Métis French." Benny stated, "I identify as a Michif person, as a Métis person," and was quick to add, "If somebody asks me to elaborate on that, I'll say that my mother is Métis and my biological father was Scottish. But an initial identification is always Métis." Shirley and Mae Louise self-identify as Métis and Ojibwe. Mae Louise said, "I am of the Métis Ojibwe culture" and "I identify myself as a Métis Ojibwe woman." Shirley asserted, "I always say that 'I'm Shirley, and I have a Métis mom and an Ojibwe dad. This is where my Métis mom is from and this is where my Ojibwe dad is from.'" She noted, "It's easier for people to recognize that I'm Métis because I work for a Métis organization and I speak French and my last name is a Métis last name.... My mom's last name is Delorme and Ducharme and Desjarlais and Cadotte and all these [Métis] names.... Even though it's easier for people to accept and recognize me as a Métis woman ... I have a Métis mom and an Ojibwe dad, which means that I am Métis and Ojibwe." Finally, when asked how she self-identifies, Sandra's response included that she was raised in the "Métis culture."

Almost two-thirds of the participants used multiple identity categories when self-identifying. Mike and Kyle, two of the youngest participants, used more identity categories than any other participant.[4] Dawnis, Ron, Running Elk, and Mike mentioned treaty and/or status when discussing their self-identification; Mike spoke of his Bill C-31 status, and Dawnis asserted that she is a member of Treaty 1. As Running Elk shared, "I identify more with my status because ... somehow it sticks out more; if you hold a card, then that's more of what you are. If I held a Métis card, then I'd probably identify more with Métis. But I do acknowledge my Métis side and know that I'm from two different types of people. So, I support Métis people, Métis initiatives, and Métis rights."[5] Ron explained that status and treaty rights were given to him by the government, but they are not his primary identity, which is Anishinaabe/Métis. He continued, "[The government] can try and change my status ... but I know what I was born as and that's how I'm going to die.... [Status] doesn't really change you; it just might change your ability to move around ... within the community as a status Indian, or as a non-status Indian, as a Métis, or as a non-Métis. Trouble is, we don't have all the White privilege that most of society tends to enjoy ... that's part of the struggle." Joe, Mike, Sandra, and Laara included First Nations in their self-identification. Sandra stated, "My legal identity is I'm First Nations with Cross Lake [Cree Nation]." Laara explained, "I will say 'Cree First Nation' or 'Nisichawayasikh Cree Nation' because I want to acknowledge the community that my maternal side is from (because I can also identify with the Pas or Opaskweyak but I went to the maternal side)." Mike, Kyle, and Joe included the term Native when self-identifying. Dawnis and Rainey also identify as spirit beings living a physical existence; and Sandra identifies as a human being. None of the participants self-identifies as non-Aboriginal or strictly Euro-Canadian today.

When asked if the way they self-identify has changed over time, many participants responded by sharing stories of their identity being defined by others, including family members, Aboriginal and non-Aboriginal community members, government, and classmates imposing labels and identity categories upon them. Rainey pointed out, "The term Halfbreed is an Other-imposed term. Métis, to some degree, is Other-imposed because it wasn't one that arose out of my family history. The term[s] Native, treaty, non-treaty, status, all of those things, they're contextual[ized] in our reality as colonized people." Tim explained that he used to self-identify as Saulteaux until he was taught the original word, Anishinaabe. Lance shared a similar story about self-identifying as Métis (also a French term) until an Elder reminded him of his original Anishinaabe identity.

Almost half the participants spoke of changes in terminology regarding their self-identification over time. Ron, Mae Louise, Mike, and Rainey no longer self-identify as "Halfbreed"; and while Dawnis was referred to as "Halfbreed" by her grandmother while growing up, she does not self-identify with that term. Tim and Lance went from self-identifying as "Saulteaux" and "Métis," respectively, to "Anishinaabe." Beginning in high school, Benny started self-identifying as "Métis" instead of "part Indian/part White." Shirley recalled an incident from high school: "My boyfriend used to tease me that, 'Well, what the heck? Are you an Indian? Are you French? Are you Métis? Are you Native? What the heck are you?' And I said, 'Well, I'm all of those things.'" She explained, "When I was a kid, I was super-proud to be an 'Indian.' Then I learned that 'Native' was a better word, so I was super-proud to be 'Native.' Then, in grade five, I learned about 'Métis' people, and I confirmed that with my mom; and, then I was super-proud to be 'Métis.'" The participants' stories highlight a connection between being labelled and defined by others and changing self-identity over time.

Running Elk, Rainey, Laara, Dawnis, and Joe now acknowledge and accept the Euro-Canadian part of their ancestry; in the past, some went as far as hiding or denying it.[6] Running Elk stated, "I think I identify more with both sides now; yeah, I identify with both sides." Rainey asserted, "I'm quite honoured by what I have inherited from my Icelandic ancestors. But ... my identity is centred there, as a Cree Anishinaabe-Kwe." Laara stated, "I'm not going to dismiss ... my [European] ancestors. That's my grandfather ... two grandfathers." She continued, "Why should I dismiss them? They're my people, too." Dawnis recalled being in grade two or three and not wanting to be "White"; in her words, "I wanted to be all Indian ... I remember facing some little things said among kids about being half." She continued, "in my life, [I've] just become more and more and more and more comfortable ... honouring both of my lineages and the strength from that." Within the past ten years, Joe has accepted that he is of "mixed descent"; before that, he used to "avoid White culture" and took offence to being identified as White. He explained, "I was actually pretty ashamed of my White culture.... I overcompensated quite a bit [laughs]: ribbon shirts, long hair, and stuff like that—the whole thing." He elaborated, "As I've become older, and really involved myself in my culture, I have to accept ... who I am in this world and part of it is accepting my heritage. I have to accept the fact that I am part White.... I'm a traditional person who's Native with some White [ancestry]—of mixed descent. I can openly say that now." I did not ask about reasons for changes to self-identification over time; however, the following patterns arose: education; obtaining Indian status; political involvement; and reclamation of Aboriginal heritage.[7]

Comparing participant and family member self-identification exposes intergenerational patterns within participant families. The most frequent identity categories among families while growing up were "Métis" and "Halfbreed," with seven and five participants mentioning these, respectively; only two participants indicated their family self-identified as "Anishinaabe."

Among participants today, the most frequent identity categories are "Anishinaabe" and "Métis," with eight and six[8] participants mentioning these, respectively; and while five participants used to self-identify as "Halfbreed," none of them use this term anymore. In other words, use of the identity category "Métis" has remained consistent across families and participants intergenerationally; on the other hand, there is a significant decrease in use of the term "Halfbreed" and a significant increase in use of the term "Anishinaabe" across these generations. The term "Halfbreed" has fallen into disuse in society at large due to negative connotations and because it no longer makes sense as a descriptive term in light of the increasing complexity in ancestry and heritage resulting from ongoing intermarriage. Factors contributing to the increase in participants' use of the term "Anishinaabe" may include the American Indian Movement (and its accompanying resurgence in pride in Indigenous identity, culture, and use of Indigenous language), the decrease in acceptance of overt discrimination in society at large, and the increase in post-secondary and traditional Anishinaabe education among Aboriginal peoples, all of which allow for increased self-esteem and the confidence to explore Aboriginal identities and traditions.

Participant family members and participants themselves used multiple identity categories in self-identification, with a slight increase among the latter—seven and eleven, respectively. Interestingly, every participant who indicated that their family used multiple identity categories while growing up also employs multiple identity categories themselves today. Mike, Joe, Kyle, and Rainey indicated that their family (or a specific family member) used one primary identity category while growing up, but that they themselves employ multiple categories today. Only Laara and her family's self-identification appear to be exactly the same over time: Cree with German and Scottish ancestry.[9]

Another pattern that can be compared across family and participant self-identification involves acknowledging Euro-Canadian identity. Rainey, Sandra, Jules, and Laara reported that their family acknowledged their Euro-Canadian ancestry (but maintained a primary Aboriginal identity) while growing up. In comparison, five participants explicitly acknowledged their Euro-Canadian ancestry today. Rainey and Laara, like their families during childhood, mentioned the importance of honouring their Euro-Canadian ancestry today. Running Elk, Dawnis, and Joe also spoke of accepting their Euro-Canadian ancestry, with the latter two discussing how they overcame shame and denial in this regard.

Feeling like others define their identity and the phenomenon of passing or trying to blend into White, Euro-Canadian culture also arose in discussions of participant and family self-identification. Eight participants indicated that their family's identity was imposed in one way or another by others; in comparison, eleven participants feel this way, at times, about their own identity today. All but one participant (Mae Louise) who mentioned their family's identity was imposed by others also spoke of their own identity in this way today.[10] Nine participants reported one or more family members trying to pass as White (or blend in with Euro-Canadian cultures),[11] but only Jules and Diane shared stories about themselves trying to pass as White when they were younger (more on this below). Today, every participant maintains an Aboriginal identity. In other words, there is a significant decrease in the phenomena of passing and blending in with Euro-Canadian cultures when comparing participant families to the participants themselves.

Two-thirds of the participants asserted that the way they self-identify is not context-specific; in other words, they identify in the same way no matter where they are. For example, Tim identifies in the same way even when people may not understand him, and Mae Louise stated, "Who I am now is who I will always be." Laara said, "I've always been one of these out Aboriginal people from the get-go.... I've been [self-identifying] way before it became sexy to do it." When asked if he identifies differently depending on where he is, Stan replied with a resolute "No," and asserted, "Do you know what I call those people? Opportunists.... [They say] 'I am Métis.' [But] the only reason they are 'Métis' is to climb the ladder. They've never been to ceremonies. They don't identify with sweetgrass, they say it stinks. But when they want to [climb the ladder], they self-identify [as Métis] ... they piss me off." There are serious negative consequences when one hides behind light skin privilege, self-identifying as non-Aboriginal in daily life, and as Aboriginal only for personal gain. Consequences include perpetuating the stereotype that Aboriginal people want everything for free; awarding scholarships and jobs to people who do not have the best interests of the Métis Nation at heart; taking opportunities away from people who have a vested interest in strengthening the Nation; and, thus, ultimately weakening the Métis Nation. However, non-opportunistic reasons do exist for identifying differently in different places, as illustrated by some of the other participants.

While their self-identification is always the same, Dawnis, Diane, Jules, and Lance assert that there are instances when they do self-identify differently. These instances involve visiting distant countries, getting caught up in academic language, participating in ceremonies with people from nations different from their own, interactions at banks, and filling out restrictive

governmental forms. While trying to explain her identity during a visit to
Hong Kong, Dawnis had to use the term "Red Indian" before she was understood.[12] As an academic, she also sometimes gets caught up in academic
language and finds herself using terms like "Aboriginal" and "Indigenous," but
ultimately finds these terms "inadequate and offensive." Diane also explained
that while her identity never changes, she is sometimes forced to self-identify
differently, due, for example, to inadequate governmental forms: "I don't like
the word 'Aboriginal' but sometimes ... that's the only square you can check."
In another example, Jules shared that he self-identifies in a traditional way
whenever he can, but that this might not be well-received—for example,
at a bank: "Binesii-gaa-gii-gwetung ndizhinikaaz. My name is The Sound
of Coming Thunder; that's how I self-identify," but "I probably wouldn't
identify myself like that when I go to the bank to get a loan [laughs]. I would
say 'My name is Alfonse Jules Lavallée, and I work at Red River College as
Elder-in-Residence.'" Finally, Lance explained that the process and protocol
of self-identifying (but not his identity) is sometimes different when participating in ceremonies from other nations in order to be respectful, especially
when visiting other territories.

The remaining participants reported that the way they self-identify is
indeed context-specific, and offered unique explanations for this. Rainey and
Shirley both indicated that the way they self-identify reflects their attempt to
relate to their audience and their audience's knowledge level and perception.
Shirley explained that she usually self-identifies as "Métis and Ojibwe," but
sometimes this depends on "what the audience will understand." She continued, "If I'm speaking to a group of kids in Scanterbury, [Manitoba,] I'll
probably emphasize more the Ojibwe part and what I know about the Ojibwe,
and how that connects to them.... I think I almost always identify the same
way, but maybe ten percent on either side; I'll slant it, depending on who I'm
talking to." She has even identified as *sauvage* in an effort to get the person
she is speaking with to understand; this is basically the French equivalent
to Dawnis's use of the term "Red Indian." According to Rainey, "a lot of the
terms by which we describe ourselves are so Other-imposed." Whether she
uses terms like "Native," "Anishinaabe," "Indigenous," or "Cree-Métis," she
feels, in her own words, like "I'm presenting myself so that other people can
relate to me. It doesn't really say who I am, because who I am is really when
I speak of myself using my spirit name." Ron shared that he self-identifies
differently when he is at ceremony from when he is at work: "When I'm in a
sweat lodge ... I use my spirit name and my clan name.... When I'm at work
... I self-identify as ... 'Métis with treaty status.' There is a growing number

of us that are declaring ourselves in that way." Running Elk self-identifies differently, whether he is visiting a Métis community or a reserve, or going for a job interview; he emphasizes his Métis identity when in a Métis community and his "Ojibwe and Cree and Irish" heritage when on a reserve. Kyle used the word "comical" when explaining his identity: "I'm Irish on St. Patrick's Day, I'm French during the Festival du Voyageur. I'm Aboriginal when it's convenient, really. I am all of those things and I'm more value-based in traditional … Aboriginal culture, but … I'm all of those things. For me to say I'm just an Aboriginal man is not completely accurate." When asked if he ever denies the Aboriginal part of his identity, he replied, "Never. Never. I'm proud of all of my ancestry and where I come from…. I never deny anything about being, I think it's Welsh and French, Irish, Aboriginal, Cree, Métis." Mike's identity is context-dependent, because he makes efforts to meet others' expectations of him—for example, whether he's on a university campus, on a reserve, or in a job interview: "I'll change … who I am to meet the expectations … it's always different; it's always a balancing act." Mike and Kyle (two of the youngest participants) seem to be the only ones whose self-identification varies significantly depending on where they are.

Most participants indicated that the way they self-identify has changed as a result of following their spiritual path. Jules's spirituality has enabled him to self-identify as Métis and Anishinaabe; he explained, "It's a transition, but, you know, Métis: I honour my people. Anishinaabe: I honour my ancestry, my Aboriginal ancestry." Diane's spiritual journey has also led her to self-identify as Anishinaabe. She shared, "Rather than being just kind of like floundering out there and just looking around, swimming around, trying to find what, who you are; right away you just identify yourself as Anishinaabe. You're not Métis, and you're not White, and you're not a Halfbreed, and you're not a dirty drunken Indian; you're Anishinaabe…. If you call yourself [Anishinaabe], everything else that you grew up with, all those names and labels, they kind of just disappear. [Be]cause the word Anishinaabe, to me … [is] such a spiritual word; a name…" Lance also shared the story of how his spiritual path led him to identify as Anishinaabe: "I started self-identifying [as Anishinaabe] when I went to see an Elder in a tipi. He asked me who I was, and I said 'I'm Lance Wood.' He says, 'Who do you belong to?' I says, 'I'm a Métis.' He says, 'You're a Métis?' And I says, 'Yes, I am a Métis.' He says, 'That's what the White people give ya; you're Anishinaabe.' He says, 'Go find yourself.' I didn't know what he meant by go find yourself. It wasn't until later in years, when I was attending a fast in Aboriginal culture, that the Elder told us, 'this is where I will find myself.' So right there, I knew that I was re-discovering myself, who I was;

being Anishinaabe rather than a Métis person who was labelled early on in my childhood days." Mike shared, "It's made me proud to be who I am ... and, you know, given me that sense of pride, sense of identity, knowing that I'm not alone.... [It has] given me a connection to a larger group of people who've struggled to maintain their identity." Dawnis's spiritual journey has led her to self-identify more with relationships and connections in Creation instead of fixating on a particular noun or identity category. She explained: "I've identified differently, not like a noun identity.... The way I identify myself (and I continue to identify my connection and my relationships in Creation) is different because I'm actively doing it ... I'm actively announcing and relating to Creation, like putting out my tobacco, saying my Name, saying my clan, announcing myself to my relatives and making that a daily practice." She continued, "It's not so much [a noun-based] identity, but relating. I identify myself and I identify my relations with each other, with others, and that's an active process that I get to participate in.... It's a source of confidence that I didn't have when I was thinking about things from a Western perspective. You know, like from 'Oh this is what an Indian is.' [Western perspective on identity is] really exclusionary; it's very definitional. You have to meet all these criteria ... it's very much like a thing.... Life is more complicated than that, and it's a lot richer than that." In these ways, spirituality influences self-identification in complex ways, which may include a sense of pride, stability, confidence, and group solidarity, in addition to a preference for identity categories like Anishinaabe, which emphasize a spiritual understanding of the world and its relationships, rather than simply a noun.

Sandra, Tim, Shirley, Stan, and Benny indicated that their commitment to spirituality has not changed the way they self-identify. Sandra and Tim responded with a straightforward "No." Shirley explained that it was her academic education along with her spirituality that most influenced her self-identification; in her own words, "my depth of knowledge is what affected how I identif[y] and that spirituality was part of my depth of knowledge. My spiritual knowledge was part of the academic knowledge and the cultural knowledge and the linguistic knowledge that I got as I got older." Stan shared that it was racism, not spirituality, that most influenced his self-identification; he asserted, "I changed [the way I self-identify] in the sixties because of the racism." Finally, when asked if the way she self-identifies has changed as a result of her spirituality, Benny had this to say: "No, not at all. I'm a Métis person, a Michif person, and I go to ceremony and I have a ceremony name that's Michif. If anything it's made me ... even prouder! I mean it's something I'm very proud of—having a [spirit] name and understanding myself in this other way. Because I'm a paradox to a lot of people and I don't think that's such a bad thing anymore.... There were moments where I would feel ashamed of the fact that I seem to not fit the expectations other people had for me as a Métis person, and now I feel very secure in my skin. I'm still aware of my skin, but I feel very secure in it."

Participant Experiences of Racism and Discrimination

Participants' experiences with racism and discrimination illustrate that colonization is alive and well in the form of stereotypes, community-specific discrimination, internalized racism, overt racism, racism at school and work, and discrimination at the hands of (non-familial) Aboriginal people.[13] These stories highlight the fact that racism is about whiteness and power in a settler society, and that it is gendered, with certain forms of discrimination targeting specifically Aboriginal men or women, and other forms affecting all Aboriginal people. While examples of racism and discrimination in the lives of the participants abound, participants' resistance and overall agency is apparent in the fact that they continue, nonetheless, to pursue Anishinaabe spirituality despite such ongoing oppression.

Over two-thirds of the participants mentioned a dozen stereotypes. Participants shared stories wherein they were assumed to be "just another dumb Indian" without a future, incapable of learning. Diane was so used to people thinking this of her that she was determined not only to graduate from high school herself, but also to make sure her children did, too. She stated, "I wanted to prove them so wrong. That's probably why I wanted to make sure I graduated from high school [and] wanted to make sure my kids all graduated from high school. And they did! I wanted to prove everybody wrong [laughs]. They weren't dumb Indians." In another example, Shirley explained that she received positive attention at school because of her lighter skin, while her darker siblings were assumed to be unintelligent and were not paid any attention. Said Shirley, "I knew when people were giving [my sister] a harder time because she was brown ... I got positive attention because of the racism towards them." Similarly, Ron recalled: "*Sans dessin* is something they used to say to us all the time. And later I found out that [means] either you don't have any brains, or you don't have any sense, or you're crazy; anyway, you're savage." Laara also shared a story wherein an academic advisor told her she would not amount to anything because she is Aboriginal: "He told me ... my goals were too high. 'You're a woman. You're Aboriginal.' He didn't specifically say, 'You're Aboriginal,' but in other words, 'People with your background won't go far. You'll end up having kids. You'll end up getting married.' So he said, 'we'll send you to secretarial school.'" In yet another example, Kyle said, "I remember teachers telling me, 'You're nothing but a stupid Indian,' and I wasn't going to do anything. Two different teachers told me I was never going to accomplish anything. And, actually, I got a MAYA [Manitoba Aboriginal Youth Achievement] award last year, and my uncle Dave's a teacher in that school and he brought the paper to school and rubbed it in their faces, so it was kind of nice." The most common stereotype experienced by participants is being told they are incapable of intelligence.

Many participants also indicated that they have had some sort of experience, personally or indirectly, with the stereotype of criminality, especially the stereotype of being a thief. Joe recalled a time when his mother "went to go get gas once. They made her, they actually had somebody watch her to fill the gas in the car, and then make her pay because they felt that she was going to take off." Joe and Mike shared stories about taxicab drivers demanding cab fare before the cab ride began because they assumed that all Aboriginal passengers will skip out on paying at the end. Mike explained,

> When I get in cabs, most cabs, they'll ask me to give them money first before they even drive away. So I still know that's racism, because they wouldn't ask someone else that. And I tell other people that, and I'm so used to them asking for money up front—and dressed the way I'm dressed right now, and I don't look like some thug or some punk or anything—and I think that's just normal for cabs to do now. And I tell [non-Aboriginal] people that, and they're like, 'we've never heard of a cab asking for money up front.' I'm like, 'yeah, they do it to me all the time, since I've been eighteen taking cabs.' And it makes me mad; I'll literally jump out of the cab and I'll make them give me every penny back and I'll walk. If it's two miles, I'll walk home.

Kyle shared a story about being at an arena for hockey practice, after which he and his teammates discovered their personal items, including car keys, had been stolen while they were practising. There were no clues as to who might have stolen the items, yet "the guy that was working there was like, 'I bet you it was a bunch of fucking dirty Indians. It was probably just fucking Indians. I guarantee you it was Indians. Yeah, it's always them. We're on Ellice [Avenue], right—it's gotta be those Indians, right!'" Jules recalled struggling to understand racism and the way a friend helped him understand:

> I really didn't know what I was experiencing, until one day a good person in my life decided to teach me about it. We went

to the States, and we went into a store, and she knew that I was struggling and trying to understand how racism looks like. And wherever we went in that store, we were followed by somebody. And "now," she said, "let's stop here and watch the next couple who come in, who are likely non-Aboriginal." Because she was Aboriginal, my friend, and I was Aboriginal, of course. And we were scrutinized. And when the next couple came in, they were non-Aboriginal; they were White. And they were greeted just like everybody is greeted by the people that work in the store, but they weren't followed around. So that was an example, and she said, "don't ever say that you don't know what discrimination or racism is all about."

Running Elk summed up this pattern: "there are a lot of stereotypes through the media, negative stereotypes that are pushed through about Aboriginal people and crime, and people on the street addicted to drugs and alcohol; so people get this stigma." Importantly, all six participants who spoke of the stereotype of criminality are male, which indicates that this racial stereotype is also gendered.[14]

Two-thirds of the participants shared stories about community-specific racism, especially pertaining to rural communities.[15] Sandra offered an example of gendered racism involving sexualized violence against Aboriginal women in the rural town of The Pas, Manitoba:

> Growing up in The Pas—that was the community where Helen Betty Osborne was killed because she was female and she was Indigenous, and only for those reasons. So I grew up with that understanding. It took eighteen years to bring the killers to justice. And of course, you know there were the whispers. [Consequently,] when I would go figure skating in the morning, it was like 6:00 in the morning, coming from a large family, I'm not getting a ride. Small community, too, so I would run to the arena in the morning. But if I saw headlights—you know, like in the winter, it's dark, right—so if I saw headlights, I'd hide in the ditch until the headlights passed. And then carry on and skate like it was a normal thing.

Laara also hinted at sexualized violence and racism directed toward Aboriginal women when she told a story about how she would spend time by herself meditating in the bushes of the rural town of Wabowden: "When my family found out I was doing this, they said 'Are you crazy? Aren't you scared of the wolves?' I never thought of wolves. I never thought of anything to come and harm me. I said, 'The only thing I would think to come and harm me is a man.' So, I was always careful no one saw me walk into the bushes."

Some participants have experienced discrimination on reserves; they shared stories of exclusion because they were not full blood, had a White parent, or did not look stereotypically "Indian." Dawnis and Mike both spoke of being called "Halfbreed" while on reserve. Dawnis also spoke of reserve residents talking down to her, sometimes in Anishinaabemowin, because of her White father. Mike was called "the Halfbreed of Gypsumville" by residents of the surrounding reserves; as he said, "So, I never really fit into the reserve[s]." KaKaKew, Benny, and Kyle each told of being excluded, denied, or questioned because of their fair skin and appearance by people who lived on reserve. Kyle recalled a time in high school when his cousin from the Sapotaweyak Cree Nation came to attend the same school as him: "I wasn't truly accepted there, either, because of my skin colour. I was that 'White guy,' that 'cool White guy,' to those [Cree] guys. So, I still didn't feel like I fit in anywhere." KaKaKew and Benny shared stories about exclusion based on their appearance in regard to participating in ceremony on reserve. In KaKaKew's case, she explained, "I still get that kind of racism from people. 'What makes you—how are you able to participate here when you're not First Nation?' You know, that kind of thing. So, it really depends on the crowd; it really depends on the people that I'm with. I mean, there's a lot of factors that come into that question." Benny shed light on one of these factors by mentioning past abuses against Aboriginal people on reserve. "However," she explains, "you feel a sense of belonging— for myself anyway—I feel like I belong in these situations [participating in ceremony on reserve], like I have a right to be there, and so, when people are skeptical of me and when people make accusations about my identity, it's very hurtful. It's so much more hurtful to be questioned by a Native person than to be questioned by a non-Native person."

Half the participants indicated that their family suffered from internalized racism while growing up and almost two-thirds said this has been true for themselves personally, at some point in their lives. Rainey explained how this happens: "I've experienced [racism and discrimination] both directly and indirectly, structurally, systemically, and from both non-Native people and Native people, Métis people. And I would say that is how racism gets internalized, you know, where we don't even value each other. We don't value ourselves." Kyle had this to say: "Growing up, it was a lot of it within myself— being racist towards myself, to other Native people—just to make myself feel better about the racism I was getting." Benny spoke of instances "where I do feel uncomfortable in my skin because of the way that I'm perceived [due to lighter skin]; one of those cases of your insides don't match your outsides."

Jules, Diane, and Mae Louise shared heartbreaking stories of internalized racism wherein they tried to pass as White or were upset when others recognized them as Aboriginal. Mae Louise explained that, after being called derogatory names so often in her youth, she began to believe the things she was hearing about herself. This persisted into her adulthood; "then, when I walked someplace on the street, and I'm an adult woman and I was around a lot of White people, right away I would go to those old tapes that played in my head: 'I'm a squaw, I'm a Halfbreed, and I know they can see me. I just know they know who I am. And I know they're talking about me.'" She went on to liken this ongoing internalized racism to "the abused woman who will leave this partner and find another abusive partner, and so on." Diane shared a story about trying to pass as White during her childhood: "We saw all these girls with all their White skin, and all these [White] people. And I used to try to cover up my arms because 'what if they see me, see my dark skin, they'll think I'm different!' I wanted so much to be like them. Well, what about my hands and my face? I didn't even think of that. I freaked out one time because I didn't bring my sweater to school, and I thought, 'Oh, they're going to see my arms!' [mimics being on the verge of tears]." Jules also spoke of internalized racism during his childhood: "There was a feeling of shame in terms of how we spoke and what we ate, and all of those things. We ate some form of bannock, and we took our lunches to school, those of us that were in day school, and it was always some kind of homemade bannock—and it was tasty, but for some reason we were ashamed that we weren't using 'bread.'" Later in life, he used to deny he was Aboriginal and instead self-identify as someone else: "I used to be Mexican, Hawaiian ... French ... when I was an adult, young man trying to make it ... probably about ten years—from the time I was about nineteen years old until the time I was about twenty-eight."

Dawnis, Joe, and Stan shared stories about internalized racism directed at the Euro-Canadian part of their ancestry. Recall that in grade two or three, Dawnis wanted to be "all Indian" and that, at one point, Joe took offence to being called "White." Also, recall that Stan used to be called spear-chucker, nigger, and wagon-burner while growing up; he explained that those experiences had created within him an aversion toward White people. In Stan's own words, "that changed me, that hardened me.... I didn't like White people, because they were so cruel. How could they do that? How could they be so cruel? When I used to get in fights with one [White] kid, I used to fight his brother, then his bigger brother, next thing his whole family."

Stories about suffering overt racism, at some point in their lives, were also common. These experiences of overt racism spanned: physical violence and rape; (death) threats; being urinated on; name-calling; loss of friends; denial of services from businesses or discrimination from police; being refused romantic dates; racist attitudes toward Aboriginal languages; hostility at work; and being paid less than White people.

Some participants shared stories about overt physical violence directed at Aboriginal men. Joe spoke of one incident that he found particularly culturally offensive: "I had really long, long hair, and I had it in braids. This one non-Aboriginal man who was a shipper/receiver ... came behind me and he grabbed my hair ... he put a knife to my braid as if he was going to scalp me.... I just asked him not to do it again, and [told him] how it made me feel. He said, 'Oh, I'm really sorry about that.' But this is something that is really ingrained in, I want to say, the average Canadian—like it's a 'joke.'"[16] Mike shared several stories about personally experiencing traumatic, overt racism, including being at a high school social when a White man got mad because Mike was sitting at the same table as him; he "told me he was going to rip my head off and kick it for a soccer ball." In another story, Mike "remember[s] hearing someone [say]—we were in a bathroom stall—they were like, 'all Indians are going to die,' or 'all Indians will die' [Then] someone penned in a date—like, scratched it in the bathroom underneath [the threat]... It's something you worry about, you question: 'Is this something you should probably take into consideration as a real threat?' And you go to school the next day, and you're wondering, 'Don't you think they should probably take this seriously?' And it was always [just] hushed up." Mike also recalled being fifteen years old and the only Aboriginal person at a party, when a twenty-two-year-old White man purposely urinated on his leg. Another difficult story was told by Rainey, who spoke about women being especially vigilant because of the racism directed toward them while she was growing up. She stated, "I know personally of women who were raped and abused ... the justification, or the sanction to do that, was because you were a Halfbreed or a Native woman."

Participants also spoke about racism and discrimination at school and work. In addition to the examples shared above, KaKaKew spoke of an experience with racism that occurred while she worked for a First Nations child and family agency that had mostly First Nations staff. She explained, "It was very, very difficult working there as a Métis person, as a person that people mistake for either Caucasian or whatever.... [They] assum[ed] that I knew nothing about Native culture, about Native spirituality, about family life." She continued, "[Even though] I was probably the only one that would practise any form of Native spirituality in that organization, in that particular office space. It was very, very difficult, when you're trying to promote culture and ... rekindling or reclaiming of your spiritual heritage, when most of the people there were either Anglican or Catholic and brought up in that way, and really did not accept Native spirituality, traditional ceremonies." Laara explained what happened at a work meeting where she suggested Aboriginal people's needs be included in the agenda. As Laara related, "One of the guys said, 'Well, I think we need to be careful. We have to be careful about what we put on this list here. We can't be making a sub-list, a laundry list,' he said, 'of special interest groups.' And I said, 'Excuse me, but I'm offended by that remark: laundry list?!' I said, 'Who do you think we are? People that you can just wash and hang out to dry?' Everything just popped out of my mouth. Of course, obviously he was embarrassed, because he realized what he had said. I mean, that's basically what it is; they're always treating us as add-ons." The same man then suggested a subcommittee be created to "deal with the issue," and that Laara head the subcommittee. Laara turned down the suggestion, pointing out that "It's almost like they're always trying to divert the work back to us," instead of having to participate in constructive solutions themselves. Sandra shared a similar experience from her job: during a meeting, an Aboriginal project came up that her boss was not willing to spend much time on, because, in his words, "We don't have many horses in the corral." Sandra explained, "We don't have a very big unit, so when he's referring to horses, he's referring to, like, me and my other staff person, and we're both Indigenous women." She continued, "A couple months later, I was told that when I come to the door I need to forget who I am, because I'm working for government." Being told that her identity, history, and heritage as an Indigenous woman were not valued at her government job was understandably incredibly offensive and hurtful for Sandra.

Slightly more than a third of the participants have experienced discrimination at the hands of other Aboriginal people (non-family members), especially having their Aboriginal identity challenged due to their appearance or their ancestry. Running Elk spoke of experiences he has had with Aboriginal people: "I've had people, because they've known that I come from a Métis and a status person, they've called me a 'not full neechi' ["friend," in Nehiyâwiwin and Anishinaabemowin]. Or I'm 'half-Native,' or something, or 'half-White,' or 'a quarter,' or something—just not 'full Native' ancestry." Shirley experienced discrimination at the hands of a fellow Aboriginal classmate for two years in a college program:

There was a girl in my class who hated the ground I walked on, everything about me: I was too French; I was too White; I didn't grow up on my reserve; I didn't speak my language; I didn't know anything about my culture—on and on and on and on. And not only was I not a "real Indian" because I didn't have treaty, I wasn't really Ojibwe because, look, you couldn't even tell by looking at me.... I really learned what it was like to have somebody hate you just because of who you are, and constant bombardment—constant—every day, twenty times a day. I'm going to the bathroom: "The little French girl needs to *oui oui*, hahahaha," you know. Or ... they were having students photographed in the students' centre for a brochure they were putting out: "Why is she going to be in the brochure? She's not even a real Indian." All the time.... It was unbelievably frustrating and maddening. And we couldn't do much to stop it; she'd get in trouble all the time from teachers. She was suspended once for two weeks from the program, but she'd just come back and start again. And start in little ways, in smaller ways, and start in Ojibwe, so I can't understand her.

In another example, Mike heard a Métis city police officer negatively stereotype a First Nation person who was out walking. Benny and KaKaKew have experienced discrimination while participating in ceremonies on reserves (Chapter 8). Also, recall the discussion above regarding community-specific (i.e., on-reserve) forms of discrimination. Finally, Rainey did not want to share specific examples of her experiences with this type of discrimination, because it is too painful.

An argument can be made that, while discrimination at the hands of other Aboriginal peoples is discriminatory, it does not constitute outright racism. As with the stories shared by participants, who discussed experiencing discrimination on reserves, the stories about discrimination at the hands of other Aboriginal people are understandably painful for the participants. However, to call this "racism" may risk obscuring the real dynamics of racism in the colonial order of a White-dominated society. When a darker-skinned, or status card–carrying, or reserve-dwelling Aboriginal person minimizes a lighter-skinned, or status-less, or off-reserve Aboriginal person's identity, it might be more accurately described as an expression of pain and racial domination by those who cannot be White in a colonial, White-dominant society that encourages them to assert power by attacking those who do not meet as many criteria for Nativeness as they do. This also calls to mind my earlier discussion on lateral/horizontal violence and the colonial mentality (Chapter 2). Ultimately, Aboriginal people cannot be victimized by other Aboriginal people in the same manner that White people (especially authority figures) can victimize Aboriginal people. It is not my intention to minimize the pain and discrimination felt in these situations. Indeed, Aboriginal people on the receiving end of such situations may at times face a virtual war on their identities, which can make it difficult to practise spirituality. I simply want to highlight the fact that racism is ultimately about whiteness and power.

In summary, all but one participant talked about having experienced racism and discrimination, often in multiple forms, in their lives. Despite such ongoing and insidious racism, the participants in this study chose nonetheless to continue pursuing a life of Anishinaabe spirituality. Future research could study more closely the effects of such racism and discrimination upon the development and maintenance of a healthy relationship with Métis and Anishinaabe identity and spirituality, or lack thereof.

CHAPTER 8

Relationship with Anishinaabe Spirituality[1]

*I'm a Michif [Métis] person that goes to ceremony. Therefore, going
to ceremony is one way of being Michif [Métis]; you can't separate
them.... There's no one way to be Michif [Métis]!*
— Benny, participant

Much time was spent with participents focusing squarely and directly upon
their relationship with spirituality. I explicitly asked the participants to tell
me the story of how they came to follow traditional Anishinaabe spirituality;
recounting their story in this way enabled them to identify whatever they felt
was significant regarding how they came to follow this path. Here, more than
at any other point during the interviews, participants spoke movingly from
their hearts, often displaying visceral reactions.

Early on, an unexpected pattern surfaced: factors contributing to the
participants' disconnection from Anishinaabe spirituality. However, participants spent much more time highlighting key factors in their journey to
spirituality that led them to commit to Anishinaabe spirituality. Patterns also
emerged regarding what it means to participants to follow this spirituality.
Moreover, reactions from others (family, friends, partners, members of spiritual communities) concerning the participants' participation in Anishinaabe
spirituality also emerged.

The topics explored in this chapter can all be understood as directly
influential to identity development; in fact, identity negotiation cannot be
understood as separate from these events and influences. This is especially
apparent in the discussions on spirit name, clan, spiritual movements, and
what it means to the participants to follow Anishinaabe spirituality.

The stories shared by participants in this chapter, perhaps more than in
any other, are marked by determination, resilience, and inspired hope. While
patterns did indeed emerge, readers will note many different paths and experiences that participants underwent in their journey to Anishinaabe spirituality.
Some of these experiences were overwhelminginly difficult and others were
transformatively encouraging. It is these experiences, the good and the bad,
taken together, that have forged the paths of the participants in finding and/
or strengthening relationships to Anishinaabe spirituality.

Disconnection Factors

I did not specifically ask about factors that have inhibited meaningful connection to Anishinaabe spirituality; however, participants identified the
following disconnection factors: Christianity; residential/boarding/day
school; government division between Métis and First Nations people; and addictions.[2] Approximately two-thirds of the participants directly or indirectly
identified Christianity as a factor that inhibits Aboriginal people from having
a meaningful relationship with Anishinaabe spirituality.[3] Many identified
fear-mongering tactics used by Christians to control Aboriginal people and
to discourage us from going to Anishinaabe ceremonies, including Christians
who refer to traditional ceremonies as "evil," "wicked," "witchcraft," or "devil's
work," and to those who participate as "heathens" and "heretics" who will
surely "burn in Hell." Joe recalled the reason why few people knew that his
uncle was in fact a medicine man: "No one really knew about that, because at
the time people didn't ever speak about that too much; it still was somewhat
notorious. Like people were notorious for having done that. My reserve was
actually a very Christian reserve, and a lot of people called them 'heretics' or
'witches,' 'evil,' 'wicked'—'wicked' was a word they used a lot." Recall Running
Elk's comment that many in his mother's community consider Anishinaabe
spirituality to be "witchcraft." He said, "[It] is surprising that people from
your own community would think that way, but I think they might have had
some influence from the church." Ron has heard Christians say, "'If you're
not reborn, then you're still of the devil. You're not clean. You haven't been
cleansed. You have to be reborn. You have to be re-baptized.'" He recalled
internalizing these beliefs while he was an altar boy, and struggling with
them for years afterward: "The Roman Catholic Church is very controlling.
They work on your psyche. It's like I felt guilty for the first fifteen years of my
life, going to mass because every time I did something wrong I felt so bad.
I thought I had done something terrible, and if I didn't get to confess to the
priest right away, I might burn in hell for the rest of my life!" Each of the
participants in question mentioned that this type of control and intimida-
tion at the hands of the Christian church, and some individual Christians,
continues to this day, and often takes aim at Aboriginal people in general and
Anishinaabe spirituality specifically.

Several participants identified a strong link between Christian fear-
mongering and government laws designed to suppress Anishinaabe people
and spirituality. Recall Jules's earlier discussion of Canadian laws against
potlatch, Sundance, sweat lodge, and pipe ceremonies, and that if a community member was caught doing ceremony, they were excommunicated by the

church—a big disgrace for the family. Laara also commented on this: "Think about at what points the ban happened, and then people became fearful of the ban, fearful of the Churches, the authority of the Churches. Look at how much authority Roman Catholic Churches have on these small communities. The priests have so much control, it's ridiculous. So, I think this is where it makes it hard for people to follow their … their traditional cultural/linguistic spirituality, because they think they are violating Christianity." Ron pointed out that "the Catholic Church and the government worked against tribal systems; they didn't like the tribal systems and they did everything they could to eliminate [them]. Our clan system—they eliminated all that, too, by giving us different names. The church and the government worked hand-in-hand to oppress us and suppress us." He shared the following horrific example: "In South America, the harvesting of souls, where the government is killing all the Indians there, but the priest is standing beside there, blessing them before they're beheaded so that they can get the soul."[4] In Canada, likewise, church and government teamed up—for example, in the form of residential schools. Given this reality, it is no wonder that Aboriginal people who have internalized these messages would not want to explore Anishinaabe spirituality!

Residential/boarding/day schools were also identified as a disconnection factor with regard to Anishinaabe spirituality. Running Elk spoke of the negative intergenerational effects of residential school upon the transmission of culture and ceremony to subsequent generations on his mother's reserve: "My grandma, on the reserve, she went to the residential schools where they told her not to speak her language or perform traditional ways, and things like that. So, I think that it kind of blocked her from passing it on to the next generation." Laara explained the displacement of the sacred medicine *asemaa* (tobacco) as another intergenerational effect: "I started realizing what happened with the residential school; that was one of the practices that was disallowed. It was displaced. You can say disallowed or displaced. Eventually, it would have been displaced out of people's experience; because, if you don't have that experience, you don't know what that's all about."

Mae Louise was not the only one who spoke of residential schools as having negatively impacted all Aboriginal people, even those who never personally attended. Mike has also been impacted by the legacy of residential schools, though he himself never attended: "I think that [learning about residential schools] has probably made me value Aboriginal culture, because I see the loss of culture. And, I see the beauty in [Aboriginal culture]. I see the pain—those stories—the pain of people who have lost the culture and for whatever reason they don't have the strength to go and regain it themselves."

Kyle wonders if his grandmother's extreme Catholicism may be a result of having attended residential school: "My grandparents went to church. They had to go to church. They were forced to—both sides. I don't know so much about my grandpa's history on my mom's side, but my grandma was very, very Catholic, which is the way they were brought up. I'm not sure if she went to a residential school or not, but she was very, very, very Catholic." Commenting on the complexity of the effects of residential/boarding/day schools, Jules said, "At one time, we weren't encouraged to feel proud.... And I knew that everything was done by the schools to make us feel inferior, [like] we would never measure up. But I think we're putting that behind us; that experience. I don't think it succeeded totally; I think [it did] partially, because [of] the colonialistic [sic] attitudes that we should do as they wanted us to do. And I think we fought against that." In these ways, residential/boarding/day schools continue to be effective in the suppression of Aboriginal cultures and spirituality, even for participants who never personally attended.

Participants also discussed divisions between Métis and First Nations peoples resulting from governmental laws and practices espoused by organized religion; while most participants did not explicitly link this division to a disconnection from Anishinaabe spirituality, I believe this connection can be made. Several examples of this forced division have already been discussed, including Ron's comments about the government's view that children born of a Métis parent and a First Nation parent are somehow "less Native," and that Bill C-31 status essentially relies upon blood quantum. Stan offered another example involving an early law banning alcohol among First Nations people but not among Métis people: "One night, an RCMP officer came to my house and told my mother that my father wouldn't be coming home for at least three months because he was 'buying beer for Indians,' he said. That's when I became confused: 'The Indians'? Well, what am I, eh? My father's friends were First Nations people; that's all he knew was First Nations people." Stan's story highlights government-imposed divisions between Métis and First Nations peoples, despite the fact that they did not make such distinctions among themselves. Effects of this division can become internalized; for instance, how Mae Louise's family tried to distance themselves from First Nations people by using "us and them" language.

Benny spoke at length about the forced division between Métis and First Nations people (caused by government and Western religion) as influencing participation in Anishinaabe spirituality. She asserted, "There is this division now that was created by the government between Métis people and First Nations people ... that division that was created by government policy," especially in communities where First Nations children were sent to residential schools and Métis children were sent to day schools. A result of this separation, according to Benny, is that "there were not a lot of Michif people that went to ceremony in these communities." Benny experienced a great deal of inner turmoil when Métis people in a specific community discouraged her from going to ceremonies, saying only First Nations people go to ceremonies. The Métis people in question struggled to accept that Benny—a Métis woman—would participate in Anishinaabe ceremony because they had internalized that Métis people only go to church. Benny shares other stories that highlight this internalized belief among some Métis people themselves: "There's Michif people I've known that have a Catholic funeral for somebody, but cut their hair off and put it in the coffin; I had an old woman once say to me, 'No, to be Michif is to be Catholic! Now, could you please pull the car over, I have to bury some medicines.'"⁵ Similarly, some First Nations people may have also internalized the belief that only First Nations people have the right to participate in ceremony. Five participants shared that they have had negative reactions to their participation in ceremony because they "are not Native enough." These experiences illustrate that government and church division between Métis and First Nations people can inhibit Métis relationships with Anishinaabe spirituality.

Many participants also spoke of addictions as impeding a connection with Anishinaabe spirituality, some of them having personally struggled with addictions at some point in their life. Tim recalled, "[I] went totally the opposite for a little while.... I started experiencing things that were killing my spirit, weakening my spirit, like the drugs, the alcohol, the fooling around, not being committed to one partner." Stan remembered his own struggle with addictions: "My mother and my father, they had a role to play in my life. They didn't play that role very well—how to nurture me, how to take care of me, how to love me.... I turned to alcohol. I was an angry young man [at] one time." KaKaKew and her ex-husband struggled with addictions for many years; unfortunately, he lost his life to alcoholism. Running Elk is the only participant to indicate that he has not completely quit drugs and alcohol; he explained, "I see myself connecting more with [Anishinaabe spirituality] some time in the future, but I don't think that I'm ready because I still ... drink alcohol on occasion and things like that, and I haven't made a solid decision to stop forever. Until I can do that, that's when I can commit myself."

Some participants spoke of battles with addiction within their own family. Rainey explained that at one time, "I distanced myself from my family because I was distancing myself from the drinking!" In another example,

Mae Louise shared, "A lot of Métis people were in residential school as well with the Sixties Scoop. We were all touched by that energy. In my family, my father—of course alcoholism ran rampant in the Métis community just as much as it did in the [First Nation] community—and so my father was one of those men who became alcoholic. And my mother became an abused woman." Mae Louise also married a man who was an alcoholic for fifteen years, half the length of their marriage. This intergenerational struggle is also true for KaKaKew's family; she married an alcoholic and her grandfather was also an abusive alcoholic.

Other participants spoke of addictions in their community. Explaining why only one other sibling follows Anishinaabe spirituality, Diane said, "[They think] it's more fun to drink and party than to go to ceremonies and be sober." When discussing her own sobriety, she spoke of discovering a world beyond alcoholism and abuse on the reserve. Tim also discussed his reserve: "You go to a house party [and] things that are not supposed to be happening are happening, like the abuses. The kids are getting abused, the women are getting abused who are passed out." He identified one historical reason for addictions among Aboriginal people: "The fur traders came around and introduced the alcohol ... when you go to a reserve and you see that, it's a reflection of how that relationship was started. The introduction of the alcohol ... that's kind of like the loss of the spirit."

Key Commitment Factors

Participants identified many key factors that catalyzed and enabled the maintenance of Anishinaabe spirituality in their lives; in decreasing order, these include: Anishinaabe ceremonies/spiritual experiences; key people and communities/places; spiritual/political movements and organizations/programs; and education.[6] These factors also directly influence identity negotiation and development.

Anishinaabe Ceremonies and Spiritual Experiences

Anishinaabe ceremonies (and/or spiritual experiences) were mentioned by every participant as influential in their journey and commitment to traditional spirituality. In decreasing order, these include: sweat lodge; spirit name and clan; lodge affiliation; medicines, smudging, and sacred pipe; drum and song; and dreams/visions and experiences with non-human beings.[7] Unlike their discussions of other types of connection factors, participants highlighted the power of these experiences and how profoundly they were moved. Indeed, while listening to these particular stories, I often found that my breath and heartbeat quickened, I broke out in goosebumps, or I felt a lump in my throat and got teary-eyed.

Almost every participant identified sweat lodge ceremony as influential in their journey and commitment to Anishinaabe spirituality; many reported their first sweat as life-altering. Mae Louise attended her first sweat one evening after helping at an Aboriginal event; in her own words, that sweat was "the most profound experience of my life." Similarly, when Benny discussed the first sweat she attended ten years ago, she said, "My whole life changed in that moment." She elaborated, "I felt like my words were being heard, that I had finally made a connection. That was really important to me, because … negotiating an urban Métis identity is a difficult thing, and I felt disconnected from the stories that I was being told at home. And in that moment, I felt connected to them. It opened up this whole new world, this whole new way of understanding."

Several participants shared that sweat lodge was influential in their journey even before they ever personally crawled in for the first time. Tim recalled being about sixteen, walking aimlessly on a reserve road and wondering, "Why am I here? What am I supposed to be doing [in life]?" Just then, his brother-in-law was driving by and stopped to ask if Tim would be firekeeper for his sweat. Tim spoke of being overcome with emotion while helping: "Wow, man, this is, I don't know what I'm doing, but I feel good doing it!" Stan shared a story about going to the United States and participating in his first ceremonies. He volunteered to be firekeeper: "Everybody was so good, so kind, and so loving. They were just beautiful people … smiling and laughing and joking." When they were finished and the conductor told them to open the sweat door, Stan witnessed a blue light leave the lodge: "I seen that blue light travel into the spirit land … I watched it travel!" When he approached the conductor with *asemaa* to ask about this, he was told, "those are the helpers that came in. That was part of that lodge, it's not uncommon." Having been close to sweats, but not yet inside, Mike also feels their power, and said, "I would be ready to make that a way of life." Laara challenged the romanticized notion of spirituality and spoke of the hard work involved with sweats (and ceremonies in general), as well as the anxiety that is not uncommon for beginners: "It's a lot of work putting things together with the preparation, the physical labour, the anxiety—the 'what [am I] doing here?' Wondering if this is the place for you? What are you supposed to say? And you don't know the prayers. [But] then when you listen to the prayer, well, anybody will know how to say that. So I try to teach people: pray from the heart. You can [say] thank [you], you're asking for prayers for people, for the earth, and what's on the earth as you start thinking consciously about that. They're not saying anything mysterious." Receiving a spirit name has also been highly influential in the spiritual journey of most of the participants. Several participants spoke of the importance of their actual naming ceremony. Laara, Lance, and KaKaKew explained that they carry two spirit names.[8] Interestingly, Laara and KaKaKew were both named by Elder Jules Lavallée, another participant in this study. As with sweat lodge, participants spoke movingly about carrying a spirit name and what this means to them.

Dawnis, Laara, Joe, and Sandra all received their spirit name at a young age. Dawnis was given her name as a baby: "I grew up knowing my Anishinaabe name: Miinawanigogiizhigook. That's my true name, and it was given to me by Ed Morgan from Red Lake... I don't remember the ceremony at all, but I always remember knowing my name." As a child, Laara was given the name Misisak (bulldog fly) by her grandfather. Joe was twelve when he received his spirit name. The experience made him "more aware of [his] Nativeness" to the point where he would try "to overcompensate by being more Native than a Native person so, like, always talking about the Native traditional ways ... growing my hair long and braiding it every day." Sandra received her spirit name at seventeen; she stated, "It's kind of like growing up with it and growing into it.... It's always, in a sense, been a part of my identity."

Benny spoke at greatest length about her naming ceremony and the events leading up to it. She explained, "I actually got my name this summer—my clan, and my colours; and that was a big test for me because of my urban existence." Benny had spent the first part of that summer in a Métis community participating in a Métis language immersion program. At the same time, she was preparing herself for her naming ceremony; she became very discouraged and conflicted when she learned that the Métis residents of that community believed that only First Nations people participate in ceremony. Thankfully, she connected with a Métis Elder who encouraged her to get her spirit name and told her that this would deepen her knowledge of herself as a Métis person. At the naming ceremony, her *gwiimeh* (namer)—a First Nations Elder—told her her spirit name in English, and instructed her to "go to your Elders and you ask them how to say this in Michif." Tim also spoke at length about receiving his spirit name. He had been having dreams about certain animals for years before approaching an Elder for help to find out his spirit name. In Tim's words, "I didn't tell the Elder I was coming. I didn't tell him about the dreams I was having about those animals. I just showed up at his place [laughs]. [We] did the ceremony and I was blown away by it! Because I didn't tell him anything, you know. And it was like he knew!" Tim explained, "Zhaawaa Makwa Inini. Maa'ingan ndoodem. In English, that means that I'm like a 'Brown Bear Man,' but the brown is kind of like how a Kodiak bear looks, it has that yellow on the fur.... And I'm from the Wolf Clan."

Most participants who spoke of receiving and carrying a spirit name also indicated that their clan has been influential in their spiritual journey. Some participants have known their clan since childhood; others have only recently learned their clan. Dawnis did not specify when in her childhood she learned that she belongs to the Waabizhayshii (Marten) Clan; Joe and Sandra were thirteen and seventeen, respectively, when they learned their clan. Six years after receiving his spirit name and clan, Tim had another experience that confirmed for him the power of Anishinaabe spirituality. He received a phone call from a relative, who said: "'I'm just phoning to let you know that we're from the Marten Clan.' I said, 'What?!' He goes, 'Yeah, we're from the Marten Clan; the Johnstones are from the Marten Clan.' I started laughing, eh, and [that] kind of pissed him off, eh, because I think he thought I was being rude. I said, 'I'm not laughing because of that.' I tell him, 'Because I know that the Wolf is a sub-clan of the Marten clan, and I already got that six years ago!' It just made me, I don't know, it was like wow!" Participants spent less time, and went into less detail, discussing their clan compared to their spirit name.

For several participants, spirit name and clan are also influential in their self-identification. Indigenous world views accord great significance to one's spirit name and clan; Ron hints at this when he stated, "I got my spirit name and my clan ... you have to if you're going to participate in those ceremonies." He explained, "I feel connected. Like once I got my spirit name and I was told, 'this is who you are spiritually, and this is how you connect to the Mother Earth, these are your colours' ... it's very empowering. And it's reassuring that you're following on the right path; that others have gone ahead of you. And when you sit down in circle and somebody says, 'My spirit name is such and such. I'm of this clan,' you can relate." Here, Ron highlights several key concepts within many Indigenous world views: an emphasis on familial relationships and interconnection in Creation; that humans are spirit beings living a physical existence; and that the spiritual path we walk in life exists for us, in part, due to the work our ancestors did. According to Anishinaabe world view, learning your spirit name and clan is just the beginning of coming to understand who you are. It is then your responsibility to search for the meaning, gifts, responsibilities, and relationships of your name and clan. Which animal is your head/chief clan? Which clans are you related to, and how closely? Which clans are distant enough to have romantic relationships with? Learning about one's name and clan—essentially who you are—is a lifelong journey.

Ron was not the only participant who spoke about his spirit name and clan as helping him to understand his identity relationally. Discussing the spirit name her grandfather gave her as a child, Misisak (bulldog fly), Laara stated, "[Spirit] names give you a job and responsibility; and, I have been a bug on the system, the European system. I've been bugging institutions, bugging them to be more aware of us [Aboriginal peoples]. Bugging them constantly, and raising the awareness of who we are, what we're about, and what we need to be in a bridging way." She also shared some of what she has learned about the spirit name she carries as an adult, White Turtle Woman: "In Ojibwe, *mikinak* is turtle.... In Cree we'd say *miskinak*—same thing. And with [turtles], symbolically they mean a pathway.... *Mikinak* is a road—literally a road. And then turtle is like a pathway. Wabowden is not a Cree word; it's named after an engineer for the Hudson's Bay Railway.... But it had its Cree [name] origina[lly].... It was called *miskinak* or *miskinaganiik*. *Miskinaganiik* is a pathway that's been developed, or a path. Wabowden is one of those stopping places that Cree people would go to Nelson House, to Cross Lake, [to] Norway House, because we always had all these different pathways." In these explanations, Laara is able to connect her spirit name with her own personality traits, unique gifts, and responsibilities to larger goals of bettering the relationships between Aboriginal and non-Aboriginal peoples in Canada, as well as to her home community and ancestral travel routes. Dawnis also touched upon relational identity when discussing her clan: "My clan ... is a recognition of my [Caucasian] father's lineage through Anishinaabe clan system. They didn't say, 'oh, well you go by your mom's clan because your dad doesn't count.' They didn't say that; they acknowledged his lineage, even though he didn't have memory of a clan ... Waabizhayshii stood up for us. So, that's how I saw that: as a recognition of the sacredness of my father's lineage." Dawnis is able to make sense of her identity in relation to Anishinaabe oral history and a clan system that honours relationships between Anishinaabe and non-Anishinaabe people.

Benny also spoke about the relationship between her spirit name, clan, and identity. Ignoring those Métis who told her that only First Nations people participate in ceremony, Benny went ahead with her naming ceremony, listened to her *gwiimeh*'s instructions, and got her spirit name translated into Michif. She had this to say about it:

> My name is Michif. I mean it's a Michif name. There are all elements of the Michif language in my name. I don't think that was

a coincidence because this name didn't come directly from this old man; it came from … a spiritual place that he had a connection with. He was speaking to the Creator. That name came from the Creator through this man to me. And so, I don't think it was a coincidence at all that my name is Michif. [Or] interestingly enough, this whole identity crisis that I was having prior to this sweat [and naming ceremony] that nobody knew about except me and this wonderful Elder that helped me find my way. [Yet] here I am in ceremony, and I found out that my name is Michif. To me, it's just … solidified the importance of ceremony in my life, because it helped me understand that it's as much a part of me as anything else. I mean, it's my spirituality, damn it. I mean, I'm a Michif person that goes to ceremony. Therefore, going to ceremony is one way of being Michif; you can't separate them…. There's no one way to be Michif!"

In these ways, participants made explicit connections between their spirit name, clan, and how they understand their own identity.

More than two-thirds of the participants reported affiliation to a traditional lodge while discussing key factors in their spiritual journey: namely, the Midewiwin lodge, the Grandmother Moon lodge, the Red Willow lodge, and the Camp Manitoo lodge. Most participants who mentioned the Midewiwin lodge were referring specifically to the Three Fires Midewiwin. A quote by Grand Chief of the lodge, Bawdwaywidun Benaise (Benton-Banai)—which can be found on regional Western Doorway ceremony posters—explains: "The Three Fires lodge is a contemporary movement of spiritual revival, renewal, maintenance, strengthening of the original teachings, ceremonies and prophecies of the Algonquian nations of the Anishinaabe (original people). The teachings, rituals, and ceremonies are vested in the Midewiwin (heart way) lodge. The Little Boy waterdrum is the teacher, *oshkaabewish* for the Grandfather waterdrum that presides over the Mide lodge." Dawnis, Running Elk, and Ron have familial connections to the Midewiwin lodge. In addition, Rainey, Diane, and Stan have been active within the lodge for several decades. Rainey has been participating in Midewiwin ceremonies since before the creation of the Three Fires lodge in the mid-1970s. She shared a story about receiving teachings from Benton-Banai at his home in Wisconsin in 1973: "We didn't have a Midewiwin lodge then. [Benton-Banai] wasn't running full Midewiwin ceremonies then. It was like he was on his path to carry out those teachings that had been left to him as a Midewiwin hereditary chief." The Three Fires lodge had been established by the late 1970s. By 1986, the

Western Doorway of the Three Fires had been established, and a lodge was also raised in Roseau River First Nation. Stan was introduced to the Three Fires Midewiwin in the late eighties, when he followed his wife to Roseau River for ceremonies.

KaKaKew, Joe, and Tim spoke of attending at least one Midewiwin ceremony. Joe found himself in Bad River, Wisconsin, where he lived with a Midewiwin family for a while. He explained, "I roofed for the man and he would give me a certain amount of money and let me live with his family. I did that for about five months, and I was taught a lot of the Midewiwin ways; and the Midewiwin ways were really close to what we were taught back home." Years later, back in Canada, Joe would become *oshkaabewis* (helper) to a Midewiwin man for three years. In Tim's case, when he was twenty-one, the same brother-in-law who had asked him to be firekeeper at the sweat invited him to a Midewiwin ceremony in Black River, Manitoba: "There was an Elder there, his name was Peter O'Chiese. He lived to be a hundred and what—seven? But the way that the ceremony is done there, it was passed down through his family, five generations. They all lived to be over a hundred years old; so the way that that ceremony happens in Black River is the way they've done it since the 1400s!"[9] At least one of Tim's children has received her spirit name through the Midewiwin lodge.

The Grandmother Moon lodge, the Red Willow lodge, and the Camp Manitoo lodge are all lodges that have been raised and activated by participants in this study. For sixteen years, Mae Louise Campbell ran the Grandmother Moon lodge on sixty acres of land in St. Laurent, Manitoba. According to Mae Louise, this lodge was "a healing place for Aboriginal women to come to; it was open to all women." Following her vision for this lodge, she and her daughter fixed up three old cabins by hand in order to offer a place for women to come and stay. Mae Louise remembered the first gathering she held there: "It was not advertised, the word was just out there, and seventy-five women came to that very first gathering.... They came from the four directions. We had women come from Toronto, from Vancouver—don't ask me how it happened, I could never explain it—from the north and from the south, even some from the States at that very first gathering. We had very profound things happening that first year. And we had a lady come all the way from the States, actually, who was our teacher." They had one such gathering every year for sixteen years; and during the final gathering 275 women participated. She continued, "We brought other grandmothers there and we did a lot of teachings around women. That's my gift. I am a grandmother, so I teach what I call women's medicine, which is the true essence, spiritual

essence, of who we are as women; to understand what makes us tick, and to
know our connection to our universe." While the lodge was still in operation, Shirley found her way there as part of her experience in the Aboriginal
Education Program through Red River College in Winnipeg.

In 1994, Jules Lavallée activated the Red Willow lodge, which is still in
operation today. According to Jules, "It's a traditional place, gathering place,
where ceremonies are done and where I used to do university courses." In
1979, Jules had the vision that eventually led to the creation of the lodge:

> I was shown that there were two circles. One of the circles was
> mostly our people, the Anishinaabe. The other circle was not us;
> it was another group of people.... I saw our people trying to get
> into the non-Aboriginal circle, but they weren't allowed to.... The
> Grandmother asked me to see which one I belong [to]—whether
> I belong in the Anishinaabe circle or whether I belong in the non-
> Aboriginal circle. I chose the Anishinaabe circle in my vision and
> they accepted me. They said, "You're welcome to be part of our
> circle for as long as you wish to be. However, there's a rule: every
> so often, we try to be accepted by that other circle. And all of us
> have to try from time to time. No one has ever succeeded ... but
> it doesn't stop us from trying." I thanked them for welcoming
> me into their circle. As I was walking out, the Grandmother
> said, "Try and see if you will be accepted by that other circle."
> I thought, "Probably Grandmother wants me to experience
> rejection," because most of us—it doesn't matter who you are ...
> whether we're White, whether we're Anishinaabe, or whatever
> nationality—we are all rejected at some point in time in our life.
> And I said, "Probably Grandmother wants me to feel rejection,
> that's the reason why she asked me to go over there." So I went
> over there, and to my surprise they accepted me into their circle.
> They said, "You're welcome to be part of our circle for as long as
> you wish to be. But there's a rule: every so often somebody from
> that other circle tries to come and join ours, and our responsibility
> is to keep those people out of here. Every member of our circle
> are committed to keep[ing] them out. That's the rule." As I was
> walking away from them, Grandmother said, "There is a third
> circle and your job is ... to find it...." And that third circle is a
> place where people—it doesn't matter what nationality, it doesn't
> matter what religion, it doesn't matter what age, it doesn't matter

what gender—all human beings, all members of the human family
will be welcome there, rich or poor.

Jules confirmed, "I carry that vision with me; I never refuse anybody from
participating in our ceremonies. I welcome everybody." He shared that over
the years people from China, Africa, India, England, Scotland, Ireland, South
America, Russia, and Germany have participated in his lodge. He said, "Every
country in the world, I believe, has come to Red Willow lodge—thousands
and thousands of people, just to spend a little bit of time."

Finally, Stan helped his teacher build Camp Manitoo, where they ran a
sweat lodge for many years. Stan and his wife continued to run this lodge
long after that teacher had moved on. Stan taught young men how to work
with the sacred fire, while his wife conducted full moon ceremonies with
the young women. According to Stan, he and his wife succeeded in putting
approximately 8,000 kids through that sweat lodge. Like the Grandmother
Moon lodge, Camp Manitoo is no longer in existence. However, for Stan,
Mae Louise, Jules, and the participants who mentioned the Midewiwin lodge,
participation in a traditional lodge has proven to be very influential in their
personal spiritual journey.

More than half the participants mentioned use of medicines and/or
smudging when discussing their journey to Anishinaabe spirituality. Several
spoke specifically about smudging; some reported it as one of the first
Anishinaabe spiritual practices they tried, and each of these people continues
to smudge in their life today. KaKaKew shared a touching story about living
at a Catholic addictions recovery centre after losing her husband to addiction:
"For one reason or another—I don't know how this was—but I had a braid of
sweetgrass in my belongings. And I don't know really where that came from.
I had no idea. And I remembered my late husband and I, we used to smudge a
lot, and so I started to smudge. I started smudging in the morning in this very
Catholic organization, their institution. And there was a nun by the name of
Sister Adrienne, and I was smudging in [my room] and she came in one day.
She thought I was smoking and [then] she realized that I wasn't, that I was
actually praying. And I told her what I needed to do. And she says 'okay....'
She asked me to move that from my room ... and to do that in the chapel."

These participants also mentioned picking traditional medicines and using them for healing; such medicines identified include sweetgrass, tobacco,
sage, tamarack, spruce gum, and *weekis* (also pronounced *weekeh*). Taught at
age five by his grandmother about his grandfather's medicine bundle, Jules
brings students from Red River College to go medicine picking. Shirley,

another participant in this study, spoke of going medicine picking while she was a student at Red River College. Laara grew up seeking medicines from medicine people in her community, and shared several stories about picking traditional medicines. In one story, Laara's mother tells her it is now Laara's responsibility to pick medicines from the tamarack tree; her mother accompanies her for support and guidance if needed, but Laara does her best to pick the medicines and teach her daughter and niece how to pick. Finally, KaKaKew and Sandra both mentioned "bad medicine."

Many of the participants who discussed medicines and smudging also discussed the sacred pipe. A third of the participants shared that they have been given a pipe and have the responsibility of being a pipe carrier. Pipe carriers KaKaKew and Joe dreamed about their pipe before they actually received it—years earlier, in KaKaKew's case, and in Joe's case one week before he received his pipe. Sandra also shared a powerful story about receiving her pipe twenty years ago. Upon receiving it, Sandra's mother made her get permission from their Bishop before she would allow her daughter to carry a pipe. Sandra went to the Bishop and he did indeed give her permission; therefore, her mother allowed her to be a pipe carrier. Sharing this story reminded Sandra about a similar story, which she also shared. The story involves former Assembly of First Nations' (AFN) National Chief Phil Fontaine, who brought the late Tobasonakwut with him to visit the Pope. Sandra explained that Tobasonakwut "presented his pipe to the Pope and the Pope blessed it, and in that blessing he had given back to our People ... the right to practise their own faith. It was almost like the church saying 'we were wrong' and 'your pipe is holy.' So that was quite amazing." KaKaKew commented on the healing powers of medicines and sacred items: "It's a very comforting feeling ... to pick up my pipe and smoke my pipe when I need to, when I need those extra prayers or strength, or to smudge and cleanse myself."

Many participants discussed at least one experience with sacred and traditional drums and songs as influential in their commitment to Anishinaabe spirituality. As with sweat lodge and spirit name, some of these participants spoke of the first time they ever heard the drum (often a water drum) as overwhelmingly powerful. Rainey recalled, "I still remember absolutely, with absolute clarity, the first time I heard a drum. The first time I seen a water drum tied." KaKaKew shared, "When I heard that drum, something opened up, something was reborn in me, and I knew that there was something more to me than just what I thought there was ... something rekindled, something awakened in me." Stan explained it in this way: "When I heard that Little Boy water drum—*doum doum doum doum doum*—that's when I found home.

That's when my spirit really started to grow." Similarly, when asked about key factors that led to his spiritual path, Tim replied without hesitation by sharing the following story:

> The drum. At the time, I was seventeen years old—this kind of blew me away—I was coming home one night, I was walking by the Catholic Church there, and it was late, man. It must have been about 12:30, 1:00 in the morning, and I heard this *doum doum doum*. And I was like, I stopped, eh, and I looked around: "What is that?!" And I heard it again, so I followed it. I followed that sound and it led me to an old cabin on the reserve. I didn't want to go inside there; I was kind of spooked out about it. It wasn't until just like maybe about five years ago, I asked that guy [who lives at the cabin] ... "Do you guys keep a water boy drum?" And he looked at me and he says, "Yeah, how do you know?" ... And, that's when I shared that with him.

Shirley has an awareness of the power of the (Grandfather) water drum, even though she has never experienced being near one. She spoke of attempting to help feast a Grandfather water drum twice, but both times something happened and she could not make it.

Others spoke of the importance in their life of personally singing with a traditional hand drum. Benny explained that joining a women's hand drumming group "was another way for me to practise what was becoming my spirituality. And so, I took to drumming really quickly and enjoyed the social aspect, as well as the spiritual aspect of that, and I learned about it." Running Elk became involved with a drum group while in high school, and ended up singing with them for seven years. He asserted, "From that first drum practice, I was ... all for it and I went there every week, practice every week, and I made it part of my life.... And I think that really tied me into getting involved with that [spiritual] side of me a lot more." Also, by age twenty-five, Tim was drumming and singing traditional Anishinaabe songs in his community and being invited to sing in sweats. Gary Raven, a late traditional knowledge holder in his community, would also invite Tim to go to the school to "help him with the kids, sing the songs with the kids and explain it to them: what it means, and how it's relevant to your life—to try to make it part of your day-to-day life."

Half of the participants indicated that one or more dreams or visions have been powerful motivators to follow Anishinaabe spirituality; almost as many spoke of influential experiences with non-human beings, including animals and spirit beings.[10] Sometimes participants spoke of non-human beings coming to them in dreams and visions.[11] As with sweat lodge, spirit name, and water drums, these types of experiences were spoken of with deep reverence and passion.

Laara explained that "when you're embedded in your way [i.e., Nêhiyaw spirituality] you have the dreams and the visions." She continued, "You hear Elders say, 'You give yourself to the Creator. You give yourself up to those ways and it will work for you.' You don't just have to go to the vision quest to get a vision. I can get visions anytime. I don't know when they'll come." She elaborated further, "It's there for all of us, that spirituality.... When the spirit ancestors know that you could become attuned to that, they come and help." Laara also shared ways that she actively participates in spirit communication: "I'm just putting it out in the air for the spirit ancestors to help, because I really believe they are there to help. Especially when you draw them with the tobacco, you draw them with the smudge. You let them know you're open. So I've had many, many dreams where I've seen things happen. And where I've been told, and I thought, 'I should have listened. I knew it! I knew it! I should have listened.' So people, of course, in the Western sense, would call it intuition. But from an Aboriginal perspective, from a Cree perspective, your ancestors are working with you, they're talking with you. And it's not just the Aboriginal ancestors; your White ancestors come and talk to you, too." Laara's explanations are helpful in understanding the participants' dreams, visions, and experiences with non-human beings.

Laara, Jules, and Mae Louise, as discussed earlier, are not the only ones who have reported dreams, visions, or visits with non-human beings as extremely influential in their journey and commitment to Anishinaabe spirituality. Stan spoke of a dream he had, which prompted him to pursue his second Midewiwin degree (he waited seven years before going forward with this). Stan shared this dream with Grand Chief Benton-Banai, who replied, "Share that dream with other people, because that dream is meant to be shared: the love the Creator has for us, the love that Gzhi Manidoo has for us." Tim also shared several dreams he has had over the years; he is a powerful dreamer (with the ability to recall dreams with vivid detail) and has been having visions since he was a young boy. More than once, while listening to Tim's stories, my skin broke out in goosebumps and my hairs stood on end.

When discussing his dreams, visions, and experiences with animals and spirit beings, Tim declared, "There were many times I had dreams about things that ... kind of directed me to being who I am: Anishinaabe." When asked to share the story of how he came to follow this path, Tim replied, "It actually happened the night my dad died; I was ten years old." One night, Tim's father had a heart attack and his mother instructed Tim to watch his little sister while she took him to the hospital; by the second night, unbeknownst to Tim, his father had had five heart attacks and had passed on to the spirit world. That night, Tim had a dream about a boy: "We were playing and then, just before he left, he tells me, 'Come here.' So I went and seen him. He says, 'Look.' He pointed to the ground and there was this rectangle, and it was made out of willow, diamond willow, and I said, 'Yeah, that's a rectangle.' He said, 'Don't forget what that is, because you're going to get another one.'" When Tim woke up, he was told his father had passed away. He did not understand the dream, but five years later he saw the boy from his dream (complete with the same outfit and red baseball cap) in a picture at his aunt's house; it was his father as a child! Tim's powerful dreams continued; he also shared a complex dream he had shortly after his daughter was born, wherein he was again shown that same rectangle. He still could not understand the meaning and significance of the shape; however, "it just so happened that my brother-in-law asked me to go with him to Black River a couple of days later, and I went. And I was at the Midewiwin lodge." On his second day at the lodge, Tim looked up and immediately recognized the rectangle he had seen twice in his dreams! He walked over to the Western Doorway within the lodge and asked the Elders sitting there what the rectangle at the top of the lodge represents. Tim shared the Elder's response: "That represents our path, that path of that good life. And I was blown away by it! I mean ... the first one I saw was when I was ten, and then again when I was twenty-one [when] my daughter was born. So, I started learning about it and started to understand that there's no wrong way to pray to the Creator." The first time Tim fasted, he wanted to learn what his role in the community would be. He explained the vision he received: "From my understanding of that vision I got is that my role is to work with the kids in regards to the songs. So that's what I've been doing. I've been doing it now for almost ten years. The first group of kids, I taught their parents now."

Several participants specifically spoke about experiences with animals and spirit beings (in waking and dream time), which have influenced their spiritual journey. Sandra shared the following: "I had a profound experience when I was fifteen. Where my grandparents lived, it was kind of in a rocky area, and so I'd go out and sit there by myself, and an eagle landed and we just sat there.... [The eagle] didn't approach me; I didn't approach it. I didn't know if it was male or female; we just sat there. And I wasn't afraid. Since then, there've been times in my life where it has actually come and got me [mimes talons picking her up by the shoulders] in my dreaming time, like just kind of picked me up.... So, that's how it started." Benny also had a powerful experience with an eagle in the time leading up to her naming ceremony, when she was struggling deeply with her identity. While driving, she spotted a "massive eagle sitting right close on the road, on this tree, and I stopped. I stopped the car completely. It was like everything, you know, I had been so flustered and in such a rush, and something about this eagle looking at me told me that I had to stop and take a moment. And so I slowed down and turned my car off on the side of the road. And I'm looking at this eagle, and it was just like this overwhelming sense of calm that filled me. And I knew that everything that was happening was good. And that this eagle had been sent to let me know that things were okay.... I felt like it was validation that I was on the right path."[12] In another example, Lance asserted that communication with animals was one factor that led him to believe in, and commit to, Anishinaabe spirituality. While discussing this, Lance shared, "That's whe[n] I came to believe in ceremonies. The Elders told us that, long ago, communication could take place with any form of God's Creation, because there is a spirit in everything.... I think we need to see to believe, and to hear to believe, before we can understand Native spirituality and the closeness ... of our way of life: being Anishinaabe people." Lance's words begin to shed light on this form of communication.

Stan, KaKaKew, and Ron each shared stories about spirit guides. Recall that during his first experience firekeeping, Stan witnessed one of the conductor's spirit guides leave the sweat lodge and travel to the spirit world in the form of a blue light. In addition, KaKaKew and Ron shared stories about coming to learn about their own personal spirit guides. In Ron's case, an Aztec woman healer first made him aware that he has three spirit guides, but at that time, according to the woman healer, they did not want to reveal their names. Some time later, Ron received a vision in the Sundance that told him to "go north." He did so, and there he met a Nêhiyaw medicine woman, who, according to Ron, almost seamlessly picked up right where the Aztec healer left off regarding his three spirit guides: "She described them exactly the way the other lady described them!" This time they were ready to share their names (or perhaps Ron was ready to hear them). Reflecting on these experiences, Ron had this to say: "A lot of what [the Nêhiyaw medicine woman] told me reinforced what the other person [the Aztec healer] had told me, and some of the stuff that my grandparents had told me, and the Midewiwin had told me. It was all in line. I couldn't have planned it that way myself—for these things to happen that way [mimes putting things in order]—they just happen that way." He continued, "It was just amazing the way they both told me the same thing, and one of them is Aztec background way out in Kenora, Ontario, and the other one is a Cree lady out in Nelson House. And yet, the connection was the same. So, you gotta give it credence. That's what I mean about this Aboriginal spirituality, it's very powerful—it's pure, it's very pure, and there's no ands, ifs, or buts. They'll tell you exactly as they see it!" For Ron and several other participants, dreams, visions, and experiences with non-human beings have been powerful encouragement to commit to Anishinaabe spirituality.

Key People and Places

Mike was the only participant who did not mention key people and places as influential on his spiritual journey; the most frequently identified key people were Elders and family members.[13] While most participants spoke of Elders, some mentioned medicine people and "teachers." The differences between Elder, medicine person, healer, and teacher were not always apparent; I try to maintain the terminology used by the participants themselves (sometimes they used two or all of these terms interchangeably). Many participants also reported rural places/communities such as reserves as influential when discussing their spiritual journey.

Many participants identified their *gwiimeh* (namer) as an Elder who continues to be influential in their lives today. Others spoke of Elders in the lodges they are affiliated with. Still others shared stories about an Elder conducting a specific ceremony they found particularly meaningful. When sexual abuse scandals in the Catholic Church came to light, Ron looked elsewhere for spiritual fulfillment. He explained, "I started to look for my spiritual guidance in some place less threatening, something more friendly. And it seemed to me that the Aboriginal Elders had that." Through the early pow wow movement and the Native Club in Winnipeg, Ron began spending time with Elders: "The Elders talked about the old days and the old ways of life, and I found that very interesting.... Then I went talking to other family Elders to learn more about spirituality." Ron identified Mr. Ed Thunderchild as his first teacher; the two often travelled together, and Ron recalled that, "if there was no sweat going on, he'd say, 'Let's go into the community here and go and find a church....' To him, it didn't matter whose holy house it was; if it was a holy house then you could get in there and you could channel your prayers to the Creator." In another example, Benny spoke at length about the Métis Elder who helped her make sense of those Métis people who claimed only First Nations people go to ceremonies; after their talk, she went ahead with her naming ceremony: "The way it was explained to me was that going to

ceremony, having that faith, means just another way of exploring who I am as
a Michif person. I have a right to that knowledge and to that spirituality. To get
a name is not to take away from who I am as a Michif person, but it's adding
to that identity that I already have. It's something that will tell me more about
myself. So, it's a positive thing. And he really helped me understand how I
was going to balance it." This Elder was travelling home from a ceremony
when she called him. According to Benny, he said, "'that was the first time
I've ever been to a thirst ceremony where the ceremony-maker was Michif.'
And I said, 'Well, who was the ceremony-maker?' And he said, 'I was.' And
it just made sense that this conversation happened.... It's a really wonderful
experience." This Elder helped Benny begin to reconcile her identity as an
urban Métis woman who participates in ceremony.

Several participants also spoke of medicine people, healers, and teachers
who have influenced their commitment to Anishinaabe spirituality. Recall
that Dawnis, Joe, and Laara all grew up with medicine people in their lives,
including within their own family. In addition to the medicine man uncle that
Joe discussed, more recently, his mother is also becoming a medicine woman
in her own right. Shirley shared a story about learning from Métis author,
playwright, and storyteller Maria Campbell while visiting petroforms. She
described Maria as a "no-nonsense Grandmother" who is not afraid to tell
you how something is supposed to be done, yet is simultaneously gentle and
loving. Shirley is also the only participant who identified a Caucasian man,
Lawrence Barkwell, as her mentor. Barkwell is a life-long honorary member
of the Manitoba Métis Federation, an ally to Aboriginal people, and has dedicated his career to Aboriginal issues. He provides Shirley with opportunities
to attend ceremonies, work with traditional medicines, and network with
traditional Native people. One participant mentioned a "bad teacher" who
made sexual advances toward the participant's teenage daughter; in the participant's own words: "I grabbed [that teacher] by the braids and I threw him
out of my house. But that didn't deter me from my culture. It was a teacher
that went bad, that's all it was—a teacher who went bad." This story reminds
us to be careful of those who abuse their position and that these individuals
are not a reflection of Anishinaabe spirituality overall.

Many participants also reported one or more family members as contributing to their Anishinaabe spiritual development. Dawnis mentioned
the largest number of family members, past and present, participating
in Anishinaabe spirituality. Other participants spoke of a grandmother
(Jules), a grandfather (Stan), an uncle (Joe and Ron), an aunt (Running Elk),
and a brother-in-law (Tim) as influential in their pursuit of Anishinaabe

spirituality. Moreover, several participants identified a partner (past or present) who has encouraged their spiritual journey. Recall that Stan's wife was involved with the Midewiwin lodge before he was, and she helped him find his way there. KaKaKew was introduced to ceremony through her late husband. She explained, "He taught me about smudging. He taught me about the sweat lodge. He talked to me about the different medicines and stuff of what he knew. My husband and I struggled with extreme chronic drug addiction and alcoholism. And when we were well, we would often use medicine to help us."

Shirley, Tim, KaKaKew, Joe, and Kyle identified their children as a catalyst or reason for ongoing commitment to Anishinaabe spirituality. KaKaKew explained that after the death of her husband while she was pregnant, "I chose to help myself and make a choice to stop using drugs and alcohol in order for me to be able to have this baby, and also for me to have a life ... it had gotten so bad that I knew that the end was pretty near." The birth of Joe's first child was motivation for further pursing spirituality in his life; in his own words, "then I became a father. I guess it became important for me to reconnect with my family because ... my immediate family was very dysfunctional. [But] my mother had a ceremony where she made amends to us for everything that happened in her past and such." The birth of Kyle's son also became a powerful impetus for strengthening spirituality in his life: "I saved up my money so I could get him some things, my new kid, and start a life and be a role model and do something with my life." Kyle smudges with his children and wants them to be exposed to Anishinaabe spirituality.

Almost every participant mentioned at least one specific community or place as significant along their spiritual journey, with more identifying rural places than urban ones. Regarding rural places, fifteen reserves were mentioned (mostly in Manitoba, but one each in Saskatchewan, Alberta, and the United States).[14] Many participants reported that the first time they ever participated in a traditional Anishinaabe ceremony was on a First Nation reserve, or that they experienced a ceremony on reserve that was particularly life-altering. Several participants identified Roseau River First Nation in Manitoba and Bad River Indian Reservation in Wisconsin as influential in their spiritual journey. KaKaKew shared, "My very first ceremony ... was on Carry the Kettle reservation in Saskatchewan." Lance identified the Community Holistic Circle Healing centre (CHCH) in Hollow Water First Nation as a key factor that led to his commitment to this way of life: "I mentioned earlier that I work for the Community Holistic Circle Healing [centre], and in our community we started using ceremonies to help oneself by smudging and going to Sundance, sweat lodges, praying for people. I think that's where I found out how to help [others]." In another example, Diane recalled that years ago people used to come from all over to participate in sweat lodge on a specific reserve because it was still a rare occurrence at that time: "People would come down in carloads, and we'd have, like, three or four sweats running ... that night to get everybody in!"

Shirley and Mae Louise spoke of participating in a ceremony in a provincial park in Manitoba: Whiteshell/Bannock Point and Birds Hill Park, respectively. KaKaKew shared that "in 2006, I received tobacco, of all places, on Vancouver Island; on a little tiny island called Gabriola, a woman passed me tobacco to go and help in their Sundance." Mae Louise also mentioned going to a ceremony "somewhere off the Number 1 Highway" in Manitoba. Likewise, several participants reported the importance of various urban locations in their journey with traditional spirituality. In terms of urban places where something significant has occurred along the participants' spiritual journeys, several participants identified the city of Winnipeg; Ron mentioned Kenora, Ontario; Mae Louise identified Brandon, Manitoba; Rainey spoke of St. Paul, Minnesota; and Stan mentioned South Dakota. Benny stated: "I think that it's in the cities where we are recreating a traditional community in the sense that our cultures are coming together and there's a dialogue there that was, for a long time, stopped by government policy. And that division that was created by government policy is becoming less defined in urban communities." Rainey identified St. Paul, Minnesota, as significant in her journey because Benton-Banai did important work there involving the creation of Anishinaabe-centred education. She recalled, "We went and visited the Red School House that Eddie [Benton-Banai] was running in St. Paul.... And I was invited with some other people over to Eddie's house for a ceremony. The first time I seen the water drum being dressed was at Eddie's house, by Eddie." Also, when asked what was happening in her life when she started becoming involved in ceremony, Laara responded, "I was involved with community work. I was working with Aboriginal women, inner city, as a volunteer." In another example, Shirley spoke about her connection to land, especially Winnipeg, as important to her as a Métis woman pursuing Anishinaabe spirituality:

> I live in Winnipeg in the heart of Red River. This is where all my family is from, all my extended family. No matter where I go in Winnipeg, I can find something [meaningful]. I really feel a strong, strong connection to the land in Winnipeg. No matter where I go, I can find something that—right now [for instance] I'm at the MMF [Manitoba Métis Federation]. When my mom

was a kid, the train station still had a tunnel you could go underneath. My mom used to come underneath from the North End
onto this side, and go down Main Street and watch movies for the
day. I'm right here, I can go further down here, there's something
about my mom. Further down [there], there's something about
my mom or my uncles....

These examples illustrate that participants are finding meaningful connections to Anishinaabe ceremony (and negotiating identity) in urban
locations; but ultimately rural locations such as reserves remain critical for
these purposes.

Spiritual/Political Movements and Organizations/Programs

Another pattern that emerged among participant responses to key factors in
their spiritual commitment and identity development is the importance of
spiritual and political movements, as well as organizations and programs. The
Red Power movement, beginning in the late 1960s and 1970s, was identified as
extremely important in spiritual development as a result of the re-emergence
of Aboriginal culture, traditional ceremonies, and pride that it made possible
for all Aboriginal people. Several participants spoke specifically about the
American Indian Movement (AIM), which was part of the larger Red Power
movement. AIM promoted Aboriginal rights and respect for traditional
Aboriginal cultures, including Aboriginal spiritual ways of life. Rainey and
Ron fondly discussed becoming involved with AIM; Ron identified this as a
time of "regrowth" for Aboriginal peoples in general. Similarly, Sandra said,
"That was really the time when there was an emergence of [Anishinaabe]
identity, and Wounded Knee was happening and Anishinaabe Park in
Kenora.... And a couple of [my friends] had become members of AIM and
travelled to wherever there was a blockade."

Alongside the Red Power movement, there was a re-emergence of interest
in traditional Anishinaabe spirituality; there was a direct connection between
AIM and the Three Fires Midewiwin lodge. Some of the most well-known,
early, influential AIM leaders were also involved with the Red School House
operated in St. Paul, Minnesota, by Benton-Banai and others. With a focus on
traditional Anishinaabe education and spirituality in the Red School House,
the Three Fires Midewiwin movement began in earnest in the mid-to-late
1970s. Reflecting upon the early Three Fires Midewiwin movement, Diane
said, "I think about this all the time: Three Fires was one of the biggest, earliest spiritual movements ... in Manitoba." She recalled, "It was so new, and
people were coming out of hiding. Our Elders were really waking up. It was

like a spiritual awakening." This spiritual awakening can also be seen in the early Morley Ecumenical Conference, mentioned by Rainey: "They were doing ecumenical kinds of youth/Elder gatherings across the country." The Red Power Movement and spiritual reawakening cleared the path for Aboriginal people to begin practising Anishinaabe spirituality again.

The resurgence of interest in Aboriginal cultures encouraged by these spiritual and political movements helped start numerous Aboriginal organizations and programs, including pow wow groups and Native Friendship Centres. Early in her search for Anishinaabe spirituality, Mae Louise began seeking out Elders and traditional knowledge holders in Aboriginal organizations and at the Friendship Centre in Brandon. Rainey and Ron spoke of becoming involved with the Winnipeg Native Club in its early days. Ron ran the club for a while in his twenties; he shared: "We started quite a movement there at the Native Club: The New Nation Chanters and Dancers, we called it. We held the very first give-away [ceremony] at the Native Club. We had probably one of the first pow wows that had been in the city for a long time." Rainey said that the Native Club was "really instrumental in trying to get more programming, culturally relevant, culturally based programming for Native youth in [Winnipeg], or [for] Native families in this city." She also spoke of being involved with the Indian and Métis Friendship Centre in Winnipeg, as well as with Waynabiig Enakamagaat, another Native youth organization. Stan explained that when he became involved with the Indian and Métis Friendship Centre in Winnipeg: "I started seeing things I had never seen in my own culture, my own Aboriginal spirituality, my own culture, my own value system." Sandra was involved with the Opaskwayak Cree Native Youth Group.

These early political and spiritual movements also proved critical in identity negotiation and development. After generations of overt colonization and attempts to "remove the Indian from the child," these political and spiritual movements openly challenged colonization and encouraged Aboriginal people to remember who they are and where they come from. Cultural programming, education, and spirituality offered ways for Aboriginal people to reconnect with themselves, their cultures, and their spirit. Métis Elder Maria Campbell explains: "Times were changing in the 1960s, especially in Indian country. The old people had become 'radicals,' or so they were called by some officials. They travelled the country holding cultural and spiritual teaching sessions wherever they could find a space, and young people came from everywhere, hungry for their knowledge. It was their stories that brought us back and launched what we now know as the Aboriginal healing movement.

Their stories taught us to decolonize ourselves and reclaim our communities" (Campbell 2011a, xviii). The ripple effects of these movements continue to be felt by all Aboriginal peoples, especially in terms of pride in identity and encouragement for learning one's culture, including spirituality.

The participants also mentioned more recent Aboriginal organizations and activism as influential in their spiritual development. Dawnis shared that her family "blockaded in support of the people at Kanesatake during the Oka Crisis." The events at Oka created further mistrust among Joe's family toward Euro-Canadians, and a desire to align more closely with Aboriginal people only. In other examples, Lance and Tim shared stories about the importance of the Community Holistic Circle Healing centre in their spiritual development. Moreover, Sandra, Ron, and Shirley all spoke of the significance of the Manitoba Métis Federation (MMF) in terms of their identity and spiritual development.

The only participants who do not appear in this pattern on spiritual/ political movements and organizations/programs are the four youngest participants: Running Elk, Mike, Kyle, and Benny. This makes sense, because the height of the Red Power movement, as well as the development of the Three Fires Midewiwin, occurred in the 1970s, before these participants were born. Coming to this realization made me wonder if there is some other key pattern that is consistently present among the younger participants. In fact, there is: education.

Education

Two-thirds of the participants reported that education (especially higher education) has been somehow influential in their spiritual journey. In addition to the four youngest participants, a majority of participants have used higher education as a way to become more involved with Anishinaabe spirituality. For some of these participants, education has been yet another tool for identity negotiation and development. As mentioned earlier, Joe worked closely with an Elder and was active with ceremonies at the Children of the Earth High School. Shirley is grateful to the Aboriginal Education Program at Red River College (RRC) for enabling her to connect with Aboriginal languages, people, and ceremonies. At the time of interview, Jules and Mae Louise were Elders-in-Residence at RRC. Jules brought classes of students to his Red Willow lodge for traditional teachings while he worked for the University of Manitoba, and then through RRC. He explained: "Gajii-maadiziyaang is a course I developed for the University of Manitoba; it's called 'A Way of Life.' And it was for ... the students who were at the 600 level. And I would take them out to Red Willow lodge. We stayed there for a whole week. And that's all I taught them [was] about the way we live, the foods, and the medicines, and the ceremonies." Laara recalled when she moved to Winnipeg: "I ended up in university. And when I came here, I always was very fortunate to connect with other Aboriginal people who led a good lifestyle; their spirituality was important for them."

The four youngest participants each clearly articulated the importance of education (especially post-secondary education) in their spiritual and identity development. Recall that Running Elk first became involved with ceremonies as a result of joining a drumming group in his high school. Running Elk continues to be involved in Aboriginal-centred organizations and events through post-secondary education. In Benny's case, attending university encouraged her to further negotiate her Métis identity and to become involved with Métis politics and Aboriginal people, which contributed to her finding her way to ceremony. She explained: "When I came to university, I began feeling like I should be political about who I was and take the steps required to give back to my community. I had this whole kind of philosophical change happen about nine years ago. So I became active in the only Métis organization that I knew about at the time; I was living in Ottawa doing my undergrad and I became involved in the Métis Nation of Ontario." Kyle also identified higher education as instrumental in his spiritual path: "That's where it really started; my traditional path was kind of nurtured here at university." He continued, "I've been to classes and teachings here at the Aboriginal Students Centre and I've been able to continue to walk that path. I'm grateful for everything that I've gone through here at school." Mike had this to say about the influence of post-secondary education upon his spiritual development: "It's made me far more confident. It's changed the way I look at the world, even at Aboriginal traditional ways. Prior to this, I probably wouldn't have went to sweats or smudged, or even maybe taken the tobacco [referring to the *asemaa* I offered him]. Those things would have been foreign to me four years ago." He continued, "The Faculty of Social Work has made me be far more accepting of Aboriginal traditional ways."

What Spirituality Means to the Participants

In order to get a better understanding of participants' spiritual commitment, they were asked to explain what it means to them to follow this spiritual path. Sandra pointed out the inadequacy of the term "to follow spirituality," and believes a more accurate way of describing it is as a way of life. The participants' responses reflect the wisdom in Sandra's words, and I agree with them;

therefore, I often use her suggested terminology. The following patterns (in decreasing order) were mentioned by at least half of the participants: giving back; relationships and connections; know who I am; found what I was searching for; and good feelings.[15]

Almost every participant emphasized that, for them, spirituality means a personal commitment to give back variously to their family, their community, their People, and all of Creation. Many spoke in terms of helping out, "doing good work," and that they viewed this as a lifelong personal responsibility and commitment. This is clearly articulated among the participants who are Midewiwin and/or Sundancers, or have been helpers in these ceremonies. Mide-Inini [Mide man] Stan shared with me how important it is to "think Anishinaabe from this day forth. 'How am I going to help my people? How am I going to help my Anishinaabe relatives?'" He elaborated, "When you do this, do it for yourself. When you're comfortable with doing it yourself, you can help your family, eh. When you're comfortable with your family, then you ... help your community." Mide-Kwe [Mide woman] Diane explained: "Being Anishinaabe, everything that I know and I believe in has helped me get to where I am today ... I have to give back ... because that's the vow I made." Similarly, Mide-Kwe Dawnis articulated that she is "committed to making sure that what I depended on is there when there's others that are seeking that same way.... As first-degree Midewiwin, I am trying to learn that length of the lodge. I spend some time at the doorway; I spend some time working with the water; I spend some time sitting by the drum, I try to learn the ties. I want to know everything that I can, so that I can be depended upon too."

A longtime Sundancer, Sandra discussed working together and "learning how to be more compassionate and empathetic, and knowing how we can all use our energy to create greater opportunity or a more positive world for our people to live in. Because when we dance, we dance for the health and happiness of all people." Ron echoed: "When I go to the Sundance and to the sweats, I'm praying there for everybody and the youth, and we make commitments to better our community." He explained that at Sundance, "it's everybody working for everybody," and that to bring healing to children, families, Elders, and the world, the dancers make sacrifices: "We're suffering like we're fasting, we're doing this, and we're doing that. You don't mind doing that because you have the power, you're empowered to do it, and you say, 'Well geez, there's 365 days a year, why can't I take four days aside and do this?' That's how we're taught: share just these few days; suffer yourself for a few days here for the betterment of everybody. And if you can do that, well you don't really realize it at the time, but once you're done all that, you feel a whole lot better yourself! You're healing yourself when you're helping heal other people." Laara also talked about giving back when she said, "I like encouraging people. I like finding ways of encouraging people, of introducing people, to connect people, to bring people together to share what I have." She encourages others who attend ceremonies to also "help out." She explained, "I tell people, 'Go and help out. Don't come and just be the spectator. Go and help out; you see someone who needs something, you go and help out,' because to me that's spirituality." She continued, "It's not just that last part— going into the sweat lodge—somebody's had to prepare that for you. It's a lot of blood, sweat, and tears, anxiety and mistakes, redo and redoing that goes into that. So if you want to help, don't just go to that part. When you leave to go home [from ceremonies] you go fight for Aboriginal people. You fight to change the system. You find a way to get it in books, find a way to make that happen." In yet another example, Lance shared that he participates in community fasting because he wants to be able to conduct fasts for his community and bring healing: "[The] Elder [is] preparing me to be a *shkawbeh* for running the fast when it is time, and he sees it is time for us to take over."

This desire and perceived responsibility to do good work and to give back is also strong among the younger participants. While completing a social work degree, Kyle would often try to "make these events ... like talk to [Elders on campus] or other people, and try to have a storytelling day, and try to have other people learn about their culture or just create awareness for people to learn and be more culturally competent." In his place of employment, he has been "advocating for more things like being able to smudge at work and, you know, maybe having an Elder that can come in and be available to some workers." For at least ten years now, Tim has been fulfilling his role in his community of helping with the traditional songs (especially teaching them to the children). Mike shared that Anishinaabe spirituality has "given me a huge, tremendous responsibility to carry on.... Because I know that I'm not doing it for myself" and that "my connection to Aboriginal spirituality now, and in the future, will help me regain who Native people are ... holistic." Similarly, traditional spirituality inspires Running Elk to keep up the good fight; he explained, "In our history, we've fought many battles in the name of our communities and cultures and protecting [our] rights. I feel like it's my duty to do that and to inspire the next generation to keep up that fight and [to remind us] that we are a strong people; that that strength flows through your blood. And that we have this in us—and it lives in you—and just to keep it going."

For many of the participants, living a life of Anishinaabe spirituality means recognizing and honouring the relationships and connections in Creation. Participants of all ages spoke passionately about their ever-deepening understanding of how they are connected to Creation, to Creator, to their ancestors, to all beings, and to the land. For example, Sandra has "a greater and more loving connection to Creation, or interconnection to Creation, and to people." In Joe's case, Anishinaabe spirituality enables him to recognize his connection to his ancestors and the land. He explained, "Sometimes I sit there, I look out, I get out of my canoe or wherever I am [on] the land somewhere, stand there and I'll look around, and I realize that this beautiful thing that's around me, or that I'm in, is actually very much a part of me; this is my ancestral home." For Benny, ceremonies helped her to feel connected for the first time in her life. Recalling her first sweat, she said: "I felt that connection to God—in the sense that my mother talked about from her kind of Christian upbringing—I felt that in the sweat and I had never felt it before." The importance of relationships can also be heard in a teaching Kyle shares with his children: "I've talked to them about sweetgrass and how it's like a kindness medicine—and the braid, and how with one strand we're weak and we can be broken, but when you tie us together, we're strong. We have to stay strong with our family and our cousins. And you know, it's important that we have each other."

Dawnis spoke at length about relationships and connections: "To be Midewiwin, and to follow that Heart Way, is to recognize the Spirit and our Mother the Earth and recognize our place in Creation; that we do have a Path and we do have a life that's for us, that's a good life. And to know, too, that we're related to all of Creation and that we have a purpose in being here; everyone that's here, we have a purpose." She continued, "I understand myself in our teachings of life, that I'm of duality; I'm physical and I'm spirit. And I'm in Creation. And I'm a woman. And I'm connected in Creation in particular ways because of who I am as a woman, [because] of my clan, [because] of my Nation, [because] of my history." Dawnis further explained, "Our Creation Story and our world view teach us about and help us to constantly identify, and we're always seeking that connection, we're always seeking to recognize that Spirit in Creation, all the different spirits, and recognize our Gzhi Manidoo: the Kind Spirit in Creation." Rainey and Mae Louise echo this understanding of relationships in Creation. According to Rainey, "To be a human being in the world ... you need to be connected to the world." She explained that, for her, living a life of Anishinaabe spirituality "puts me on a string of lives.... So I can look in every direction and never forget how my feet are connected to the earth." She continued, "[Anishinaabe spirituality] taught me how to have relationships with everything, and everybody, and every being, both physical and spiritual. And, I'm still learning, learning all the time. It gave me a way to ... be centred in that.... Because I think what we experienced as Native people was a great disconnect that's still making so many of our people sick." Mae Louise seems to pick up where Rainey left off: "We are spiritual beings, and if we disconnect from that then we're separated from our truth; so that's what I teach. That's really what our problem is in the world today.... The most important separation of all is us individuals separating from the unique truth of who we are as humans. We get separated from the soul of us, from the spirit of us, from the true essence of who we are: we are spiritual beings." She elaborated, "If we go back generations, that's what the Elders would have taught us from the time we were born. We would have been taught how we are so connected spiritually to every living thing. Nothing was done without ceremony. Your birth was a celebration. Your rite of passage as a young woman was a celebration. Everything was to celebrate your life and who you were and how you're connected to every living thing on this earth.... That was very much a part of who we were; that's how we lived. We didn't just say it, we lived it every day. So that's what we're separated from, you see." Most of the participants recognize the ultimate significance of connection and relationships in Creation; such an understanding directly influences participants' identity, enabling them to come to know their own identity.

Two-thirds of the participants indicated that because of Anishinaabe spirituality they now know who they are in Creation; this is directly connected to themes of giving back and relationships in Creation.[16] According to participants, knowing who one is in Creation and how one relates to all other beings helps one to know how to give back using one's own unique gifts and responsibilities. Sandra asserted, "My spiritual practice is about deeper understanding of myself and the world I live in" and "how I relate to the world." Mae Louise also spoke of gaining a deeper understanding of herself because of Anishinaabe spirituality: "I've connected with my spirit; I've connected with the soul of me and the true essence of who I am as a woman." For Ron, Anishinaabe spirituality (especially Sundance and Midewiwin) means "a rejuvenation; it's a rekindling. You just reaffirm everything. Every year you go back there, you reaffirm: This is me. This is who I am. This is what we're doing." Anishinaabe spirituality is helping Tim learn who he is: "[I'm] just trying to find out who I am as a person." He clarified: "In order for me to move forward in my life, I need to know where I come from. I need to understand who I am." When asked what it means to him to follow this spiritual path, Stan exclaimed: "It's who I am. What it means to me to follow this path? [Pauses] I wish everybody could find out who they are. Who am I? Where did I come from? Why am I here? Where am I going? Think of those four simple questions; if you can answer those four simple questions, then you know who you are."

Anishinaabe spirituality enables participants to come to know who they are; therefore, it directly influences their self-identification. This influence on self-identification has more to do with the process of self-identifying as opposed to their use of any particular noun. Joe said, "[Anishinaabe spirituality] means a lot, it's my identification, really. It's how I identify myself, I suppose, really, if I actually think about it. My spirituality pretty much identifies myself as a First Nations person in this country." Benny shared, "[Thanks to my spirituality] I came to understand myself in a completely different way. A way that was really healthy. For a long time, I had very negative, very negative perceptions of myself. And all of a sudden, who I was was just completely accepted, unequivocally accepted, no questions. There was a sense of belonging that I felt when I was in ceremony, regardless of how I looked." As mentioned earlier, Dawnis also points out the importance of the process of self-identification and our relationships in Creation, as opposed to focusing on a noun-based identity (see Chapter 7). She elaborated further: "There's lots of books about Native identity that are very list-based, and those kind of things make people feel left out, and excluded, and ashamed just being where we are ... in history. I think that it's important that we have people who aren't limited by that kind of thinking framing these kinds of questions [about self-identification]. You know, like thinking about it not really [in terms of] who belongs and who doesn't, but [instead], how are we related? Because it's not a question in Anishinaabe thought; we're related to every being of Creation. There's always a relation. So it's not 'do you belong, do you not belong?' It's 'how are we related?' I think that's an important part of how we identify with each other." Dawnis is quick to point out that she has come to this understanding in large part due to being Midewiwin and living her life according to Anishinaabe ways and thinking.

Several participants spoke of an intense feeling of searching for something (but not knowing what they were searching for) early in their lives as a motivating factor for exploring Anishinaabe spirituality. Diane explained that she was "trying to find, [or] looking for something ... I knew there was something out there, but trying to look for it and trying to find it." Shirley shared, "As I became an adult, I was just desperate, desperate, desperate for knowledge. I remember I went to the Centennial Library [in Winnipeg] and I read—it took me about two years—but I read every single book in the Aboriginal Interest section." At a young age, KaKaKew also became aware of this sense of searching for something missing from her life: "I can remember as a young child always feeling like the black sheep, always feeling like there's something missing, there's something that's not quite right. That I don't feel part of this kind of nuclear family, I never understood what it was about. I think it might have something to do with that missing heritage, that something that got left behind or pushed away or something. I don't think that that dies. I don't think it just goes away [just] because you don't want it to be around in your family." KaKaKew's family continues to struggle with internalized racism and passing as White; she feels that denying one's Aboriginal heritage leaves one incomplete and ever-searching to fill the void. Stan also felt this void early in his life, and began searching to fill it. The empty feeling continued even after he joined the Pentecostal Church. He recalled, "Even back then, I knew there was something missing; there was something lacking in my life," and "I thought [church] was filling my spirit but ... there was still something missing ... even though I went for about a year.... [It] didn't fill me as I should be filled." Stan pinpointed this relentless feeling: "I felt lonesome, my spirit felt lonesome." Mae Louise also described this feeling in her life: "I had a restlessness and an anxiety, or whatever you want to call it, in the spirit of me; and I said, 'there's something missing in my life, and I have to find out what it is.'" Like the others, Mae Louise went in search of this missing piece:

> I went in search—and by this time, like I said, my children are born and they're older and kind of on their own—and I had this loss inside of me. And I said, "I have to find out what it is." And what I did, as a woman on a journey of searching, I explored everything. I said, "Well, maybe if I go to this church, maybe if I go to this church, maybe I'll try this group, and I'll go to this group." Searching, searching, searching—I was searching for a spiritual identity is what I was searching for. And no matter where I went, I couldn't find it. It never felt right; nothing felt right to me, and so I continued to search.... I was being attracted to the Aboriginal culture and I didn't know it was Aboriginal spirituality [that] I was searching for.

Many participants indicated that, for them, Anishinaabe spirituality means they found what was missing in their life; this is also true for some who did not explicitly mention the phenomenon of searching. Diane stated, "It's just that I always knew there was something else out there. And I found it." Shortly after participating in her first Anishinaabe ceremonies, KaKaKew knew that she, too, had found the missing piece: "There was just something resonating inside of me," and "It just made sense to me; it's like putting on a pair of gloves that fit properly.... It just fits right with how I feel about me." She emphasized that the timing needed to be right for this to occur: "I mean you don't receive your [spiritual] tools until you're ready. You don't say ... you want it because it looks nice; that just is not the way that it works. You get it when you're ready; when you've ... earned it." When she experienced her first sweat lodge, Mae Louise remembers feeling like she had finally found what she had been so desperately searching for, and described it as "the most profound experience of my life." In her own words, "I remember after it was all over—and I can't even really describe what happened in there or anything—and I knew when it was over, I just took my blanket and—I still get emotional when I think about it—and I ran into the bush and I laid on the ground in the blanket, and I remember just sobbing and sobbing. And I said, 'Oh my god! This is what I've been looking for, this is what I've been looking for!' I felt that in that lodge, the first time I was there. It was absolutely awesome. And then, from that time on, I said, 'This is what it is! This is what's missing!' And it's that connection, that connection to the Earth Mother and all our relations that brought me to my, what I call Aboriginal spirituality." For a majority of the participants, practising Anishinaabe spirituality means discovering what was missing in their life and filling the void.

Half the participants spoke about good feelings resulting from a life of Anishinaabe spirituality, including: happiness, joy, gratitude, pride, love, peace, freedom, optimism, positivity, empowerment, enlightenment, hope, and rejuvenation. Many also spoke of a rekindling or reaffirmation of these feelings, even in times of adversity. Kyle explained that, for him, spirituality "means being happier. My whole life I just believed in being happy and people try to get in the way of that, prevent you from being happy. I don't know why people like to do that. To me, living this lifestyle is just about being happy and enjoying everything that life has.... It's just about being positive and happy in life. There's not much better than that." Dawnis shared: "I liked the sound of [ceremonies]. And I liked that people were happy; people were happy at ceremonies and they were talking about things that were important. A lot of times, people just talk about school and job and, you know, like those kinds of things—but it doesn't touch to the heart of where you are and what life is about [the way ceremonies do]." Ron had this to say: "For me it's empowering. It's enlightening. It gives me a lot of hope, a sense of hope.... It's very good, very positive." He explained that spirituality informs the work he does in life:

"Through my work, I focus a lot [on] educating the youth and reinforcing that they're good, their character is good, that they shouldn't put themselves down." In another example, Stan recalled the powerful dream that eventually prompted him to go for his second Midewiwin degree, and that his spiritual teacher told him was meant to be shared with others. He said, "That old lady went over to where I was sitting, in this dream. As she was dancing to me, I felt this love. But that love that I feel, you could multiply that by fifty thousand times, that's how much love I felt.... That emotion is what I will feel when I go home to the spirit world: I already know what's up there. I already know the feeling that I will feel in my final destination, in that spirit realm where my ancestors are." For Stan, feeling this love in his dream and recognizing it to be the love that Creator has for all Creation inspires him to be grateful in life and to encourage others to be more grateful in their lives. He clarified: "Life is good. Be grateful, be grateful. When I get my age, I'm grateful for another season like this one here [motions to the colours of fall out his office window]. I'm grateful I'm seeing another season. I'm grateful for another winter when that new blanket of snow covers Mother Earth while Mother Earth is resting.... We've got to be grateful for life, eh: Bimaadiziwin—this beautiful, beautiful, sacred life."

Participants also highlighted that Anishinaabe spirituality helps them to focus on the good in life, even amidst adversity and hardship. Joe asserted, "[Spirituality] brings me joy.... My spirituality brings me peace; a great deal of peace. It makes me much more of an optimist than I used to be; before, I was very pessimistic." KaKaKew shared the following: "[Sundancing] this year, I have to tell you that it was completely about the joy in my life. Absolute joy, even in the worst suffering that was going on during those two-and-a-half days [of fasting and dancing], it was overwhelming joy and gratitude that I had, that I felt." Dawnis also spoke of focusing on the good during difficult times: "I feel that positivity. I feel that optimism, even when I'm clouded in grief. I know that there's a way to move out of the grief, because the lodge helped me." She also said, "I think we can move beyond that larger grief from the Sixth and the Fifth Fire as a people. And even I see grief in my [Caucasian] dad's line, too, and loss; and I think that it even helps me for that." Dawnis is highlighting the power of Anishinaabe spirituality to heal intergenerational grief existing not only among Aboriginal peoples today, but also among Euro-Canadians.

Curiosity, Hostility, or Support?

Finally, I was curious about others' reactions to the participants' involvement with Anishinaabe spirituality. Were participants more often met with curiosity? Hostility? Support? At the end of the interview, I asked participants about reactions they have received from their own families, as well as from members of their spiritual communities (e.g., affiliated lodges, ceremony conductors, and others who participate). Patterns arose in the types of reaction (positive, negative, and neutral), as well as in reactions by families and members of spiritual communities. The variety of reactions reported is noteworthy, with many mentioning unique reactions.[17]

Participants reported a greater number of positive reactions toward the pursuit of their spiritual path than they did negative or neutral reactions. Reported in each case by two-thirds of the participants the most common reactions have been positive: support, acceptance, and pride. A third of the participants indicated the following reactions: participation or desire also to participate in ceremonies (positive); lack of understanding (negative); and no opposition (neutral). Other types of positive reactions included: respect; understanding; "positive"; happy; "put me to work"; and welcoming.[18] Other types of negative reactions mentioned were lack of acceptance/disapproval; critical/judgmental; distrust; ridicule/not taken seriously; fear; suspicious/ hesitant; "not Native enough"; and a partner ending their romantic relationship with them due to the participant's pursuit of Anishinaabe spirituality.[19] Neutral reactions reported were: curiosity; shocked/surprised; and not surprised.

The participants who reported a negative reaction by one or more family members spoke of tension caused by a lack of understanding on the part of the family member in regard to Anishinaabe spirituality. Lance and Sandra explained that a family member was fearful and distrustful of traditional spirituality due to a lack of understanding. Rainey, Kyle, and Diane shared that upon discovering they were pursuing Anishinaabe spirituality, one or more family members mocked and ridiculed their pursuit. In most of these cases, participants reported that this negative reaction occurred early on in their spiritual pursuits, and that their family member no longer holds that negative view. Interestingly, a few of the participants who reported a negative reaction from a family member shared that, early on in their spiritual journey, they themselves tried to push their family to accept Anishinaabe spirituality and go to ceremony, which worsened their family's reaction. Rainey shared an insight she had learned from trying to force people, especially her sister, to embrace ceremony: "When I was younger, I would have taken a more, almost militant stance, to saying, 'Why aren't you accepting who you are?!' But I think that's a stage.... What I was pressing on her had more to do with me than it had to do with her.... I learned that if you try and press your stuff on somebody, it has more to do with you than them. It's not worth what it costs your relationship when it's people that you love.... Respect is respect. And sometimes it takes experiencing the negative impact of something for you to realize—for me to realize, anyway—that I dishonoured a fundamental value of respect if I try to impress something on somebody. It's not theirs, it's mine. It's theirs if they want it." Similarly, Diane, KaKaKew, and Kyle were also quick to note that they no longer feel the need to convince their families to adopt Anishinaabe spirituality in their own lives.

Upon closer inspection of the participants' families' reactions, it becomes obvious that twice as many positive reactions were reported than negative or neutral reactions. Two-thirds of the participants shared positive reactions from at least one family member in regard to their spiritual pursuits, while only a third mentioned negative reactions; only one participant mentioned a neutral reaction. Significantly, half of the participants who shared a negative family reaction also shared a positive reaction from a different family member. In terms of positive family reactions, participants used terms such as proud, happy, accepting, and supportive. Ron said, "I think by and large we support each other. They support me in what I'm doing; they're very happy that I'm happy. And so long as they're happy, I'm happy." Benny had this to say: "My family was very proud of the progress, not the 'progress,' but they see how ceremony has changed me for the better. And they are very happy that I've found a way to connect with the Creator, with God, and it's very, it's very accepted. In my family, there are no judgments as far as going to ceremony instead of going to church—not at all, because they're seen as the same thing. They're seen as close to the same thing." Others mentioned that one or more family members have shown interest and curiosity in the participant's spiritual pursuits. Also, more than half of the participants who reported positive reactions from one or more family members indicated that a family member has participated in ceremony with them.

When it came to reactions from others who participate in ceremony, the only negative pattern that arose has to do with participants being judged "not Native enough"; this issue also impacts identity negotiation. KaKaKew, Benny, and Shirley shared similar stories about being questioned or distrusted at ceremony because their appearance is not stereotypically Aboriginal. KaKaKew sometimes feels unwelcome at ceremonies because, she explained, "my skin tone is not dark enough" for some people's liking. She pointed out that this reaction is context-specific: "If I'm in, let's say, a different community and participating in ceremony, or whatever, I still get that kind of racism from people: 'How are you able to participate here when you're not First Nation?'"

Benny also spoke of sometimes feeling uncomfortable at ceremonies because of the way she is perceived due to her skin colour, and that this can be a very painful experience; she believes that one time an Elder did not accept her tobacco for this reason. She also spoke of times when she was not invited to ceremony, and other times when she was treated poorly at ceremony. One story involved a traditional teacher of hers cautioning her before going to a thirst dance, saying that her presence would worry people there and not to walk around like it was her right to be there; she did not end up going to the ceremony. On the other hand, Benny has also received positive reactions regarding her participation in ceremony from others in spiritual communities.

Shirley also reported being made to feel unwelcome at ceremonies because of her appearance, as well as receiving positive reactions from spiritual community members. When asked about what others' reactions have been, she said, "Six of one, half a dozen of the other. Some people are really open, really inviting, really 'of course you don't know anything, my girl, come, we'll teach you. This is why you're here.'" She explained that half the time people at ceremonies are open, inviting, welcoming, and understand that she does not know much about ceremonies and are willing to teach her; the other half of the time, they give her the "evil eye." In her own words, even if they come to accept that she is not a "White girl," they say, "'But still, you're not actually really a Native.' Because what I get all the time (which drives me nuts) is: 'You didn't grow up on the reserve. You don't speak your language. You don't know any of this stuff.' Of course I don't, which is why I'm trying to learn!" This reaction seems to be especially true for people who do not see a place in ceremony for those who were not raised with ceremonies.

While not stated in the context of ceremonies, Adese's (2010) words shed some light on this issue: "The hairs on my arms stood up when I was faced with the cautionary acceptance of FBIs (full-blooded Indians), whose skepticism towards my increasingly pale skin was fuelled by an understandable fear that my mixed-ness might also mean that I was being 'mixed in the mind' and behave predominantly in Eurocentric, disrespectful or appropriative ways of thinking and ways of being" (240). Such skepticism is sometimes also present at ceremonies, as illustrated above. As a result of colonization, many Aboriginal people do not know their language, teachings, and ceremonies but nonetheless have the desire to learn. At the same time, Aboriginal people who have managed to hold on to these ways have learned to be cautious and protective of them in the face of suppression and persecution by institutionalized religion and government, and commodification by non-Aboriginal (and sometimes Aboriginal) people. The situation may become even more complex when an unfamiliar person, especially one who can be mistaken for White, wants to participate. These are highly complex situations, and issues which must be approached with respect.[20]

Nonetheless, as with family reactions, participants reported more positive than negative or neutral reactions to their participation in ceremony from other members of spiritual communities. Half the participants who reported a positive reaction explained that this is because traditional people want everyone to go to ceremonies. They mentioned that people who are serious about ceremony understand the importance of everyone finding ceremony and sharing in this way of life. Joe stated, "They want everyone there. Well, they don't want everyone there, but the people who want to be there; it doesn't matter really your ethnicity or where you come from, you're always welcome because, again, we're all related. They take that to heart. I'm very happy about that." The participants mentioned terms such as "acceptance" and being "welcomed" by others who also participate in ceremonies. Benny explained that traditional people recognize that participating in ceremony is "a commitment. It's a commitment to a way of living your life. So, people have been very positive, very happy for me, excited for me that I have this new understanding of what my responsibilities are in the world."

Kyle, Ron, and Sandra all explicitly stated that they consciously surround themselves with people who are supportive of them and their (spiritual) choices in life. Ron shared, "I've had a lot of support because I hang out with people that respect what I'm doing. If they don't have respect for what I'm doing, then I have no use for them either. Why would I hang out with somebody that's negative all that time?" Shirley commented on the acceptance and respect for her spiritual choices that she has felt in the broader Métis community:

> In a Métis community, if we were all sitting right here [motions to the big boardroom table and points to each seat, in turn]: this guy's super-Catholic, this guy's super-Cree spirituality, this guy's a mix, this guy does a little bit of things, this guy's a shaman, this guy's a priest, and it's all accepted as Métis. That's one of the cool things about being Métis, right, is you're part of this and part of that, so you get to have whichever parts you want. So, in the Métis community, [it's] not a big deal. And in the Métis community, whatever I do, somebody else in the room will recognize, so I'm in community anyways. And vice versa; whatever somebody else does, I'll understand or get. Or even if I don't, I can respect it, because I know it's part of that sphere.

Overall, according to the participants, positive reactions to their pursuit of Anishinaabe spirituality are twice as common as negative ones, and neutral reactions are rare. Despite the occasional negative reaction, each participant continues to participate in ceremonies and has not been deterred from living a life of Anishinaabe spirituality.

CHAPTER 9

Conclusion: Lighting the Eighth Fire

In following this way of life and being a Métis (what they called me), it's very important to find out who you are, like that Elder said, "any which way that you want." You need to [pauses] do it on your own. You gotta ask for direction in life. And to seek out those Elders; they're not gonna come to you. You need to go to them to find your way of life. I have done that. And now the little knowledge that I [have gained from] going to Elders, sweat lodge, Sundance—I pass that on because it's only [in] that [way that] I can help the people; by sharing my true life experience [and] what I went through, or what I have seen through dreaming and visions in the sweat or visions in the fasting.

—Lance, participant

There exists a long history of suppression of Anishinaabe spirituality among the Métis (and other Aboriginal people) at the hands of church and government. Such suppression has been especially effective in the forms of mobile missionaries, residential/boarding/day schools, and government legislation, including laws that were in effect for a century, which prohibited Anishinaabe ceremonies. As I have tried to illustrate, this legislation was also designed to divide and conquer Anishinaabe peoples by creating false distinctions between us—for example, by giving us different legal identities. This history continues to influence all Aboriginal peoples today, including the names we call ourselves, as well as with regard to the fact that Métis people who follow Anishinaabe spirituality are an exception to larger patterns among the Métis population. Over the generations, as Aboriginal people have internalized such colonial beliefs (often in an effort to escape discrimination and simply survive), we have denigrated our own teachings; in some cases, entire communities continue to believe that Anishinaabe spirituality is devil worship.

According to Sundance Chief David Blacksmith, "It is our own people that go against it [Sundance/Anishinaabe spirituality], Indians against Indians, Aboriginal people against Aboriginal people and that is so sad. The Christians don't work with the traditional people, the traditional people don't work with the Christians and all that stuff. And I don't believe that. We should all work together. I'll even go to Church to prove that I can work with you; I can pray in your Church. You should not take your belief and call my Sundance down or my traditional beliefs" (quoted in Robinson 2013c). For these reasons, Sundance Chiefs David and Sherryl Blacksmith and Elder (Grandpa Joe) Esquash have made it their life's work to welcome those who lost the tradition back into the circle, because they believe this way means the survival of Native People, and if even one youth learns to value their life, their efforts are worthwhile (Robinson 2013a; 2013b; 2013c). In the words of Sherryl Blacksmith, "We are free to practice our culture and our beliefs. It's not something to be ashamed of; it's not something to pretend that it doesn't exist. It's something to be honoured, pursued, to be proud of" (Robinson 2013c).

The experiences shared by the eighteen participants in this study illustrate the ongoing effects of this colonial history. Through their stories, we glimpse ways in which this history lives on through our thoughts, behaviours, actions, and relationships. Each participant also highlights the tenacity and resistance of Aboriginal people in overcoming the historical suppression of our cultures, the forced divisions between our peoples, as well as the power of spirit, which calls us to reconnect with our Anishinaabe spiritual ways of life. Indeed, in ceremony we are taught that our ancestors are waiting for us to reconnect in these ways.

To undertake this study on the relationship between people with Métis ancestry and Anishinaabe spirituality, and its impact upon self-identification, I employed a Métis Anishinaabe methodology and research design unique to this project. I fashioned this methodology from my own life experiences as Métis Anishinaabe-Kwe, as well as from knowledge that I have learned from other Anishinaabe scholars. I drew most heavily upon Anishinaabe knowledge and teachings that have been shared with me in ceremonial settings, especially through the Three Fires Midewiwin lodge. In this sense, my methodology is not unique at all; it is influenced by ancestral understandings. Especially influencing my Métis Anishinaabe approach to research are key principles within my world view and my relationship to knowledge, as well as within my values and ethics. These principles include the Anishinaabe Creation Story, the Seven Fires Prophecy, *mino-bimaadiziwin*, Anishinaabe sources of knowledge, relational accountability, and the ethic of reciprocity. I sought understanding of the participants' stories using, in part, intuitive and prayerful analysis. I succeeded in this way by working with sacred medicines such as *asemaa* and *mushkodaywushk*, and by participating in ceremony throughout this process. I began and ended this journey with ceremony (traditional fast and sweat lodge, and sweat lodge and night ceremony, respectively) and I prayed daily with *asemaa* for guidance and direction from Gizhi Manidoo and Spirit to do this research and write this book in a good way and to share those messages that need to be shared in order for this work to benefit others.

I also chose to incorporate select Euro-Canadian research practices and tools (quota sampling, thematic analysis, and NVivo8 software). My blending of Métis, Anishinaabe and Euro-Canadian concepts and tools is an asset to this study just as it was for my ancestors long ago; my life experience reflects both. With these tools, I have been able to uncover several important patterns within the richness and complexity of the stories participants so generously shared through their interviews.

As we have seen, older generations within participants' families can speak one or more Aboriginal languages, but most participants themselves cannot speak an Aboriginal language; however, most participants are making efforts to learn. Participants spoke of their family relationships with Aboriginal cultures in terms of cultural values, subsistence practices, and ways of relating to Aboriginal cultures, among others. Most indicated that their family's relationship with Aboriginal cultures is improving. In terms of family relationships with Euro-Canadian cultures, education, and employment, Euro-Canadian control, and a desire to fit in were common themes. Most participants feel that their family's relationship with Euro-Canadian cultures has not changed over time.

Every participant experienced significant Christian influence during their upbringing, with Roman Catholicism being the most common primary religion while growing up. On the other hand, for most participants, Anishinaabe spirituality was not a significant influence during upbringing; however, more than half discussed individual Anishinaabe ceremonies and practices within their family during their childhood. For many, their family's relationship with spirituality has been more or less the same for three or more generations. However, most participants themselves no longer practise Christianity; in other words, Christianity is becoming less and less of an influence upon participant families with each subsequent generation. Many families are now participating in Anishinaabe spirituality (sometimes combined with Christianity). Anishinaabe spirituality is now the primary faith in the lives of most participants themselves.

Issues of family and participant self-identification, including a comparison of both, were also explored. Significantly, most participant families self-identified as Métis and/or Halfbreed (and only two as Anishinaabe) while growing up; in contrast, most participants themselves self-identify as Anishinaabe and/or Métis (and none as Halfbreed) today. Common themes that arose within participant families while growing up, as well as among participants themselves, include use of multiple terms when self-identifying; the phenomenon of trying to pass as White; and feeling like others define their identity. Acknowledging Euro-Canadian ancestry and feeling like others define their identity remain mostly consistent across these groups; however, there is a decrease in the phenomenon of passing as White when comparing younger generations to older ones.

Most participants' identity is not context-specific; however, sometimes circumstances and audience make this next to impossible. Participants who indicated that their self-identification is context-specific usually do not offer a wholly different self-identification, but rather emphasize certain parts of their identity depending on context (especially audience). It was also highlighted that there are indeed non-opportunistic reasons why someone might self-identify differently depending on context. Most also reported that their spiritual journey has indeed influenced their self-identification in some way or other. Participants' experiences with racism and discrimination, as potentially influential upon spirituality, revealed patterns, including: stereotypes and community-specific, internalized, and overt racism. Experiences of racism and discrimination are also gendered—for example, with Aboriginal males more likely to be labelled a "criminal" and to experience physical violence, and Aboriginal women experiencing a disproportionate amount of sexualized violence and threats to their safety, including rape and murder.

I spent considerable time focusing on participants' own relationships with spirituality, including disconnection factors that have threatened to inhibit connection with Anishinaabe spirituality, especially: Christianity; residential/boarding/day schools; government division between Métis and First Nations peoples; and addictions. According to the participants, the factors most influencing their commitment to Anishinaabe spirituality are Anishinaabe ceremonies (such as sweat lodges and spirit names), key people and places (such as Elders and reserves), political and spiritual movements (such as the American Indian Movement), and education (especially post-secondary). For the participants, living a life of Anishinaabe spirituality means giving back (e.g., to one's community); an emphasis on relationships and connections in Creation; knowing who they are; good feelings; and having found what they had been searching for. Finally, others' reactions to the participants' pursuit of Anishinaabe spirituality were briefly explored, with positive reactions from family and spiritual community members being reported twice as often as negative reactions.

Taking a closer look at how spirituality has influenced the participants' self-identification, it became apparent that learning their spirit name and coming to know who they are in Creation significantly influences identity. Participants' involvement with Anishinaabe spirituality has resulted in changes to their process of self-identification and relating (as opposed to just a noun-based identity). In other words, many participants indicated that they now focus more on how they relate to everyone and everything in Creation, as opposed to fixating on calling themselves by this or that specific noun or name; the names themselves (e.g., Cree or Métis) have become less important than the relationships. Taken together, these findings paint a picture, in broad brushstrokes, of the participants' lives in relation to Anishinaabe spirituality and self-identification. The purpose of looking at such a wide range of areas is to begin to take notice of which ones may be indirectly and directly influencing relationships with Anishinaabe spirituality among people with Métis ancestry.

As the conversations documented in this book show, the historical context of colonialism continues to thread its way through the lives of Métis people today. In this regard, most participants spoke of the ongoing effects of residential schools, Christianization, government and church suppression of Anishinaabe spirituality, as well as government division between Métis and First Nations people. These effects are being experienced (at one time or another) within the lives of the participants themselves or among their family members—for example, in the form of struggles with internalized racism and/ or addictions. Consequently, some participants shared painful experiences of feeling unwelcome at ceremonies where people were suspicious of their identity because of their fair appearance, questioning whether or not they were "really Native" or had the "right" to be there. The fact that each participant continues to participate in Anishinaabe ceremony contributes to breaking down these colonial divisions and overcoming these barriers. In addition, the effects of the suppression of Anishinaabe ceremonies are still being felt by many participants, especially in the form of residual fear and distrust of Anishinaabe spirituality among family and community members. Thankfully, this trend also appears to be abating with each subsequent generation; today, most participants' families are encouraging of their involvement in ceremony, if not participating to some extent themselves.

The political and spiritual movements of the 1960s and 1970s have had a resounding impact on the older participants in this study in terms of identity and spirituality. The Red Power Movement, the American Indian Movement, the birth of the Three Fires Midewiwin society, and the empowering environment of the times served as catalysts for many Anishinaabe people to stand up for their rights, a renewed sense of pride in their identity, and a return to their ancestral cultural and spiritual ways. Almost without exception, participants aged fifty and older spoke of the power of those times as positively and powerfully influencing their self-identification and healing journey to wholeness (i.e., Anishinaabe spirituality). Some of the younger participants also spoke of being influenced by these movements through their family's involvement.

A similar phenomenon appears to be happening today for younger people through higher education. Without exception, the youngest participants in this study each spoke of the importance of higher education as a catalyst for strengthening their sense of Aboriginal identity and group belonging, as well as their journey to Anishinaabe spirituality. Through higher education, these participants have access to Elders, cultural teachings, events, and even ceremonies that they would not have access to otherwise (often because their family and/or community remains highly assimilated). In many cases, participants have begun their journey with Anishinaabe spirituality, thanks in part to their university education and experiences, and are now committed to pursuing it as a way of life.

Yet another larger-scale theme arising throughout this study is the fact that people have transformative experiences that change their spiritual path and identity; and, despite obstacles, they keep going and do not give up. Each participant shared at least one major event or experience in their life (sometimes negative, but often empowering) that forever changed them in some way and eventually contributed to their strengthened Aboriginal identity (however they choose to self-identify) and commitment to Anishinaabe spirituality. For some, this transformative experience came in the form of a significant struggle with addiction or abuse, a devastating loss such as the death of a loved one, or a suicide attempt. For others, it came in the form of ceremony, for instance hearing the Little Boy Water Drum for the first time, or experiencing their first sweat lodge ceremony, or receiving their spirit name. Whether the event was heartbreaking or overwhelmingly positive, the participants used the experience to better their lives and become healthier human beings through their commitment to Anishinaabe spirituality. They spoke of turning even the most traumatic experiences into a fierce and unyielding determination to turn their life around and commit to a healthier life informed by Anishinaabe spirituality; or, if they had already committed, of remaining unwavering in their dedication to this path. Each of these participants illustrates the power of Anishinaabe spirituality in overcoming adversity.

The intergenerational movement away from Christianity and toward Anishinaabe spirituality occurring within the participants' families is yet another "bigger picture" that emerged. It is significant that almost every participant was raised in a Christian faith (and none in a solely Indigenous faith); however, many of the participants themselves now adhere to an Anishinaabe spiritual path and are raising their children in this way. Among these participants, there also appears to be a pattern whereby people with Métis ancestry who follow Anishinaabe spirituality seem more likely to self-identify as Anishinaabe (or Métis Anishinaabe), as opposed to strictly Métis. This is also true for me personally. Does it have to do with the Anishinaabe teachings themselves? Or the particular spiritual communities to which the participants belong? Is it a combination of these factors? It would be interesting to explore this topic further and to compare the patterns within this study to a group who pursue Anishinaabe spirituality and staunchly self-identify solely as Métis.

As there exists almost no research to date on the relationship between Métis ancestry and Anishinaabe spirituality and its influences upon identity, this book is meant to begin the discussion. The key themes and patterns that have emerged within this book will come into sharper focus as future research is conducted on this topic, contributing to the discussion. I hope future research will grow from the seeds I have tried to sow with this book; for example, a deeper look into the relationship between higher education and Anishinaabe spirituality or between racism and Anishinaabe spirituality. A more in-depth investigation of contemporary factors that continue to disconnect Métis (and other Aboriginal) people from traditional Anishinaabe spirituality is also needed. Or, perhaps an examination of the factors that motivate some people with Aboriginal ancestry to choose to self-identify as non-Aboriginal today. Another possible study that could build upon this one would be an exploration of contemporary syncretism of Anishinaabe spirituality and Christianity in well-adjusted Aboriginal (or maybe even non-Aboriginal) people, perhaps including a look at historical forms of this syncretism. Yet another interesting and important avenue for future research might be a study looking at efforts of contemporary Euro-Canadian, non-Aboriginal people seeking to remember their own ancestral Original Instructions.

I would like to conclude by highlighting the final comments shared by three participants at the end of their interview. Sandra noted the sensitive nature of spirituality in general, especially in relation to Métis people who choose to live according to Anishinaabe spirituality. She stated, "I think your research in this area is very important. I think that spirituality in any context is a difficult subject, and in this [context] ... it's almost political. It's almost political when we talk about the identification of Métis people and Indigenous [spiritual] practice, because I think some people like to hold that snapshot of the Red River in 1870 as that is who a Métis person is: [a] French-speaking, Catholic person. We're not that anymore; there may be a few, but that's not who we are as People." Ron seems to echo this in his final remarks: "I think the Métis community is very diverse, and that's part of our strength, I think, because I've met Métis right across Canada." Keeping this diversity in mind, I would like to repeat Lance's closing words: "In following this way of life and being a Métis (what they called me), it's very important to find out who you are, like that Elder said, 'any which way that you want.' You need to [pauses] do it on your own. You gotta ask for direction in life. And to seek out those Elders; they're not gonna come to you. You need to go to them to find your way of life. I have done that. And now the little knowledge that I [have gained from] going to Elders, sweat lodge, Sundance, I pass that on because it's only [in] that [way that] I can help the people; by sharing my true life experience [and] what I went through, or what I have seen through dreaming and visions in the sweat or visions in the fasting." Throughout this book, I have tried hard to emphasize the diversity among people with Métis ancestry (and other Aboriginal people), but also that we share commonalities, including in our journeys to and with Anishinaabe spirituality.

I realize that I have been irrevocably changed by the work of recording and discussing these stories. For much of this work, I was simultaneously on a spiritual journey as Midewit (a Midewiwin Initiate). I became first-degree Midewiwin near the end of my research journey; therefore, my research study, writing this book, and being Midewit will forever be inextricably connected for me. Separately, each of these journeys can be tremendously demanding, time-consuming, and emotional; together, they felt overwhelming at times. Having said this, I would not have changed a thing. Not even being para-lyzed with worry for months at the beginning of my fieldwork stage for fear that people might think I was only at ceremonies for research purposes; or accidentally revealing a participant's identity; or not initiating after my first year as Midewit. While those were by far the most personally challenging things I had to deal with on this journey, they also provided me invaluable teachings about honesty and speaking from my heart; learning to love myself, mistakes and all; and learning to deeply trust myself, others, and spirit. For me, travelling both the research and Midewit journeys at the same time has meant both journeys have been heightened and enriched.

My life will forever be changed by the generosity, kindness, and sincerity of the participants in this study, some of whom I met through this study, all of whom I now know on a much deeper level. Whether I knew the participant previously or not, each participant freely shared their innermost feelings, passions, and experiences with me. While it is not likely that I will be able somehow to repay them for their generosity, they have given me permission to share their stories and I have committed to this. I have faith that the stories and experiences within these pages will positively impact others in their own journey to and with Anishinaabe spirituality and *mino-bimaadiziwin*. Every participant in this study is a most beautiful role model; I believe their stories will inspire others, as they have so profoundly inspired me.

The participants in this study have chosen the path of spirituality. They show us that we can empower ourselves and others by the way we live our lives and the choices we make each day. They encourage us to think beyond ourselves to the future for our families, communities, nations, and our Mother Earth. The participants remind me of the Anishinaabe concept *ayangwamezin*: be focused, be determined, but be careful, and do not give up. To quote Three Fires Midewiwin Grand Chief Bawdwaywidun Benaise on this concept: "To have courage isn't to be without fear; fear is a natural human feeling and it helps us to be more careful. But we shouldn't let the fear stop us from doing what we know needs to be done." This is good advice to keep in mind and heart throughout one's spiritual journey in life, as are the following words from Ernest Lerat, a fourth-year Sundancer who has committed to dance another four years: "This [Sundance/Anishinaabe ceremony] is where you get your strength, don't be scared. So many people are scared because they don't understand. Come and learn and understand. And don't be scared. Be as happy as all these guys [motions all around him]; look, everybody is giggling, laughing. No drugs, no alcohol, nothing; just pure emotion and that's the greatest" (Robinson 3012c).

A word of advice to those interested in going to a ceremony for the first time: there are protocols that need to be followed when approaching ceremony, participating in ceremony, and around the ceremony grounds. The Blacksmiths have extended an open invitation to everyone to come participate in their ceremony regardless of age, race, religion, etc., but it is important to note that not all ceremony leaders have extended a similar invitation. Try to talk to others who have gone to the ceremony you wish to participate in. Important things to consider include: Is this ceremony open to the public?

 How can I approach ceremony in a good way (i.e., with an offering or gift of tobacco, cloth, or food)? What is appropriate to wear (i.e., women are often expected to wear long skirts, but sometimes two-spirit women are exempt from this)? How do I enter the lodge in a good way (which way do I walk, where am I allowed to sit)? If you make a mistake and someone corrects you (hopefully in a kind way), do not take it personally; instead, try to see it as a learning opportunity. Finally, the protocol is different depending on the ceremony conductor, the traditional territory you are on, etc.; be respectful of the protocol where you are (even if you were taught to do it differently).

   With this work, I have sought to raise awareness about the relationships between Métis people and Anishinaabe spirituality, especially those factors that hinder and nurture such a spiritual commitment. I have sought to break down colonial divisions between Métis and First Nations people and encourage the healing of our familial relationships while celebrating our differences. A deeper goal of this work is to encourage people with Métis ancestry (and other Aboriginal people) to reconnect with Anishinaabe spirituality in order to contribute to fulfilling the work of the Oshkibimaadiziig spoken of in the Seven Fires Prophecy. I believe this prophecy has much to teach us today, as humanity and the environment are facing increasing destruction—for example, in the form of global warming. The prophecy encourages all of us, as descendants of the four Original Peoples, to choose the path of spirituality:

> The prophet of the Fourth Fire spoke of a time when "two nations will join to make a mighty nation." He was speaking of the coming of the Light-skinned Race and the face of brotherhood[/sisterhood] that the Light-skinned brother[/sister] could be wearing. It is obvious from the history of this country that this was not the face worn by the Light-skinned Race as a whole. That mighty nation spoken of in the Fourth Fire has never been formed.
>
> If we natural people of the Earth could just wear the face of brotherhood[/sisterhood], we might be able to deliver our society from the road to destruction. Could we make the two roads that today represent two clashing world views come together to form that mighty nation? Could a nation be formed that is guided by respect for all living things? (Benton-Banai 1988, 93)

   I want to remind us all of the good work our ancestors—Shingwauk, Mistahimaskwa (Big Bear), Pitikwahanapiwiyin (Poundmaker), Minahikosis (Little Pine), Kamiscowesit (Beardy), and Louis Riel, to name a few—did to encourage Anishinaabeg (including Métis) to stand together united without giving up our unique cultures. Indeed, let us go one step further and heal our relationships with settlers, so that coming generations (and all our relations in Creation) can have a brighter future. Viewed from a certain angle, we can see progress being made by Canadian society in terms of recognizing the importance of Aboriginal cultures and of bettering relationships with Aboriginal peoples. As Siggins writes, "It is only recently that our society has slowly taken off its blinkers of prejudice and come to understand ... that Native cultures have their own uniqueness and value—great value in a world polluting itself to death.... [W]hat makes Louis Riel so intriguing is that he managed to straddle two cultures, Native and white, and came as close as anyone to envisioning a sympathetic and equitable relationship between the two. That Canadians may someday achieve this vision remains Louis Riel's legacy" (Siggins 1995, 448). Likewise, Payment notes that "it is only in the last decade or so that profound changes have taken place in the views of the clergy towards Aboriginal cosmology. The Catholic Church has developed a more open attitude towards Aboriginal spirituality and integrated indigenous traditions in its ministry. Métis priests, such as the late Oblate Guy Lavallée [from St. Laurent, Manitoba], have celebrated Métis spiritual values and culture in prayers and rituals that are meaningful. Riel has also been recognized as a prophet, and his legacy has been celebrated rather than condemned or belittled as in the past" (Payment 2009, 122). Indeed, the Idle No More movement is the most recent incarnation of Indigenous resistance, this time with greater support from non-Indigenous allies; it brings renewed hope because it shows us these very options. Our ancestors and the participants in this study show us the possibility that, together, we can endeavour to form that mighty nation and light the eighth and final fire of eternal unity and ensure *mino-bimaadiziwin* (healthy, balanced, good life) for all those who are yet unborn.

Miigwetch, Niikaanigaana! (Thank you, all my relations)!

Gichi Miigwetch *(Acknowlededgements)*

I will forever be grateful to the participants themselves for choosing to work with me and for so generously sharing their stories, experiences, and time; I hope the wisdom you share in these pages will reach many others. This work would not have been possible without each of you; *gichi miigwetch*!

Special thanks to my biological parents, Donna and Renald, for your unconditional love and support and for letting me stay in your home for impromptu writing retreats; and to my traditional adoptive parents, Charlie and Violet, for your generosity of spirit, kindness, and gentleness. Thank you to Sylvie and Gina for being proud of me and always rooting for me. Kevin, thank you for our many work sessions at cafés, your good advice, and for our collective venting which kept me sane! Amanda, *miigwetch* for your un-faltering confidence in me and my work, for your patience and constructive feedback, and for not letting me work through mealtimes (how could I with your delicious cooking?!). A heartfelt *miigwetch* to all my loving biological and Midewiwin family and friends for your unwavering encouragement, support and confidence in me and helping me learn who I am.

I give thanks for, and honour, my Midewiwin teachers including Rainey Gaywish (Riverton, MB), Charlie Nelson (Roseau River First Nation, MB), Eddie Benton-Banai (Lac Courte Oreilles Reservation, WI), Jim Dumont (Shawanaga First Nation, ON), Dorene Day (St. Paul, MN), and countless others. I have learned a lot from Marcel, Bernie, and Norbert Hardisty, and the late Gary Raven (Anishinaabe from Hollow Water First Nation). I also have great respect for what I learned from Wilton Goodstriker (Blackfoot from Alberta), Shirley Williams and Edna Manitowabi (Odawa from Wikiwemikong First Nation, Ontario), and Michael Thrasher and Rebecca Martell (Nêhiyaw from Waterhen Lake First Nation, Saskatchewan). Most re-cently, I have had the honour of learning from David and Sherryl Blacksmith (Nêhiyaw from Cross Lake First Nation and Anishinaabe from Swan Lake First Nation, respectively). I am still learning and it is with humility that I say, any errors in this book are my own.

Miigwetch to Dr. Lynne Davis for her keen attention to detail, tireless guidance, and her persistence in keeping me on task and on time, and for encouraging me to publish this book! *Miigwetch* to Dr. David Newhouse for his patience and kind-hearted support. I am indebted to Dr. Rainey Gaywish for her enthusiastic encouragement, for being my good friend and trusted spiritual advisor, and for being ever generous with her time and wisdom.

Thank you to Jean Wilson for her insightful help in navigating the initial stages of the academic publishing process. My thanks also to the wonderful (and friendly!) team at the University of Manitoba Press including David Carr for his spirited support and vision for my book and Glenn Bergen for his patience and persistence in editing and his sharp eye for detail. A big *miigwetch* to Christi Belcourt for generously allowing her beautiful artwork to grace the cover of my book.

I am also thankful for helpful financial support from the National Aboriginal Achievement Foundation, the Ontario Graduate Scholarship, the Stephen Stohn and Family Bursary, and the Jean Evelyn Graves-Canadian Studies Graduate Scholarship.

Last, but not least, I want to say *gichi miigwetch* to Gizhi Manidoo and Spirit for directing this work from beginning to end and for all the blessings of my good life.

Glossary

Aatsokaanag	Sacred stories, legends
Aazhoodena	Stony Point First Nation
Algokowin	Entirely
Asemaa	Tobacco
Abiding	First
Anishinaabe(g)	Ojibwe person (people) [Original people]
Anishinaabe-Kwe	Ojibwe woman
Anishinaabe-Inini	Ojibwe man
Anishinaabemowin	Ojibwe language
Ayangwamezin	Be focused, determined, careful; do not give up
Baaskaandibewi-Ziibiing	Brokenhead First Nation
Bimaadiziwin	Life
Biizhew	Lynx
Doodem	Clan
Endaso-giizhigaad	Every day
Gaa-wiikwedaawangaag	Sandy Bay First Nation
Gagii-maajiiyaang	A way of life
Gichi Manidoo	Creator
Gichi Miigwetch	Thank you very much
Gwiimeh	Namer
Inini	Man
Kiimoochly [Giimooji]	Secretly
Kwe	Woman
Ma'iingan	Wolf
Makwa	Bear
Manidoo(g) [Manitoes]	Spirit(s)
Mide-inini	Midewiwin man
Mide-kwe	Midewiwin woman

Midewit	Midewiwin initiate
Midewiwin	Way of the heart
Mikinaakwajiw-Ininiwag	Turtle Mountain, ND
Miinawa	And, also
Mikwayndaasowin	Recalling, remembering that which was there before
Mino-bimaadiziwin	Good, balanced life
Miskwaadesiins	Little red turtle
Mooneyash [Mooniyaa]	White person
Mushkodaywushk	Sage
Ndaaw	I am
Ndizhinikaaz	I am called (my name is)
Neeshwaswi' ishkodaykawn	Seven fires (prophecy)
Nêhiyaw	Cree person
Nêhiyawêwin	Cree language
Niikaanigaana	All my relations/relatives
(O)shkaabewis	Helper
Oshkibimaadiziig	New people
Oshki-Ishkonigan	St. Peters/Peguis First Nation
Waabishkizi	It is white (White person)
Waabizhayshii	Marten
Waanibiigaaw	Hollow Water First Nation
Wemittigozhi [Wemitigoozhi]	White person (French person)
Wiigwas	Birchbark
Wiisaakodewikwe(g)	Metis woman (women)
Wiisaakodewinini(wag)	Metis man (men)
Wiiwkwedong	Kettle Point First Nation
Zaagaate	The sun is coming out, shining
Zaaskajiwaning	Dauphin River First Nation
Zhaawaa [Ozaawaa]	Yellow
Zhiibaashkodeyaang	Roseau River First Nation

Notes

CHAPTER 1: Seven Fires Prophecy and the Métis: An Introduction

1   Noteably, more recent texts on Métis studies that are proving helpful include St-Onge, Podruchny, and Macdougall, *Contours of a People: Metis Family, Mobility, and History* (2012), and Adams, Dahl, and Peace, eds., *Métis in Canada: History, Identity, Law and Politics* (2013).

2   Throughout this book, my examples often refer to the Anishinaabeg and the Midewiwin because of my own ancestry and personal experiences.

3   In 2011, 451,795 people identified as Métis. They represented 32.3 percent of the total Aboriginal population; Aboriginal people account for 4 percent of the total Canadian population (Statistics Canada 2013a). These are the most recent population statistics available at this time.

4   According to APTN (16 August 2013), "Shanneen's story was not the first time cameras were allowed into a Sundance, the [television show] Sharing Circle aired an American Indian Sundance several years ago and our current affairs show Contact showed some of it and discussed it."

5   In the late 1980s, Three Fires Midewiwin Grand Chief Eddie Benton-Banai faced similar reactions for publishing sacred Anishinaabe teachings and knowledge in a book he wrote called *The Mishomis Book*. Today, this book is widely regarded as "the Anishinaabe Bible," and is often included in university course reading lists. When individuals are interested in becoming involved in ceremony, they are often first encouraged to read this book when learning how to approach traditional teachers in a good and respectful way.

6   European settlers called the Nêhiyawak by the name "Cree" and the Anishinaabeg by the names "Ojibwe/Ojibwa/Ojibway" in central/eastern Canada, "Saulteaux" in central/western Canada, and "Chippewa" mainly in the north-central United States. According to oral history, the Anishinaabeg and Nêhiyawak used to be one and the same (Benton-Banai 1988, 108). As they became distinct nations, they maintained extensive trading and intermarrying, and similarities in their cultures and languages persist. It is not uncommon to have a complex interweaving of Anishinaabe and Nêhiyaw ancestry and heritage in a single family, especially in Métis families in central/western Canada.

7   Bostonnais's father, Peter Pangman, participated in the early development of the North West Company (owning two shares). Not much is written about his relationship with Bostonnais's Anishinaabe mother (for example, her name, whether she was married to Peter *à la façon du pays* and then later abandoned for

a white wife, which was common at the time), but sometime after Bostonnais's birth, Peter moved to Montreal and married a Scottish woman (Grace MacTier) with whom he had more children; one of their sons would become a member of the legislative assembly of Lower Canada in 1837.

8   In 1811, Thomas Douglas, Fifth Earl of Selkirk (a.k.a. Lord Selkirk), reached an agreement with the Hudson's Bay Company to found the Red River Colony (a.k.a. District of Assiniboia or the Selkirk Settlement, located in and around present-day Winnipeg) with Miles Macdonnell as the first governor. The settlers would arrive in the Red River region in 1812. Métis and First Nation habitation of the area predates the settlers' arrival. Also note that, technically, bison roam North America, South America, and Europe, while buffalo are found in Asia and Africa; however, the terms are often used interchangeably when referring to the bison of the Canadian plains.

9   The Battle of Seven Oaks is often recognized as one of the first instances of external recognition of distinct Métis nationhood.

10 The same is true of the European ancestors on my mother's side. Interestingly, the name Fiola actually comes from a German ancestor whose last name was Vignola (in German, the letter "v" sounds like an "f"); the name went through various transformations upon coming to Canada until it settled into its current form.

11 At that time, the area was known as "Saltel" after one of a handful of founding families, which also included the Legals and Fiolas. A cross and two plaques still mark the spot where the first mass in the region was held (in the home of Norbert and Adèle Saltel on 24 October 1904, in what would become the parish of Sainte-Geneviève). The cross was erected during the twenty-fifth anniversary of that event in 1929.

12 Known historically as Ste. Anne des Chênes (or Oak Point), Ste. Anne was an early Métis settlement in what would become Manitoba. At one point, it was headquarters for the crew building the Dawson Trail, one of the first overland fur trade routes in the West. When the Canadian government began sending surveyors, led by Colonel John Stoughten Dennis, to divide up the land for incoming settlers, they attempted to survey Ste. Anne first, but were intimidated off the land by the strong Métis resistance and promptly left. They decided to begin surveying near the American border instead; when they approached St. Vital, they would again be kicked off Métis land—this time by Louis Riel and several others; it is at this point that the Red River Resistance began (Siggins 1995, 89, 96).

13 Social locations refer to the complex intersections of race, class, sexuality, ability, and religious affiliation (among others) within interlocking systems of power and oppression.

14 More of my spiritual teachers are identified in the acknowledgment section of this book.

15 Through my research and Midewiwin oral history, I have learned that historically the Saulteaux (Anishinaabeg) people across Manitoba followed the Midewiwin way of life (Gaywish, pers. comm.). This would have included my own Anishinaabeg (and possibly Nêhiyawak) ancestors.

16 Much has been written about Métis identity politics; instead, I focus on Métis relationships with Anishinaabe spirituality (and how this influences self-identity). I will say that there is little agreement about the definition of Métis—who belongs,

and who is excluded. It is a controversial and sensitive topic for many. Some believe that the true Métis are descendants of the original Métis of the Métis Nation (French and Cree and/or Ojibwe ancestry), with roots in the fur trade and the bison hunt, and in the forced dispersal from the Métis homeland (north-central North America, especially Manitoba and Saskatchewan), a shared culture and history, self-identification as Métis, and acceptance as Métis by the Métis of the Métis Nation (i.e., Red River Métis). Before the Manitoba Act (1870) there were two main groups of Métis: descendants of the French and Cree/Ojibwe, who often worked for the North West Company and would coalesce into the Métis Nation in Red River by the early nineteenth century (they were called "Métis," "Bois-Brûlés," or "Michif"), and the descendants of the English/Scottish and Cree/Ojibwe, who often worked for the Hudson's Bay Company (they were called "Halfbreeds," "Country-Born," or "Rupertslanders") and would become part of the Métis Nation by the time of the Manitoba Act of 1870 (Peterson and Brown 1985). After the passing of the Indian Act in 1867, some First Nation individuals who were prevented from obtaining registered Indian status (i.e., non-status Indians) came to be seen as Métis by the government and non-Aboriginal Canadians, and some eventually intermarried with the Métis and came to see themselves as Métis. Then, after the passing of the Constitution Act in 1982, when the Aboriginal Peoples of Canada became constitutionally recognized as First Nations, Métis, and Inuit in section 35, more persons whom the government prevented from being recognized as First Nations status Indians, or Inuit, came to be seen as Métis by others and sometimes called themselves Métis in an effort to gain recognition as an Aboriginal People of Canada. It is important to remember that after the Métis were defeated in the 1885 Resistance, we lost self-determination and control over our own membership and had no choice but to accept the new members who were excluded from the other groups. Today, groups like the Métis Nation of Ontario argue that they should be able to determine their own membership (Belcourt 2013). Importantly, nowhere in these discussions is biological determinism a key factor in defining the Métis. In other words, being Métis is more than simply Indigenous plus European ancestry/blood; it is also distinct nation, culture, history, language, traditions, dress, artistic expression, and importantly homeland, among other characteristics (Andersen 2014; Shore 1999).

CHAPTER 2: Spirituality and Identity

1 Benton-Banai knows the name(s) of the famil(ies) who took in Louis Riel (pers. comm.).

2 An "oblate" identifies a person who has dedicated himself/herself to the service of God through religious life (Huel 1996, 305). They associated themselves with monastic orders, even though they were not formally monks or nuns themselves.

3 Personal communication with Nêhiyawak speaker Neal McLeod, 2006.

4 Content taken from Harrison's book, but spelling taken from Patricia Ningewance's *Talking Gookom's Language*.

5 *Gichi-miigwetch* to one of my peer reviewers for reminding me of the important ideas in this paragraph.

6 Leading up to this, distinct mixed-blood identities and communities were already in existence in eastern Canada and the northern United States (J. Peterson 1985)

sometimes refered to as proto-Métis. These communities are not to be confused with the Red River Métis and the Métis Nation that would emerge later. It is becoming increasingly common to distinguish between the original Red River Métis Nation and other metis with capitalization and an accent above the "e" for the former but not the latter. Also, despite the common misconception, Métis are no more "mixed(-race)" than other Indigenous groups; the difference is that we are a post-contact Indigenous group like the Seminole, Comanche, Oji-Cree and Lumbee (Andersen 2014, 208). The racialized view of "Métis as mixed" has enabled anyone with Aboriginal and European ancestry to claim a Métis identity, to the point where "Métis" has become an umbrella term, or dumping ground, for identity, which obscures the distinct nationhood, history, culture, and language of the original Métis and their descendants. Serious consequences of this include the prevention of Métis Nation self-determination and sovereignty. For an articulate and passionate explanation of these issues see the work of Chris Andersen (2014).

7   It is also important to keep in mind that relations between Aboriginal peoples were not always smooth. "Traditionally, the Sioux were rivals of the Cree and Saulteaux Indians. The Cree and Saulteaux had slowly driven the Sioux out of the Plains in what is presently Manitoba and Saskatchewan. A 'No-man's Land' formed between the rival groups. The Métis... [in these regions] thus became a rival of the Sioux" (Sealey and Lussier 1975, 53). According to Siggins, "With the exception of the Sioux, who resided primarily in the United States, the relations between the mixed-bloods and Indians were most often peaceful and accommodating. The Métis in particular acted as a buffer, a link between Natives and whites" (9). However, she mentions that the Saulteaux and Métis were sometimes rivals during the fur trade (ibid., 170). Sealey and Lussier also comment on difficult relations between the Cree, Saulteaux, and Métis. "The Cree Indians objected to the fact that the Saulteaux Indians were grandly selling land to Selkirk when the Saulteaux were interlopers in the area. Traditionally, for perhaps 1500 years, the Cree and Assiniboine had owned the Red River area. Indeed, one reason [Chief] Peguis was so helpful to the settlers was to gain allies, for at no time did the Cree or Assiniboine Indians fully accept his intrusion into the valley. It was, however, a sign of the times. The Saulteaux Indians slowly but surely drove the Cree and the Assiniboine out of much of southern Manitoba and Saskatchewan. The battle was still being waged when the Saulteaux rather arrogantly resold the land to the Canadian government in 1871. In selling the land to Lord Selkirk, Chief Peguis noted that he didn't recognize that the Métis had any claim to the land. It is reported that Bostonnais Pangman, a Métis with a reputation for violence, told chief Peguis that if he continued to talk in such a matter [sic] the Métis would settle the argument by killing all the Saulteaux. Apparently, it settled the argument. Such was the violent tenor of the times" (ibid., 43). While these (sometimes contradictory) explanations are likely simplistic (and, in the passages by Sealey and Lussier, decidedly unsympathetic towards the Saulteaux and Métis), they are useful for pointing out that relations between Aboriginal people were not always peaceful and disputes did occur over land, resources, hunting territory, encroaching settlers, and colonial divide-and-conquer strategies. One wonders about the extent to which these relationships were impacted by incoming settlers and the spread of colonization, as well as how spirituality was impacted.

8   McCarthy ignores the possibilities that it was the Métis who were absorbed into the Saulteaux and Cree population, or that distinguishing amongst themselves in these ways was never a priority.

9 Mihesuah does not explain why one must choose to self-identify with only one of many identities available to multiheritage persons, and she fails to ask who benefits when such a choice is made. Also, she does not consider the choice to self-identify as a new racial group as a legitimate decision arrived at through critical agency. Many people who self-identify as metis, especially Red River Métis people, would likely feel offended hearing Mihesuah describe Métis identity as a failure to pick one heritage, as it denies that Métis Nation heritage is complete and legitimate in and of itself.

10 For more on identity theories relevant to mixed-race peoples, see works by Ali 2003; Lawrence 2000, 2004; Restoule 2004; Root 1992; Penn 1997; I. Peterson 1997; Spencer 1997; Schouls 2003; Strong and Barrik 1996; Van Kirk 1980; Weaver 2001; T. Wilson 1992; Womack 1997; Yellow Bird 1999; and Zack 1995.

11 Not all European cultures have enjoyed the same degree of white privilege. At various points in history, some European groups faced discrimination and oppression from other European groups who considered themselves "whiter" and superior (e.g., White Anglo-Saxon Protestants), in Europe as well as in North America. An examination of this history goes beyond the scope of this book. However, it is important to remember that racism is about whiteness and power; the greater the perceived whiteness, the greater the privileges and power. It is with this understanding that some Métis people tried to identify with whiteness and downplay their Nativeness after 1885 in an effort to escape discrimination. For more on racism as being about whiteness and power, consult the reference page for works by Sherene Razack.

12 For an example of the devastating effects that passing and trying to assimilate into British English settler culture can have on a mixed-race family, see Van Kirk's (1985) chapter entitled " 'What if Mama is an Indian?': The Cultural Ambivalence of the Alexander Ross family."

13 Collections reflecting this include: Christine Miller and Patricia Chuchryk's (1997) *Women of the First Nations: Power, Wisdom and Strength;* William Penn's (1997) *As We Are Now: Mixblood Essays on Race and Identity;* Maria Root's (1992) *Racially Mixed People in America;* and Joyce Green's (2007) *Making Space for Indigenous Feminism.* These collections reject simplistic and oppressive identity categories and contribute to the discussions around evolving, contradictory, and multiple identities.

CHAPTER 3: Understanding the Colonial Context of Métis Spirituality and Identity

1 For more on Métis history, see Dickason 1985; Shore 1999; Peterson and Brown 1985; Mercier 1974; Lavallée 2003; Gordon 2005; St. Onge 2004; Campbell 2011b; and Barkwell, Dorion, and Prefontaine 2001.

2 The "one-drop rule" has also significantly influenced identity in America, mostly in relation to African Americans. In keeping with the savage/civilized continuum, anyone with one drop of African blood/ancestry is simply Black; also, the principle of "hypodescent" automatically assigns children of mixed unions to the subordinate social group. These concepts were meant to protect the rights of slave owners. According to Hollinger (2005), "Some slave-era and Jim Crow governments did employ fractional classifications, providing distinctive rights and privileges for

'octoroons,' 'quadroons,' and 'mulattoes,' " but eventually went the way of Virginia, "whose miscegenation statute as revised in 1924 classified as white only a person 'who has no trace whatsoever of blood other than Caucasian' " (20–21). In 1964, the Civil Rights Act was passed; then in 1967, the Virginia statute and all racial restrictions on marriage were invalidated in the U.S. Supreme Court case of *Loving v. Virginia*. This led to a "bi-racial baby boom" in the 1970s (Khanna 2010, 99). Interestingly, since the civil rights movement, African Americans began using the "one-drop rule" as a tool of inclusivity to promote unity and numerical strength among the Black community; once used as a tool of white oppression, the one-drop rule is now used to unify Black Americans (Khanna, 99, 114). Other minority groups, including Native Americans, have followed suit. Also, see footnote 5 in Chapter 4.

3   On the flip side, the same arbitrary process decided when Halfbreed families were recorded as taking treaty and likely got their names onto the general lists—which, together with the band lists, would eventually become the Indian Registrar in 1951 (Gilbert 1996, 15)—thereby subjecting them to all the rules of the Indian Act, including suppression of spirituality and the forced removal of children to residential schools.

4   Protection for religion meant the right to denominational schools: "provision was made for public support of both a Protestant and Roman Catholic school system" (Manitoba Project 2011, 5). This clause did not appear in the original List of Rights agreed upon by the Red River provisional government; rather, it seems to have been added sometime between when the three representatives of the provisional government were en route with the List to negotiate in Ottawa and their arrival there. Evidence suggests that Bishop Taché was instrumental in this sleight of hand (Siggins 1994, 169). It is difficult to determine whether this provision reflected that a majority of Métis, by 1870, were following Christian religions, or whether it is a reflection of the religions of choice of only those involved in the negotiations, or whether it is the work of the clergy alone.

5   For more on the swindling of Métis land via the scrip system, see: Sealey 1978; Fillmore 1978; Barkwell 2002; Chartrand 2002b; Santin 2007; and Ens 1996. For an excellent article on Métis (land and other) rights, see Chartrand and Giokas 2002.

6   Throughout his entire life, Riel fought for Métis and First Nation rights. By 16 October 1870, Riel and others had democratically formed the National Committee (which would replace the HBC's Council of Assiniboia as the governing body of Assiniboia, eventually leading to Riel's Provisional Government, which would successfully negotiate Manitoba's entry into confederation). Each parish was to democratically select a representative as a delegate to form a council to discuss important issues; Henry Prince, Chief of the Saulteaux residents in St. Peter's Parish, was one such delegate (Siggins 1995, 111). Riel was also instrumental in the List of Rights (or Bill of Rights) designed by the Executive of the Provisional Government; it voiced the Red River inhabitants' terms for annexation to Canada. It sought to protect Métis, First Nation, and even White settler rights (those who had already been living in the region for some time); clause 13 stipulates "That treaties be concluded between Canada and the different Indian tribes of the Province of Assiniboia, by and with the advice and cooperation of the local Legislature of the Province" (ibid. 450). Riel continued his activism for Métis and First Nation rights during his stay in Montana after having been exiled from Canada. He met with

several First Nations and spoke of creating a country that Métis and First Nations could call their own; he met with Chief Sitting Bull, Crowfoot's people, and Chiefs Little Pine and Big Bear (Siggins 1995, 293–95). Riel also wanted protection for Métis, First Nations, and already established White settlers during his participation in the Northwest Resistance in Saskatchewan. Chief White Cap of the Sioux Nation was a member of the Exovedate (within the democratically elected Provisional Government formed by Riel and others) there. As in Manitoba, the Provisional Government of Saskatchewan passed a Bill of Rights (8 March 1885); clause 7 states "That better provision be made for the Indians, the parliamentary grant to be increased and lands set apart as an endowment for the establishment of hospitals and schools for the use of whites, half-breeds, and Indians, at such places as the provincial legislatures may determine" (ibid. 452). Riel continued to fight for Métis and First Nation rights even while he was on death row! While awaiting his execution, with the help of his lawyer, Riel smuggled a letter to the U.S. President (Grover Cleveland) from his jail cell proposing that "Métis and Indian territory be made one vast region under the protection of the U.S. government" (ibid. 437).

7 . Indeed, throughout their book *Loyal till Death: Indians and the North-West Rebellion*, the authors work hard to distance the First Nations from the Métis during the Northwest Resistance. While they are correct in stating that there was no grand alliance, they seem to go too far in the opposite direction. We must keep in mind that, at the time, many settlers and the Canadian government feared such an alliance, the latter often encouraging such fears through propaganda in the newspapers. Many argue that Prime Minister John A. Macdonald purposely stirred up these fears to justify continued spending on the transcontinental railway (which could quickly transport Canadian militia to the Northwest and crush Aboriginal dissenters). With the defeat of the Métis at Batoche, the government also punished First Nations, especially the Cree, in an effort to quash any remaining hopes of an alliance or resistance against the Canadian government. The oppression faced by Aboriginal peoples in the West after 1885 was utterly devastating; many Métis would change their names and try to pass as white, and many First Nations would try to separate themselves from the Métis in an effort to lessen the persecution they received as a result of the "Métis Rebellion." These survival tactics, and their effects, persist to this day.

8 "The basis for entitlement to a First Nation membership list maintained by the Department [AANDC] is whether the applicant is entitled to be registered as an Indian" (Gilbert 1996, 64). Even though the 1985 Indian Act attempts to give First Nations an opportunity to control their own membership codes, the Department sets out a lengthy list of rules and laws by which the band must abide in determining membership. Just like the heavy hand of the American government in determining tribal membership (discussed at the beginning of this chapter), "the courts, however, seem to be assuming an increasing role in supervising the application of these new laws" (ibid. 4–5). To date, out of 614 First Nations in Canada, only 253 control their own membership (AANDC 2010).

9 Please note that this section relies mainly on secondary sources and that many primary church records remain locked in private archives. "Permission ha[s] to be obtained to examine these collections and their facilities [are] limited. The private nature of these archives ma[kes] it difficult for lay persons and especially scholars in nondenominational universities to undertake serious research on the

missionary activities..." (Huel 1996, xxi–xxii; Daniels 2006, 101). (Indeed, the Truth and Reconciliation Commission and the general public are demanding that the churches and especially the government honour the apology for residential schools by handing over all documents detailing the abuses at the schools; however, the most damaging documents remain under lock and key). Moreover, researching this topic is made more difficult because in many of the documents Métis people are also referred to as "halfbreeds" or "non-treaty," and it is possible that some non-Native people were lumped into the category "non-treaty." Many people identified as "non-treaty" have last names that are frequently identified as long-standing Métis family names (Daniels 2006, 102).

10 Many Anglicans viewed Native peoples as nothing but "Savages" (Widder 1999, xx).

11 Examples include: St. Norbert, St. Boniface, Ste. Agathe, Ste. Geneviève, St. Eustache, St. François Xavier, St. Malo, Ste. Anne, Ste. Theresa Pointe, Ste. Rose du Lac, St. Lazare, St. Alphonse and St. Pierre-Jolys. Île-à-la-Crosse, Lake St. Martin, and Cross Lake also point to Christian influence in settling the province.

12 The residential school system would come to be "one of the most notoriously under-funded programs in Canadian history" (J. Miller 1996, 38).

13 This statistic is part of a set that states that, out of 105,000 to 107,000 former residential school students alive in 1991, approximately 80 percent were registered Indians, 6 percent were non-status Indians, and 5 percent were Inuit (Logan 2008, 84–85).

14 At the St. Laurent day school, clergy called my uncle Bob Normand Jr. the Devil for being left-handed, and the priest would bless him daily in front of the other children. They tied his left arm behind his back (only untying him for recess) so he would be forced to learn how to write with his right hand; he was six years old (pers. comm.).

15 This class structure continued after graduation; Indian Agents reported female students as doing well when they were married to a White man and doing poorly if they had married a Métis man or had returned to their homes (Logan 2008, 82).

16 In February 2000, the MMF started its "Lost Generations Project," one of the first AHF Métis-specific projects in Canada (Logan 2006a, 3) in an effort to counter the fact that attendance of Métis students at residential schools continues to be overlooked (Logan 2008, 72–73).

17 The mandatory long-form census has been replaced in Canada by the National Household Survey; the change brings with it several obstacles, including an increase in incompletely enumerated communities and shakier insight into Aboriginal issues ("Lost Long-Form Census" 2013).

18 *Miigwetch* to the peer reviewer of this manuscript who suggested this argument in no uncertain terms.

CHAPTER 4: A Métis Anishinaabe Study

1 Paradigm essentially means a particular world view underlying theories and methodology (system of methods, e.g., interviews) used to understand the world, undertake research, and create new knowledge.

2 Mi'kmaq scholar Marie Battiste (1986) popularized the term "cognitive assimilation"; using the myth of the illiterate Indian, Europeans have pushed to make Aboriginal people literate in European languages, using European methods and values, which amounts to a colonization of the minds of Aboriginal people (23).

3   For more on Indigenous methodologies, see: Guba and Lincoln 1998; Steinhauer 2001; Gaywish 2008; Weber-Pillwax 2001; S. Wilson 2001, 2003, 2008; and Kovach 2009.

4   These "colours" do not necessarily represent what we understand today as "races."

5   TallBear (2003) points out that one drop of Indian blood should not determine enrollment in a tribe/Indianness, because it ignores the importance of tribal cultural knowledge, life experience, and/or political affiliation (97–98). While I agree with TallBear, it can be very welcoming for previously (or legally) excluded mixed-blood persons to feel included by the "one-drop rule" when it is used as a tool of inclusion—for instance, when Grand Chief Eddie Benton-Banai says that it only takes one drop of Anishinaabe blood to claim your birthright as Anishinaabe, including the Midewiwin lodge. I do not believe Benton-Banai means to say that blood is the sole connection/requirement for an Indigenous identity. Instead, in the Three Fires Midewiwin Lodge, I have learned from teachers, including Benton-Banai, that being Midewiwin comes with responsibilities that include ongoing participation in ceremony, passing the teachings on to subsequent generations, and living life according to Midewiwin principles. In other words, I interpret this to mean that with one drop of blood, you are welcome to claim your birthright, but this only has meaning if you make a life-long commitment to live your life according to Anishinaabe ways.

6   Sherryl reminded me that David never went to school and has no formal education; he was raised in the bush by his grandparents. David understands the importance of Indigenous and Western education; he encouraged his wife to get a degree (he was a stay-at-home dad so she could get a degree in education) because he wanted his children, especially their four daughters, to retain their independence, help themselves, and be "strong, educated Indian women." When I started going to ceremonies, a trusted confidante gave me advice on how to spot good/trustworthy male traditional teachers. She said, "pay attention to how they think/speak about and treat women; do they work with their wife (or other female teachers) and share responsibilities for leading?" As an Indigenous woman, I always pay close attention to this; women make up half the population, so it is important that we see women in leadership roles (including the divine feminine). This is especially critical given the degradation of our women that is an ongoing effect of colonization (our men also suffer from internalized European patriarchy). David and Sherryl are a wonderful example of sharing authority, responsibility, and leadership in ceremony; I have seen this with my own eyes.

7   For more details on quota sampling, see Bryman and Teevan 2005, 228. Non-probability sampling makes the most sense for this project given the fact that no research has been conducted to date regarding the relationship between people with Métis ancestry and Anishinaabe spirituality; therefore, it is impossible to know how many such people exist.

8   My aim was to focus on descendants with Indigenous and European ancestors who have a connection to the original Métis Nation. Almost every participant in the study is such a descendant through one or both parents. Three participants are not, but they have been included in the study because they nonetheless have a connection to the original Métis Nation—for example, by growing up in a predominantly Métis town, or through oral family history of taking Métis scrip and being kicked off reserve, or because their own family referred to them as a

"Halfbreed" while growing up—and they meet the other criteria for participation. Importantly, self-identification as "Métis" was not necessary for participation in this study; and it is not my intention to impose a Métis identity on participants. Indeed, some of the participants are descendants of the Métis Nation, but do not self-identify as Métis. The range of participants highlights the historic and ongoing complexity of Métis ancestries and identities and our nuanced relationships with other Aboriginal groups.

9   Half the interviews for this book were completed by the time Bill C-3 was implemented, and its consequences remain largely unknown; therefore, only Bill C-31 is examined in the lives of the participants.

10 Four participants were aged eighteen to thirty (one female, three males); four were aged thirty-one to forty-four (two females, two males); and ten participants were aged forty-five or older (six females, four males).

11 Miigwetch to Odawa Midewiwin Elder Shirley Williams for sharing this teaching with me in my first year at Trent University. Also see Anderson 2011.

12 An exception might be pow wows, but some argue that these are no longer ceremonial in nature (especially competition pow wows as opposed to traditional pow wows).

13 Six have Bill C-31 status, one has 6(2) status, one has 6(1) status, and one participant gained status through marriage.

14 Thirteen out of eighteen participants were born in Manitoba; the remaining five moved to Manitoba at a young age and were raised here. Two participants spent a portion of their childhood on a reserve.

15 This is in contrast with the tendency in Western academia to privilege "outsiders" (often non-Aboriginal people) as experts on all things "Aboriginal" (L. Smith 2001, 79).

16 I conducted one interview per participant lasting approximately one hour each. Interview locations included community centres, university campuses, reserves, participant homes, my own home, and one took place over the telephone due to geographic distance.

17 I was on my "moontime" (menses) during two interviews (one female, one male). I have been taught that women on their moon are very powerful and do not need to smudge (or work with *asemaa*) because their body is already in ceremony. Knowing this, I explained to both participants that I wished to offer them a tobacco tie at a later date and gave them the options of proceeding with the interview, smudging with or without me, or rescheduling the interview; both chose to proceed. The female participant prepared and lit a smudge for us both; the male chose to smudge only himself with his own sweetgrass.

18 For this study, I adhered to "Section 6: Research Involving Aboriginal Peoples" of the Tri-Council Policy Statement (TCPS): Ethical Conduct for Research Involving Humans (PRE 2005), and "Chapter 9: Research Involving the First Nations, Inuit, and Métis Peoples of Canada" of the TCPS2 (PRE 2011a, 2011b).

19 The consent form gave participants the choices to remain anonymous, to review their transcript and direct quotes appearing in the final draft, to keep the digital recording and written transcript of their interview, and to let their interview be used for future research. Thirteen out of eighteen chose to review their transcripts; eleven opted to keep their files; and all agreed to let their interview be used for

future research. Importantly, I also returned to the participants for confirmation regarding permission to be included in this book.

20 Four participants chose to remain anonymous for personal reasons.

21 Themes are determined by "how often certain incidents, words, phrases, and so on that denote a theme recur. This process may also account for the prominence given to some themes over others" (Bryman and Teevan 2005, 318). After transcribing each interview, I proceeded with coding using the qualitative research software NVivo8, which helped me create a database of interviews and patterns.

22 Please note that the information that follows (such as ages) reflects the time of the interview; interviews were conducted from late 2009 to late 2010.

23 This participant has chosen to remain anonymous and has asked to be referred to in English by his spirit name. Some information is purposely vague for anonymous participants in an effort to protect their anonymity.

24 This is a pseudonym.

25 Her family has historical connections to Manitoba, Saskatchewan, and Ontario.

26 There is also unknown European ancestry on her mother's side very far back in their family history.

27 She is unaware of her biological father's ancestry.

28 This participant has also chosen to remain anonymous, and has asked to be referred to by her spirit name in Cree.

29 Diane is the final participant who asked to remain anonymous; she chose her own pseudonym.

30 She has retained her status even after her divorce.

31 Jules' spirit name translates as "the Sound of Coming Thunder" (phonetic spelling).

32 Mae Louise's spirit name translates as "Fire Heart Woman" (phonetic spelling).

CHAPTER 5: Residence, Education, Employment, Ancestry, and Status

1 Populations in both The Pas and Riverton are 40 percent Aboriginal and 60 percent non-Aboriginal. Ste. Rose du Lac, Manitoba, fell 4 percent short of being identified as a Métis community in the 2006 census.

2 According to the 2011 National Household Survey, the largest Métis population in Canada exists in Winnipeg, at 46,325 (Statistics Canada 2013a). As previously mentioned, there are challenges with the NHS and it provides less reliable data, especially concerning Aboriginal statistics ("Lost Long Form Census" 2013). Some scholars also caution against using the NHS because it was not mandatory (increases rate of non-response), thirty-six reserves were incompletely enumerated, it is not as thorough as the 2006 long-form census, and its methodology is new and largely untested. For these reasons, I continue to rely on the 2006 census data throughout this book.

3 Camperville; Eddystone; St. Laurent; St. Labre; Manigotagan; Cold Lake (a.k.a. Kississing Lake); Duck Bay; Winnipegosis; St. François Xavier; Cranberry Portage; Cross Lake; Seymourville; Dauphin River; Wabowden; Ste. Rose du Lac; Fisher Branch; and Spy Hill, Saskatchewan. Note that not all of these places are considered "Métis" according to Statistics Canada (i.e., at least 25 percent of the population);

some may have had larger Métis populations historically, but today have more non-Aboriginal residents.

4   Gaa-Wiikwedaawangaag (Sandy Bay); Zhiibaashkodeyaang (Roseau River); Baaskaandibewi-Ziibiing (Brokenhead); Misipawistiks (Grand Rapids); Pinaymootang (Fairford); Ochekwi-Sipi (Fisher River); Zaaskajiwaning (Dauphin River); Chemewawin (Pine Bluff/Easterville); Nisichawayasihk (Nelson House); Kinosawi Sipi (Norway House); Opaskwayak (The Pas); Waanibiigaaw (Hollow Water); Oshki-Ishkonigan (St. Peter's/Peguis); Wiiwkwedong (Kettle Point); and Aazhoodena (Stony Point), Ontario; Mississauga (Blind River), Ontario; and, Mikinaakwajiw-Ininiwag (Turtle Mountain), North Dakota.

5   St. Peter's reserve—part of the Peguis First Nation—was illegally taken by Canada in 1907. In 1998, the Government of Canada finally admitted this and entered into negotiations for outstanding Treaty Land Entitlement (TLE) with Peguis regarding that land (Peguis First Nation 2008, 2009).

6   In Canada, the Aboriginal population aged 25 to 64 with a university degree has increased slightly since 2001 (from 6 to 8 percent); however, we still lag far behind the non-Aboriginal population (23 percent) and the gap between the two populations continued to widen between 2001 and 2006 (AANDC 2008a). The highest level of education (university degree) attained by the participants in my study (44 percent) far outweighs that of the overall Canadian population (25 percent), the urban Aboriginal population (15 percent), and the reserve population (7 percent) (UAPS 117).

7   The primary sector includes agriculture, fishing, mining, etc. The secondary sector comprises manufacturing jobs. Finally, the tertiary sector—also known as the services sector or the services industry—includes jobs in the fields of government, health care, public health, waste disposal, education, banking, consulting, hospitality, tourism, sales, legal services, retail sales, etc.

8   The terms Saulteaux, Ojibwe, Chippewa, and Anishinaabe are different names for the same nation. When discussing their ancestry, six participants used the term "Ojibwe," five used the term "Saulteaux," one used the term "Anishinaabe," one used the term "Anishinaabe Ojibwe," and one used the terms "Ojibwe" and "Saulteaux" interchangeably.

9   Thirteen participants identified Saulteaux/Ojibwe/Anishinaabe (alone or in combination) as their Aboriginal ancestry; and eleven participants identified Cree (alone or in combination).

10 A process by which individuals voluntarily, or through coercion, were forced to give up Indian status and accompanying rights in exchange for "regular" Canadian citizenship and the right to vote. As part of the Canadian government's assimilative agenda, enfranchisement was designed to remove status from as many people as possible and apply pressure to assimilate into mainstream society (Sealey 1978; Sealey and Lussier 1975; Shore 1999; Santin 2007; and Murray 1993). Also, see Chapter 3.

11 Of the participants who do not have Indian status, Shirley, KaKaKew, Benny, and Rainey each have a Métis card (or had one at one point in their life). This card denotes citizenship/membership in the Métis Nation, and is issued, for example, by the Manitoba Métis Federation (MMF).

12 Sandra was president of the Métis Women of Manitoba (MWM) for approximately ten years, and served on the board of directors of the Manitoba Métis Federation

(MMF); in 1993, she was also national president of the MWM and vice-president of the MMF.

CHAPTER 6: Family History

1 The United Nations Educational, Scientific, and Cultural Organization's (UNESCO) *Atlas of the World's Languages in Danger* (Moseley 2010) has developed a scale for language vitality ranging in decreasing order from "safe" (language is spoken by all generations; intergenerational transmission is uninterrupted), to "vulnerable" (most children speak the language, but it may be restricted to certain domains, including homes), to "definitely endangered," to "severely endangered," to "critically endangered" (the youngest speakers are grandparents and older, and they speak the language partially and infrequently), and finally, "extinct" (there are no speakers left). Northwestern Ojibwe, Plains Cree, and Oji-Cree, all spoken in Ontario and Manitoba, are classified as "vulnerable," as is Western Ojibwe (a.k.a. Saulteaux or Plains Ojibwe), which is spoken in Manitoba and Saskatchewan; Michif is classified as "critically endangered."

2 The following terms were used in decreasing order: "Ojibwe" (five); "Saulteaux" (three); both of these terms interchangeably (two); and "Anishinaabe" (one).

3 While I did not specifically ask about relationship to European languages, Benny mentioned an ancestor who spoke Cree, French, and English; Tim's maternal grandfather spoke Anishinaabemowin, French, and English; and Laara's father spoke Cree, German, and English.

4 The term "Aboriginal cultures" is pluralized, here, to emphasize the heterogeneity of Aboriginal cultures; however, I often use the term in its singular form to promote better flow. This also goes for the term "relationships." Participants discussed their family's relationships with one or more Aboriginal cultures simultaneously; the same is true regarding the Euro-Canadian cultures.

5 I discuss a pattern when five or more participants mentioned it. Values that were identified but had fewer than five people mention them include: self-sufficiency/ resourcefulness/self-determination; hospitality; resilience/adaptation/survival; reciprocity/thanksgiving/sharing; storytelling/oral tradition; and restorative justice.

6 Subsistence practices mentioned by fewer than five participants were: trading; farming; baking/cooking; making clothing/sewing; leatherwork; beadwork; craft-making; net-making; and basket-weaving. This work was often for the purpose of sale.

7 Smaller patterns that arose include: Euro-Canadian holidays; having a family member in the military; "Canadian citizenship"; sports; "mainstream culture"; relationships marked by conflict and disassociation from Euro-Canadian cultures; Euro-Canadian family; and daily life. One person each mentioned: bagpipes; funerals; Indian Act; material stability; taxes; urbanity; and Western medicine.

8 Other stories of Euro-Canadian control are discussed elsewhere in the book and will therefore not be repeated here. These include residential/boarding/ day schools (Chapters 2 and 8); Indian status (Chapters 3, 4, and 5); religion and language (Chapter 6); use of medicines (Chapter 8); scrip, land theft via treaties, and suppression of the pow wow and other ceremonies (Chapter 3); and racism (Chapter 7).

9 Joe is referring to the violent land dispute in 1990 between the town of Oka, Quebec, and the Mohawk community of Kanesatake, which lasted seventy-eight days; the

town wanted to expand a golf course onto sacred Mohawk pineland and their cemetery. The expansion was cancelled, but one person died by gunfire early in the standoff (a corporal from Quebec's provincial police force).

10 Several participants reported more than one Christian denomination: Laara (Anglican/Catholic); Lance (Protestant/Anglican); Rainey (Lutheran/Anglican/ Mennonite); Tim (Anglican/Catholic); Mike (Pentecostal/United); Kyle (United/ Catholic); and Sandra (Protestant/Catholic).

11 Ten Catholic, one Pentecostal, and one United.

12 Recall that the Indian Act made Christian churches the only places where three or more "Indians" could legally gather.

13 The following spiritual practices were mentioned by fewer than five participants each: oral history stories about ceremonies in past times; Midewiwin; spirit name; Sundance; sweat lodge; shake tent; pow wow; dancing; drumming; smudging; chanting; midwifery; and one story about Little People. The belief that there are many paths to Creator, and the importance of respect and non-interference, were also discussed.

14 In fact, the ban against Sundance and Potlatch was removed with the 1951 amendments to the Indian Act; however, as was the case in Jules's family, many Aboriginal people were under the impression it was still illegal for several more decades. In general, Indian agents, the government, and church representatives did nothing to correct this impression; rather, the lack of awareness worked to their benefit in promoting assimilation.

15 Shirley, Running Elk, Ron, Lance, and Laara mentioned that one or more family members have participated in ceremonies with them or because of them; this number climbs to fifteen when participants' own children and grandchildren are included. Kyle, Running Elk, Tim, Mike, and KaKaKew reported "no change" in their family's relationship with spirituality since their upbringing. Despite Christianity being the most significant spiritual influence in their family during their upbringing, Diane's two sisters, Lance's mother, Ron's family, Tim's immediate family, and Joe's grandparents today enjoy a significant blend of Christianity and Anishinaabe spirituality. On the other hand, Rainey's siblings, Shirley's family, Diane's siblings, and Mike's mother no longer adhere to any spirituality (they all used to follow Christianity). Laara and Jules explicitly mentioned that their family no longer adheres to Christianity; the same goes for Stan's siblings. Mike's father was never spiritual, but is even more opposed to Christianity now. Sandra and Benny both explained that their family is prayerful and has faith today, but does not adhere primarily to Christianity or Anishinaabe spirituality. Laara's sister was the only family member identified as solely Christian today (though she continues Nêhiyaw practices like making offerings in the lake when harvesting medicine).

CHAPTER 7: Self-identification and Personal Experiences

1 Mae Louise also appears in the previous category. (i.e., family self-identification as Métis/Michif).

2 Smaller self-identity categories included: non-status Indians; neither Indian nor White; Anishinaabe; First Nation; Native; not White but want to be; part Indian/ half Native or not Indian; Ojibwe; Cree; Aboriginal; Indigenous; and Treaty 1.

3 Family feelings and ways of relating to identity mentioned by fewer people included: "standing up for Aboriginal rights"; being "vocal" about identity; "acceptance"; being "made to feel inferior" to non-Aboriginal people; feeling "different" than others; feeling "normal"; denial; shame; confusion; importance/appreciation; connection; conflict with Euro-Canadians; and acknowledgment that there was some "good" within their Aboriginal identity.

4 Kyle included the following: Canadian, Aboriginal, English, French, Welsh, Irish, Cree, Métis, White, and Native. Mike mentioned: First Nations, Aboriginal, Native, Bill C-31, "mixed," and "Indian."

5 Running Elk does not use multiple identity categories.

6 Other changes included going from a primarily non-Aboriginal identity, for a time, to a primarily Aboriginal identity (Kyle, KaKaKew, and Jules), and feeling like their identity is still changing (Benny and Shirley).

7 Reasons mentioned by fewer participants included: decolonization; employment; honouring Aboriginal ancestry; family history research; lack of connection to Euro-Canadian family; grandparents' influence; and geographical move.

8 Seven if Sandra is included; recall that when asked how she self-identifies, her response included being raised in "Métis culture."

9 Laara uses the term First Nation; she did not mention whether her family also used this term while she was growing up. This term was not in general use until the 1980s.

10 The participants are: Shirley, Benny, Tim, Dawnis, Lance, Stan, Ron, KaKaKew, Rainey, Joe, and Mike.

11 Diane, Kyle, Shirley, Mae Louise, Benny, Laara, Tim, KaKaKew, and Jules.

12 *Miigwetch* to Dr. Lynne Davis for reminding me that this is consistent with education in other countries colonized by Britain; "Red Indian" is how the peoples of North America were distinguished from peoples of the Indian subcontinent.

13 Smaller patterns included: a belief among participants that Euro-Canadian people are racist due to being culturally unaware/uneducated; discrimination at the hands of Aboriginal family members; white privilege (self, siblings, children, extended family); and racism at the hands of police, military, government (Aboriginal Affairs and Northern Development Canada, immigration and justice departments), and the service sector. Lance was the only participant to report that he has never experienced racism or discrimination.

14 Other stereotypes identified include: the gendered stereotype of the Indian squaw; the Savage; all Native people want free handouts; the dirty Indian; the Hollywood Indian; the Indian addict; the Indian servant; all Indians war dance; the lazy Indian; and stereotypes regarding Aboriginal appearance (i.e., "real Indians" have dark skin, hair, and eyes).

15 Only Jules and Mike spoke of racism in an urban location (Winnipeg); both grew up in rural locations and then moved to Winnipeg in their late adolescence/early adulthood. Mike experienced exceptionally less racism in Winnipeg than in Ashern, Manitoba; however, Jules experienced racism much more frequently (almost daily) in Winnipeg than in the rural communities where he had lived previously.

16 Joe explained that "in Native culture, you never touch a man's hair unless asked, to my understanding. In my culture, I've been taught that the people who mend or

take care of your hair are you, your children, maybe your daughter, your wife, your mother, your grandmother—but that's it, really. No one else should take care of it but yourself after that."

CHAPTER 8: Relationship with Anishinaabe Spirituality

1   Due to the sheer magnitude of data collected for this chapter, unless otherwise indicated I discuss only those patterns that apply to at least half of all participants in the study (nine). (I discussed patterns with a minimum of five participants in the previous findings chapters.)

2   Disconnection factors mentioned by fewer than nine participants include: government suppression/laws against ceremony; lack of connection to ceremony conductors/opportunities for ceremony; community-specific disconnection from ceremonies; physical distance from homeland/community/family; abuse; contemporary Euro-Canadian cultures; discrimination against fair-skinned Métis people at the hands of First Nations people; loss of connection to spirit; disconnection from Anishinaabe spirituality as a survival tactic; sexism in ceremony (male domination); and free will/choice.

3   As I have already spent a considerable amount of time discussing Christianity and residential schools, I will examine these here only briefly. In addition, some participants spoke of their relationship with Christianity today, including: having a relationship with Christianity only through their family; parallels between Anishinaabe and Christian spirituality; and following Anishinaabe and Christian spirituality simultaneously. Those who spoke of the latter mentioned that it is challenging to incorporate both into their lives; in fact, it appears that the stronger the participant's relationship with Christianity, the more challenging it becomes to follow both. No participant in this study identifies as solely Christian today.

4   Here, I believe Ron is alluding to the work of Bartolomé de las Casas, a sixteenth-century Dominican friar and one of the first settlers in the "New World." He converted countless Indigenous people to Christianity on their deathbeds before the Spanish conquistadors murdered them. In his words, "our first purpose was... to convert them to our holy Catholic faith, and to send to the islands and Tierra Firme [northern end of South America], prelates and religious... to teach the inhabitants our Catholic faith" (quoted in Vickery 2006, 107). Writing in 1542, de las Casas denounced the violent actions of the conquistadors and estimated the death toll of Indigenous peoples at the hands of the conquistadors since contact some fifty years earlier to already be 15 million (de las Casas 1552). Instead, he advocated for conversions instead of killing in order to bring about the "greatest harvest of souls since apostolic times" (Vickery 2006, 107). While de las Casas was a vocal opponent of slavery and violence against Indigenous peoples, I caution against being quick to praise the so-called "Protector of the Indians" as he was personally responsible for oppressing Indigenous spirituality and ways of life among so many people.

5   Among the Anishinaabeg and Nêhiyawak, cutting off one's hair and placing it in the casket is a way to honour and mourn a close loved one who has passed on. "Burying medicine," or making offerings, is a form of prayer and thanksgiving.

6   Key factors mentioned by fewer participants, in decreasing order, include: upbringing; the phenomenon of searching; employment; Euro-Canadian spiritual traditions; moving; addictions recovery; death/loss/illness/suicide attempt; good

parenting/role model; family history research; relationship with land; marriage; artwork; world view; recreation; and cultural events.

7 Ceremonies and spiritual experiences mentioned by fewer participants include: Sundance; pow wow; traditional feast; fast/vision quest; *oshkabewis* (helper); sacred feathers; traditional funeral; traditional wedding; Yuwipi; sharing circle; sacred fire; medicine wheel; Elderhood/Elderwork; and personal spirit colours. The following were also mentioned: traditional adoption ceremony; ancestors; birthing ceremony; dark room ceremony; full moon ceremony; Jiibaay; Mexican moon dance; prophecy; seasonal ceremonies; shake tent; traditional tipi construction; Warrior Dance; and women's teachings.

8 Lance was the only participant to mention that he also has two clans. In his own words, "My clan is the Squirrel. And the second clan given to me by my Elder is the Eagle. I follow that Eagle on my mother's side."

9 The late Peter O'Chiese was a revered and central Elder and Midewiwin teacher within the (pre-Three Fires) Midewiwin lodge; he was one of the current Grand Chief's main teachers.

10 Joe, Lance, Ron, Sandra, Tim, and Stan appear in both patterns.

11 By "dreams" I am referring to those ones that come to us while we are asleep and by "visions" I am referring to those ones that come to us in our waking states; these encounters are not always cut and dry.

12 I have personally heard teachings from the Three Fires Midewiwin lodge about the way eagles will sometimes show themselves to you with the purpose of telling you that you are on the right/good path, headed in the right direction (in life).

13 Also mentioned were priests (and one nun); Aboriginal education resource persons; and community members.

14 Opaskwayak; Cross Lake; Nelson House; Dakota Tipi; Poplar River; Berens River; Bloodvein; Brokenhead; Hollow Water; Fisher River; Black River; Roseau River; Carry the Kettle, Saskatchewan; Saddle Lake, Alberta; Bad River, Wisconsin.

15 Patterns mentioned by fewer people (in decreasing order) include: daily way of life; faith in higher power; instructions on how to be human; healing; many paths to Creator/how to pray the Anishinaabe way (i.e., there is no one way); understanding; respect; lifelong learning; no judgment; parenting; clean and sober living (maintaining sobriety); strength/support; balance; cannot imagine life without spirituality; inherent rights; thinking Anishinaabe/focused mind; fulfilling prophecy; Heart Way; welcoming all; reclaiming; and empowerment.

16 A few participants also raised the following interrelated issues: know where I came from; know why I am here; and know where I am going.

17 Unique negative reactions included: Christian conversion attempt, disbelief, jealousy, discomfort, resentment, and that Aboriginal spirituality is useless. Unique positive reactions included: approval, blessings, excitement, interest, and recognition.

18 Here, "positive" refers to the fact that participants used the term positive to describe a reaction by one or more people in their life. "Put me to work" refers to a member of a spiritual community encouraging the participant to participate in ceremonies upon learning of their interest in Anishinaabe spirituality.

19 "Not Native enough" refers to a reaction whereby someone claims the participant is not Native enough to have the right to participate in ceremony.

20 Also recall my earlier discussion on participant experiences with racism and discrimination (Chapter 7).

Bibliography

"9 Questions about Idle No More." CBC News. 5 January 2013. http://www.cbc.ca/news/canada/story/2013/01/04/f-idlenomore-faq.html (accessed 3 August 2013).

AANDC (Aboriginal Affairs and Northern Development Canada). 2008a. *Fact Sheet: 2006 Census Aboriginal Demographics.* http://www.aadnc-aandc.gc.ca/eng/1100100016377 (accessed 30 June 2011).

———. 2008b. *Treaty 3 between Her Majesty the Queen and the Saulteaux Tribe of the Ojibbeway Indians at the Northwest Angle on the Lake of the Woods with Adhesions (1875).* http://www.aadnc-aandc.gc.ca/eng/1100100028675 (accessed 15 July 2011).

———. 2010. "Frequently Asked Questions about Aboriginal People." http://www.aadnc-aandc.gc.ca/eng/1100100016202/1100100016204 (accessed 18 April 2013.).

———. 2011. *Alberta (Aboriginal Affairs and Northern Development) v. Cunningham.* Judgments of the Supreme Court of Canada. http://scc.lexum.org/en/2011/2011scc37/2011scc37.html (accessed 26 October 2011).

Aboriginal Healing and Wellness Strategy. 2006. Ontario Ministry of Community and Social Services. http://www.mcss.gov.on.ca/en/mcss/programs/community/programsforaboriginalpeople.aspx (accessed 9 November 2011).

Aboriginal Justice Inquiry (AJI). 1991. *Report of the Aboriginal Justice Inquiry of Manitoba.* Aboriginal Justice Inquiry Commission. Vol. 1, Ch. 14. http://www.ajic.mb.ca/volumel/chapter14.html (accessed 7 May 2013).

"Aboriginal Self-Government in the Northwest Territories." n.d. Government of Northwest Territories. Supplementary Booklet 1. http://www.gov.nt.ca/publications/asg/pdfs/abor.pdf (accessed 19 August 2014).

Acoose, Janice. 1992. "Iskwekwak—Kah' Ki Yaw Ni Wahkomakanak: Neither Indian Princess Nor Squaw Drudges." MA thesis. University of Saskatchewan.

———. 1994. "Knowing Relations is Knowing Oneself." *Windspeaker* 11(24): 4.

———. 1999. "The Problem of 'Searching' for April Raintree." In *In Search of April Raintree: Critical Edition,* edited by Beatrice Culleton Mosionier and Cheryl Suzack, 227–36. Winnipeg: Portage and Main Press.

———. 2008. "Honouring Ni' Wahkomakanak." In *Reasoning Together: The Native Critics Collective,* edited by Janice Acoose, Craig S. Womack, Daniel Heath Justice, and Christopher B. Teuton, 216–33. Norman: University of Oklahoma Press.

Adams, Christopher, Gregg Dahl, and Ian Peach (eds.). 2013. *Métis in Canada: History, Identity, Law and Politics.* Edmonton: University of Alberta Press.

Adams, Howard. 1989. *Prison of Grass: Canada from a Native Point of View.* Calgary: Fifth House Publishers.

_____. 1999. *Tortured People: The Politics of Colonization*. Penticton: Theytus Books.

Adese, Jennifer. 2010. "My Life in Pieces." In *Other Tongues: Mixed-Race Women Speak Out*, edited by Adebe DeRango-Adem and Andrea Thompson, 238–42. Toronto: Inanna Publications.

Alberta. 1978. Alberta Federation of Métis Settlement Associations. *The Metis People of Canada: A History*. Toronto: Gage Publishing.

Ali, Suki. 2003. *Mixed-Race, Post-Race: Gender, New Ethnicities and Cultural Practices*. New York: Berg.

Allen, Paula Gunn. 1992. *The Sacred Hoop: Recovering the Feminine in American Indian Traditions*. Boston: Beacon Press.

Andersen, Chris. 2014. *Métis: Race, Recognition, and the Struggle for Indigenous Peoplehood*. Vancouver: University of British Columbia Press.

Anderson, Kim. 1997. "A Recognition of Being: Exploring Native Female Identity." PhD diss. University of Toronto.

_____. 2000. *A Recognition of Being: Reconstructing Native Womanhood*. Toronto: Second Story Press.

_____. 2011. *Life Stages and Native Women: Memory, Teachings, and Story Medicine*. Winnipeg: University of Manitoba Press.

Anzaldúa, Gloria. 1987. *Borderlands/La Frontera: The New Mestiza*. San Francisco: Aunt Lute Books.

"APTN Viewers React to Sundance Broadcast." 2013. APTN (Aboriginal Peoples Television Network), 16 August. http://aptn.ca/pages/news/2013/08/16/aptn-viewers-react-to-sundance-broadcast/ (accessed 20 August 2013).

Atleo, Richard. 2004. *Tswalk: A Nuu-chah-nulth World View*. Vancouver: UBC Press.

Augustus, Camie. 2008. "Métis Scrip." *Our Legacy*. University of Saskatchewan Archives. http://scaa.sk.ca/ourlegacy/exhibit_scrip (accessed 4 April 2012).

Bailey, Aimee. 2005. *Anishinaabe 101: The Basics of What you Need to Know to Begin your Journey on the Red Road*. Golden Lake: The Circle of Turtle Lodge.

Barkwell, Lawrence, ed. 2002. *Métis Rights and Land Claims: An Annotated Bibliography*. Winnipeg: Louis Riel Institute.

Barkwell, Lawrence, Leah Dorion, and Audreen Hourie, eds. 2006. *Métis Legacy II: Michif Culture, Heritage and Folkways*. Winnipeg: Pemmican Publications.

Barkwell, Lawrence, Leah Dorion, and Darren Prefontaine, eds. 2001. *Métis Legacy: A Métis Historiography and Annotated Bibliography*. Winnipeg: Pemmican Publications.

Barkwell, Lawrence, Lyle Longclaws, and David Chartrand. "Status of Métis Children Within the Child Welfare System." *Canadian Journal of Native Studies* 9, 1 (1989): 1–21. http://www3.brandonu.ca/library/cjns/9.1/metis.pdf (accessed 7 May 2013).

Battiste, Marie, ed. 1986. "Micmac Literacy and Cognitive Assimilation." In *Indian Education in Canada: The Legacy*, edited by Jean Barman, Yvonne Hébert, and Don McCaskill, 23–44. Vancouver: University of British Columbia Press.

_____. 2000. Introduction. "Unfolding the Lessons of Colonization." In *Reclaiming Indigenous Voice and Vision*, xvi–xxx. Vancouver: University of British Columbia Press.

Beck, Peggy. 1977. *The Sacred: Ways of Knowledge, Sources of Life*. Tsalie: Navajo Community College.

Belcourt, Tony. 2013. "FOR THE RECORD… On Métis Identity and Citizenship Within the Métis Nation." *Aboriginal Policy Studies* 2, 2: 128–141.

Benton-Banai, Edward. 1988. *The Mishomis Book: The Voice of the Ojibway.* Hayward: Indian Country Communications.

Berger, Lawrence, and Eric Rounds. 1998. "Sweat Lodges: A Medical View." *The HIS Primary Care Provider* 23, 6: 69–75.

Bizzaro, Resa Crane. 2004. "Shooting Our Last Arrow: Developing a Rhetoric of Identity for Unenrolled American Indians." *College English* 67, 1: 61–74.

Blackstock, Cindy. 2003. "First Nations Child and Family Services: Restoring Peace and Harmony in First Nations Communities." In *Child Welfare: Connecting Research Policy and Practice*, edited by Kathleen Kufeldt and Brad McKenzie, 331–42. Waterloo, Ontario: Wilfrid Laurier University Press.

Bourassa, Carrie. "Summary Review of the Manitoba Child Welfare System for the Saskatchewan Child Welfare Review." Submitted to the Saskatchewan Child Welfare Review Panel. 18 August 2010. http://saskchildwelfarereview.ca/Review-Manitoba-Child-Welfare-System-CBourassa.pdf (accessed 7 May 2013).

Bowden, Jeanne Wismer. 1998. "Recovery from Alcoholism: A Spiritual Journey." *Issues in Mental Health Nursing*, 19, 4: 337–52.

Brown, Jennifer S.H. 1983. "Woman as Centre and Symbol in the Emergence of Métis Communities." *Canadian Journal of Native Studies* 3, 1: 39–46.

Bruchac, Joseph. 2010. "Elder's Meditation of the Day." *White Bison Centre for the Wellbriety Movement.* http://mountzion144.ning.com/profiles/blogs/elder-s-meditation-of-the-day-august-15?xg_source=activity (accessed 15 August 2011).

Bryman, Alan, and James J. Teevan. 2005. *Social Research Methods.* Toronto: Oxford University Press.

Burnett, Kristin, and Geoff Read, eds. 2012. *Aboriginal History: A Reader.* Don Mills, ON: Oxford University Press.

Campbell, Maria. 2011a. Foreword. In *Life Stages and Native Women: Memory, Teachings, and Story Medicine*, edited by Kim Anderson, xv–xix. Winnipeg: University of Manitoba Press.

_____. 2011b. *Halfbreed.* Toronto: McClelland and Stewart.

Canada. 2010. *Bill C-3.* Ottawa: House of Commons. http://www.parl.gc.ca/HousePublications/Publication.aspx?Language=E&Mode=1&DocId=4340270&File=24#1 (accessed 20 December 2011).

Cardinal, Harold, and Walter Hildebrandt. 2000. *Treaty Elders of Saskatchewan: Our Dream Is That Our Peoples Will One Day Be Clearly Recognized As Nations.* Calgary: University of Calgary Press.

Castellano, Marlene Brant. 1998. "Updating Aboriginal Traditions of Knowledge." In *Indigenous Knowledge, Global Contexts*, edited by George Dei and Budd Hall, 21–53. Toronto: University of Toronto Press.

_____. 2008. "A Holistic Approach to Reconciliation: Insights from Research of the Aboriginal Healing Foundation." In *From Truth to Reconciliation: Transforming the Legacy of Residential Schools*, edited by Marlene Castellano, 385–96. Ottawa: Aboriginal Healing Foundation Research Series.

Charmaz, Kathy. 2006. *Constructing Grounded Theory: A Practical Guide Through Qualitative Analysis.* London: Sage Publications.

Chartier, Clément. 2010. "Métis still waiting for their apology." *Winnipeg Free Press*, 18 June: A17. http://www.winnipegfreepress.com/opinion/westview/metis-still-waiting-for-their-apology-96636889.html (accessed 30 October 2011).

Chartrand, Paul L.A.H. 2002a. Introduction. In *Who Are Canada's Aboriginal Peoples? Recognition, Definition, and Jurisdiction*, edited by Paul Chartrand, 15–26. Saskatoon: Purich Publishing.

_____. ed. 2002b. *Who Are Canada's Aboriginal Peoples? Recognition, Definition, and Jurisdiction*. Saskatoon: Purich Publishing.

_____. 2006. "Métis Residential School Participation: A Literature Review." In *Métis History and Experience and Residential Schools in Canada*, edited by Paul Chartrand, Tricia Logan, and Harry Daniels, 9–51. Ottawa: Aboriginal Healing Foundation.

_____. "The other side of the Métis story." *Winnipeg Free Press*. 3 December 2013. http://www.winnipegfreepress.com/opinion/westview/the-other-side-of-the-metis-story-197265771.html (accessed 18 April 2013).

Chartrand, Paul, and John Giokas. 2002. "Who Are the Métis? A Review of the Law and Policy." In *Who Are Canada's Aboriginal Peoples? Recognition, Definition, and Jurisdiction*, edited by Paul Chartrand, 268–304. Saskatoon: Purich Publishing.

Chartrand, Paul, Tricia Logan, and Harry Daniels, eds. 2006. *Métis History and Experience and Residential Schools in Canada*. Ottawa: Aboriginal Healing Foundation.

Chemawawin Cree Nation. 2011. "Community Profile." http://www.chemawawin.ca/about/about.htm (accessed 30 June 2011).

Chrisjohn, Roland, and Sherri Young, with Michael Maraun. 1997. *The Circle Game: Shadows and Substance in the Indian Residential School Experience in Canada*. Penticton: Theytus Books.

Coates, Ken. 1999. "Being Aboriginal: The Cultural Politics of Identity, Membership and Belonging Among First Nations in Canada." In *Aboriginal Peoples in Canada: Futures and Identities*, edited by Michael Behiels, 23–41. Canadian Issues, Vol. 21. Montréal: Association for Canadian Studies.

Cole, Yolande. 2010. "Indian Act Reforms Don't End Fight for Aboriginal Women's Equality, Activists Say." Straight.com: Vancouver's Online Source. 23 December. http://www.straight.com/article-365785/vancouver/indian-act-reforms-dont-end-fight-aboriginal-womens-equality-activists-say (accessed 18 December 2011).

Crawford, Amy. 2011. "Pursuit of Higher Self: Stories of Personal and Spiritual Transformation shared by Adventure Athletes." PhD diss. California Institute for Integral Studies.

Crosby, Marcia. 1991. "Construction of the Imaginary Indian." In *Vancouver Anthology: The Institutional Politics of Art*, edited by Stan Douglas, 267–94. Vancouver: Talonbooks.

Dalai Lama. 2010. *My Spiritual Journey: The Dalai Lama*. New York: HarperLuxe.

Daniel, G. Reginald. 1992. "Passers and Pluralists: Subverting the Racial Divide." In *Racially Mixed People in America*, edited by Maria P.P. Root, 91–107. London: Sage Publications.

Daniels, Judy. 2006. "Ancestral Pain: Métis Memories of the Residential School Project." In *Métis History and Experience and Residential Schools in Canada*, edited by Paul Chartrand, Tricia Logan, and Harry Daniels, 86–149. Ottawa: Aboriginal Healing Foundation.

Daniels v. Canada. 2013. Federal Court (decision). 8 January. http://bcmetis.com/wp-content/uploads/Daniels-Decision-January-2013.pdf (accessed 9 April 2013).

Daschuk, J.W., Paul Hackett, and Scott MacNeil. 2006. "Treaties and Tuberculosis: First Nations People in late 19th Century Western Canada, a Political and Economic Transformation." *Canadian Bulletin of Medical History* 23, 2: 307–30.

Deerchild, Rosanna. 2004. "Tribal Feminism is a Drum Song." In *Strong Women Stories: Native Vision and Community Survival,* edited by Kim Anderson and Bonita Lawrence, 97–105. Toronto: Sumach Press.

Dei, George Sefa. 2000. "Rethinking the Role of Indigenous Knowledges in the Academy." *International Journal of Inclusive Education* 4, 2: 111–32.

de las Casas, Bartolomé. (1552) 1992. *A Short Account of the Destruction of the Indies.* Toronto: Penguin Classics.

Dickason, Olive Patricia. 1985. "From 'One Nation' in the Northeast to 'New Nation' in the Northwest: A Look at the Emergence of the Métis." In *The New Peoples: Being and Becoming Métis in North America,* edited by Jacqueline Peterson and Jennifer S.H. Brown, 19–36. Winnipeg: University of Manitoba Press.

_____. 1992. *Canada's First Nations: A History of Founding Peoples from Earliest Times.* Toronto: Oxford University Press.

Dickason, Olive Patricia, and William Newbigging. 2010. *A Concise History of Canada's First Nations.* Toronto: Oxford University Press.

Dorion, Leah, and Darren Prefontaine. 2001. "Deconstructing Métis Historiography." In *Métis Legacy: A Métis Historiography and Annotated Bibliography,* edited by Lawrence Barkwell, Leah Dorion, and Darren Prefontaine, 13–36. Winnipeg: Pemmican Publications.

Dumont, Jim. 1979. "Journey to Daylight-Land: Through Ojibwe Eyes." *Laurentian Review* 3, 2: 31–43.

_____. 1990. "Justice and Aboriginal People." A Paper Prepared for the Public Inquiry into the Administration of Justice and Aboriginal People. Unpublished essay. University of Sudbury.

Duncan, John. 2013. "Statement from Minister Duncan—Daniels Court Decision." *Aboriginal Affairs and Northern Development Canada (AANDC).* 6 February. http://www.aadnc-aandc.gc.ca/eng/1360168626906/1360168661069 (accessed 9 April 2013).

Duran, Eduardo. 2006. *Healing the Soul Wound: Counselling with American Indians and Other Native Peoples.* New York: Teachers College Press.

Duran, Eduardo, and Bonnie Duran. 1995. *Native American Postcolonial Psychology.* New York: State University of New York.

Dusenberry, Verne. 1985. "Waiting for a Day that Never Comes: The Dispossessed Métis of Montana." In *The New Peoples: Being and Becoming Métis in North America,* edited by Jacqueline Peterson and Jennifer S.H. Brown, 119–36. Winnipeg: University of Manitoba Press.

Eberts, Mary. 2010. "McIvor: Justice Delayed—Again." *Indigenous Law Journal* 9, 1: 15–46.

Ellinghaus, Katherine. 2008. "The Benefits of Being Indian: Blood Quanta, Intermarriage, and Allotment Policy on the White Earth Reservation, 1889–1920." *Frontiers: A Journal of Women Studies* 29, 2–3: 81–105.

Ens, Gerhard J. 1996. "Métis Scrip." In *The Recognition of Aboriginal Rights*, edited by Samuel Corrigan and Joe Sawchuk, 47–56. Case Studies 1. Brandon: Bearpaw Publishing.

Ermine, Willie. 1995. "Aboriginal Epistemology." In *First Nations Education in Canada: The Circle Unfolds*, edited by Marie Battiste and Jean Barman, 101–12. Vancouver: University of British Columbia Press.

Ethics Guidelines for Ph.D. Program in Indigenous Studies of Trent University. 2004. Trent University. http://www.trentu.ca/indigenousstudiesphd/ethicsguidelines.php (accessed 6 August 2011).

Fanon, Frantz. 1963. *The Wretched of the Earth*. New York: Random House.

Fillmore, W.P. 1978. "Half-Breed Scrip." In *The Other Natives: The-Les Métis*, edited by Antoine Lussier and D. Bruce Sealey, 31–36. Vol. 2. Winnipeg: Manitoba Métis Federation Press.

Fiola, Chantal. 2004. "Are Critical Feminism and Spirituality Mutually Exclusive?" BA thesis. University of Manitoba.

———. 2006. "Decolonizing the Social Sciences: Aboriginal-Centered Theorizing and Aboriginal Relationships with Postcolonial Theories." MA thesis. Ontario Institute for Studies in Education, University of Toronto.

———. 2010. "Stories from a St. Laurent Founding Family: Experiences in Red River Métis Family History Research." In *The Land between the Lakes: R. M. of St. Laurent*, edited by St. Laurent and District History Book Committee, 506–11. Altona: Friesens Corporation.

———. 2012. "Re-Kindling the Sacred Fire: Métis Identity, Anishinaabe Spirituality and Identity." PhD diss. Trent University.

Fontaine, Nahanni. 2001. "Neither Here, Nor There: A Reflection on Aboriginal Women and Identity." MA thesis. University of Manitoba.

Freire, Paulo. (1970) 2006. *Pedagogy of the Oppressed*. New York: Continuum International Publishing Group.

Garroutte, Eva Marie. 2003. *Real Indians: Identity and the Survival of Native America*. Los Angeles: University of California Press.

Gaywish, Rainey. 2008. "Prophecy and Transformation in Edward Benton-Banai's Revitalization of the Midewiwin Heart Way. 'Neegawn I-naw-buh-tay Aynnayn-duh-mawn.' My Thoughts Flow forward to the Future." PhD diss. Trent University.

Ghostkeeper, Elmer. 1986. *Spirit Gifting: The Concept of Spiritual Exchange*. The Artic Institute of North America. Calgary: University of Calgary.

Gibson, Dale. 2002. "When Is a Métis an Indian? Some Consequences of Federal Constitutional Jurisdiction over Métis." In *Who Are Canada's Aboriginal Peoples? Recognition, Definition, and Jurisdiction*, edited by Paul Chartrand, 268–304. Saskatoon: Purich Publishing.

Gilbert, Larry. 1996. *Entitlement to Indian Status and Membership Codes in Canada*. Carswell/Thompson Professional Publishing.

Giokas, John, and Robert Groves. 2002. "Collective and Individual Recognition in Canada: The *Indian Act* Regime." In *Who Are Canada's Aboriginal Peoples? Recognition, Definition, and Jurisdiction*, edited by Paul Chartrand, 41–82. Saskatoon: Purich Publishing.

Gordon, Irene Ternier. 2005. *The Battle of Seven Oaks and the Violent Birth of the Red River Settlement*. Canmore: Altitude Publishing.

Grant, Agnes. 2004. *Finding My Talk: How Fourteen Native Women Reclaimed Their Lives After Residential School.* Calgary: Fifth House.

Green, Joyce. 1997. "Exploring Identity and Citizenship: Aboriginal Women, Bill C-31 and the 'Sawridge Case.'" PhD diss. University of Alberta.

Green, Joyce, ed. 2007. *Making Space for Indigenous Feminism.* Winnipeg: Fernwood Publishing.

Green, Lesley L. 1998. "Stories of Spiritual Awakening: The Nature of Spirituality in Recovery." *Journal of Substance Abuse Treatment* 15, 4: 325–31.

Guba, Egon G., and Yvonna S. Lincoln. 1998. "Competing Paradigms in Qualitative Research." In *The Landscape of Qualitative Research: Theories and Issues*, edited by Norman K. Denzin and Yvonna S. Lincoln, 195–220. California: Sage Publications.

Guimond, Eric. 2003. "Changing Ethnicity: The Concept of Ethnic Drifters." In *Aboriginal Conditions: Research as a Foundation for Public Policy*, edited by Jerry White, Paul Maxim, and Dan Beavon, 91–107. Vancouver: University of British Columbia Press.

Hamill, James. 2003. "Show Me Your CDIB: Blood Quantum and Indian Identity Among Indian People of Oklahoma." *American Behavioral Scientist* 47, 3: 267–82.

Harmon, Alexandra. 2001. "Tribal Enrollment Councils: Lessons on Law and Indian Identity." *The Western Historical Quarterly* 32, 2: 175–200.

Harrison, Julia D. 1984. *Metis: People between Two Worlds.* Toronto: The Glenbow-Alberta Institute.

Hart, Lisa. 2011. *Children of the Seventh Fire: An Ancient Prophecy for Modern Times.* Granville: The McDonald and Woodward Publishing Company.

Henry, Keith. 2013. "Daniels Case—Initial BC Métis Federation Overview and Comment." BC Métis Federation. 11 January. http://bcmetis.com/2013/01/daniels-case-initial-bc-metis-federation-overview-and-comment/ (accessed 9 April 2013).

Howard, Joseph. (1952) 1974. *Strange Empire: Louis Riel and the Métis People.* Toronto: James Lewis and Samuel.

Howrich, Jeff. 2001. "How Indian Are You?" Minnesota Public Radio. http://news.minnesota.publicradio.org/projects/2001/04/brokentrust/horwichj_quantum-m/index.shtml (accessed 3 December 2011).

Huel, Raymond. 1996. *Proclaiming the Gospel to the Indians and Métis.* Edmonton: University of Alberta Press.

Hurl, Lorna. "The Politics of Child Welfare in Manitoba, 1922–24." *Manitoba History* 7 (1984). http://www.mhs.mb.ca/docs/mb_history/07/childwelfare.shtml (accessed 7 May 2013).

Interagency Advisory Panel on Research Ethics (PRE). 2005. "Section 6: Research Involving Aboriginal Peoples." In *Tri-Council Policy Statement (TCPS): Ethical Conduct for Research Involving Humans.* 18 October. http://www.pre.ethics.gc.ca/english/policystatement/section6.cfm (accessed 7 September 2011).

_____. 2011a. "Chapter 9: Research Involving the First Nations, Inuit and Métis Peoples of Canada." In *Tri-Council Policy Statement 2 (TCPS2): Ethical Conduct for Research Involving Humans.* 2nd ed. 7 April. http://www.pre.ethics.gc.ca/eng/policy-politique/initiatives/tcps2-eptc2/chapter9-chapitre9/ (accessed 7 September 2011).

_____. 2011b. *Tri-Council Policy Statement 2 (TCPS2): Ethical Conduct for Research Involving Humans.* 2nd ed. 7 April. http://www.pre.ethics.gc.ca/eng/policy-politique/initiatives/tcps2-eptc2/Default/ (accessed 7 September 2011).

Jaime, Angela M. 2003. "A Room without a View from within the Ivory Tower." *American Indian Quarterly* 27, 1: 252–63.

"James Ray Found Guilty over Arizona Sweat Lodge Deaths." 2011. BBC News: U.S. and Canada, 22 June. http://www.bbc.co.uk/news/world-us-canada-13884063 (accessed 24 October 2011).

"Judge Nixes Massive Metis Land Claim." 2007. CBC News, 7 December. http://www.cbc.ca/news/canada/manitoba/story/2007/12/07/metis-claim.html (accessed 7 September 2011).

Julian, Steve. 2011. "Are You Indian Enough? The Hierarchy of Aboriginal People." 3 September. http://thevoiceoftheindigenous.wordpress.com/2011/09/12/are-you-indian-enough-the-hierarchy-of-aboriginal-people/ (accessed 3 December 2011).

King, Thomas. 1990. "Godzilla vs. Post-Colonial." *World Literature Written in English* 30, 2: 10–16.

Kirby, Sandra L., Lorraine Greaves, and Colleen Reid. 2006. *Experience Research Social Change: Methods beyond the Mainstream.* 2nd ed. Toronto: Broadview Press.

Kovach, Margaret. 2009. *Indigenous Methodologies: Characteristics, Conversations, and Contexts.* Toronto: University of Toronto Press.

Laenui, Poka. 2000. "Processes of Decolonization." In *Reclaiming Indigenous Voice and Vision*, edited by Marie Battiste, 150–60. Vancouver: University of British Columbia Press.

LaFromboise, Teresa D., Anneliese M. Heyle, and Emily J. Ozer. 1994. "Native American Women." In *Native American Resurgence and Renewal: A Reader and Bibliography*, edited by Robert N. Wells Jr., 463–94. London: The Scarecrow Press.

LaRocque, Emma. 2001. "Native Identity and the Metis: Otehpayimsuak Peoples." In *A Passion for Identity: Canadian Studies for the 21st Century*, edited by David Taras and Beverly Rasporich, 381–99. 4th ed. Ontario: Nelson Thomson Learning.

_____. 2007. "Métis and Feminist: Ethical Reflections on Feminism, Human Rights and Decolonization." In *Making Space for Indigenous Feminism*, edited by Joyce Green, 53–71. Winnipeg: Fernwood Publishing.

Lavallée, Guy. 2003. "The Métis of St. Laurent, Manitoba: Their Life and Stories, 1920–1988." MA thesis. Winnipeg: University of Manitoba.

Lawrence, Bonita. 1999. " 'Real' Indians and Others: Mixed Race Urban Native People, The Indian Act, and the Rebuilding of Indigenous Nations." PhD diss. Ontario Institute for Studies in Education, University of Toronto.

_____. 2000. "Mixed-Race Urban Native Identity: Surviving a Legacy of Genocide, Regulating Native Identity." *Kinesis.* Native Women's Issue. December 1999/January 2000: 15, 18.

_____. 2004. *"Real" Indians and Others: Mixed-Blood Urban Native Peoples and Indigenous Nationhood.* Vancouver: University of British Columbia Press.

_____. 2005. "Colonization and Indigenous Resistance in Eastern Canada." In *Race, Space and the Law: Unmapping a White Settler Society*, edited by Sherene Razack, 21–46. Toronto: Between the Lines.

_____. 2012. "Identity, Non-Status Indians, and Federally Unrecognized Peoples." In *Aboriginal History: A Reader*, edited by Kristin Burnett and Geoff Read, 196–205. Don Mills, ON: Oxford University Press.

Leblanc, Daniel. 2014. "List of Missing, Killed Aboriginal Women involves 1,200 cases." *Globe and Mail*. 1 May. www.theglobeandmail.com (accessed 19 December 2014).

Leonard, Alison. 2003. "Journey Towards the Goddess." *Feminist Theology* 12, 1: 11–35.

Logan, Tricia. 2006a. Introduction. In *Métis History and Experience and Residential Schools in Canada*, edited by Paul Chartrand, Tricia Logan, and Harry Daniels, 1–8. Ottawa: Aboriginal Healing Foundation.

_____. 2006b. "Lost Generations: The Silent Métis of the Residential School System. Revised Interim Report." In *Métis History and Experience and Residential Schools in Canada*, edited by Paul Chartrand, Tricia Logan, and Harry Daniels, 61–85. Ottawa: Aboriginal Healing Foundation.

_____. 2007. "We Were Outsiders: The Métis and Residential Schools." MA thesis. University of Manitoba.

_____. 2008. "A Métis Perspective on Truth and Reconciliation: Reflections of a Métis Researcher." In *From Truth to Reconciliation: Transforming the Legacy of Residential Schools*, edited by Marlene Brant Castellano, Linda Archibald, and Mike DeGagné, 69–88. Ottawa: Aboriginal Healing Foundation Research Series.

"Lost Long-Form Census means Shakier Insight into Aboriginal Issues." *Globe and Mail*, last modified 9 May 2013. http://www.theglobeandmail.com/commentary/editorials/the-lost-long-form-census-means-shakier-insight-into-aboriginal-issues/article11837320/.

Lussier, Antoine. 1985. "Msgr. Provencher and the Native People of Red River, 1818–1853." *Prairie Forum*. 10, 1:1–15.

"Manitoba Metis Appeal Judgment Rejecting Land Claim." 2008. CBC News, 16 February. http://www.cbc.ca/news/canada/story/2008/02/16/metis-judgment.html (accessed 8 March 2011).

MMF (Manitoba Métis Federation) v Canada (Attorney General). 2013. Judgments of the Supreme Court of Canada. http://scc.lexum.org/decisia-scc-csc/scc-csc/scc-csc/en/item/12888/index.do (accessed 18 April 2013).

Manitoba Project. n.d. "Birth of Manitoba." http://manitobia.ca/content/en/themes/bom (accessed 6 August 2011).

Maracle, Lee. 1996. *I Am Woman: A Native Perspective on Sociology and Feminism*. Toronto: Press Gang.

Martin-Hill, Dawn. 2004. "She No Speaks and Other Colonial Constructs of 'The Traditional Woman.' " In *Strong Women Stories: Native Vision and Community Survival*, edited by Kim Anderson and Bonita Lawrence, 106–20. Toronto: Sumach Press.

Mason, Roger Burford. 1996. *Travels in the Shining Island: The Story of James Evans and the Invention of the Cree Syllabary Alphabet*. Toronto: National Heritage.

Mawani, Renisa. 2002. "In Between and Out of Place: Mixed-Race Identity, Liquor, and the Law in British Columbia, 1850–1913." In *Race, Space, and the Law: Unmapping a White Settler Society*, edited by Sherene Razack, 47–70. Toronto: Between the Lines.

McCabe, Glen. 2008. "Mind, Body, Emotions and Spirit: Reaching to the Ancestors for Healing." *Counselling Psychology Quarterly* 21, 2: 143–52.

McCarthy, Martha. 1990. *To Evangelize the Nations: Roman Catholic Missions in Manitoba 1818–1870.* Winnipeg: Manitoba Culture Heritage and Recreation Historic Resources.

McCormick, Rod. 1997. "Healing through Interdependence: The Role of Connecting in First Nations Healing Practices." *Canadian Journal of Counselling* 31, 3: 172–184.

McIvor, Sharon, and Jacob Grismer. 2010. *Communication Submitted for Consideration Under the First Optional Protocol to the International Covenant on Civil and Political Rights.* Geneva. 24 November. http://www.socialrightscura.ca/documents/legal/mcivor/McIvorPetition.pdf (accessed 18 December 2011).

McLeod, Neal. 2007. *Cree Narrative Memory: From Treaties to Contemporary Times.* Saskatoon: Purich Publishing.

Memmi, Albert. (1957) 1965. *The Colonizer and the Colonized.* New York: Orion Press.

Mercier, Soeur Pauline. 1974. "St-Laurent Manitoba." Unpublished manuscript. Elie, Manitoba: White Horse Plain School Division.

"Métis Nation Applauds Supreme Court's Decision on Alberta Métis Settlements." 2011. *Canadian Newswire*, 21 July. http://www.metisnation.ca/index.php/news/metis-nation-applauds-supreme-courts-decision-on-alberta-metis-settlements (accessed 26 October 2011).

"Métis Present Land-Claim Case to Supreme Court." 2011. CBC News, 13 December. http://www.cbc.ca/news/canada/manitoba/story/2011/12/13/manitoba-metis-supreme-court-hearing.html (accessed 20 December 2011).

Michell, Herman. 1999. "Pakitinâsowin: Tobacco Offerings in Exchange for Stories and the Ethic of Reciprocity in First Nations Research." *Journal of Indigenous Thought.* Regina: First Nations University of Canada (formerly Saskatchewan Indian Federated College).

Mihesuah, Devon A. 1999. "American Indian Identities: Issues of Individual Choice and Development." In *Contemporary Native American Cultural Issues*, edited by Duane Champagne, 13–38. London: Altamira Press.

Miller, Christine, and Patricia Chuchryk, eds. 1997. *Women of the First Nations: Power, Wisdom and Strength.* Winnipeg: University of Manitoba Press.

Miller, J.R. 1989. *Skyscrapers Hide the Heavens: A History of Indian-White Relations in Canada.* Toronto: University of Toronto Press.

_____. 1996. *Shingwauk's Vision: A History of Native Residential Schools.* Toronto: University of Toronto Press.

Milloy, John. 1999. *A National Crime: The Canadian Government and the Residential School System, 1879 to 1986.* Winnipeg: University of Manitoba Press.

Milne, Brad. 1995. "The Historiography of Métis Land Dispersal, 1870–1890." *Manitoba History* 30: 30–41.

Moore, James T. 1982. *Indian and Jesuit: A Seventeenth-Century Encounter.* Chicago: Loyola University Press.

Morse, Bradford W., and Robert K. Groves. 2002. "Métis and Non-Status Indians and Section 91(24) of the Constitution Act, 1876." In *Who Are Canada's Aboriginal Peoples? Recognition, Definition, and Jurisdiction*, edited by Paul Chartrand, 41–82. Saskatoon: Purich Publishing.

Moseley, Christopher, ed. 2010. *Atlas of the World's Languages in Danger*, 3rd ed. Paris, UNESCO Publishing. http://www.unesco.org/culture/en/endangeredlanguages/atlas (accessed 24 December 2014).

Murray, Jeffrey S. 1993. "Métis Scrip Records: Foundation for a New Beginning." *The Archivist* 20, 1: 12–14.

National Aboriginal Law Section (NALS). 2010. *Bill C-3: Gender Equity in Indian Registration Act*. Ottawa: Canadian Bar Association. April. http://www.nwac.ca/sites/default/files/imce/WEBSITES/201105-06/Bill%20C-3-eng1.pdf (accessed 18 December 2011).

Nicks, Trudy, and Kenneth Morgan. 1985. "Grande Cache: The Historic Development of an Indigenous Alberta Métis Population." In *The New Peoples: Being and Becoming Métis in North America*, edited by Jacqueline Peterson and Jennifer Brown, 163–84. Winnipeg: University of Manitoba Press.

Ningewance, Patricia M. 2004. *Talking Gookom's Language: Learning Ojibwe*. Lac Seul, Ontario: Mazinaate Press.

Owens, Louis. 2002. "As If an Indian Were Really an Indian." In *Native American Representations: First Encounters, Distorted Images, and Literary Appropriations*, edited by Georges M. Bataille, 11–24. Lincoln: University of Nebraska.

Payment, Diane. 2009. *The Free People—Li Gens Libres: A History of the Métis Community of Batoche, Saskatchewan*. Calgary: University of Calgary Press.

Peguis First Nation. 2008. "The Illegal Surrender of the St. Peter's Reserve." 31 August. http://www.peguisfirstnation.ca/pdf/PFN_SC_Au08.pdf (accessed 30 June 2011).

———. 2009. Treaty Land Entitlement. http://www.peguisfirstnation.ca/tle.html (accessed 30 June 2011).

Penn, William S., ed. 1997. *As We Are Now: Mixblood Essays on Race and Identity*. Los Angeles: University of California Press.

Peters, Evelyn, and Mark Rosenberg. 1991. "The Ontario Metis: Some Aspects of a Metis Identity." *Canadian Ethnic Studies* 23, 1: 71–85.

Peterson, Inez. 1997. "What Part Moon." In *As We Are Now: Mixblood Essays on Race and Identity*, edited by William S. Penn, 82–86. Los Angeles: University of California Press.

Peterson, Jacqueline. 1985. "Many Roads to Red River: Métis Genesis in the Great Lakes Region, 1860–1815." In *The New Peoples: Being and Becoming Métis in North America*, edited by Jacqueline Peterson and Jennifer Brown, 37–72. Winnipeg: University of Manitoba Press.

Peterson, Jacqueline, and Jennifer S.H. Brown, eds. 1985. *The New Peoples: Being and Becoming Métis in North America*. Winnipeg: University of Manitoba Press.

Pitawanakwat, Brock. 2008. "Bimaadziwin Oodenaang: A Pathway to Urban Nishnaabe Resurgence." In *Lighting the Eighth Fire: The Liberation, Resurgence, and Protection of Indigenous Nations*, edited by Leanne Simpson, 161–74. Winnipeg: Arbeiter Ring Publishing.

Pompana, Yvonne. 2009. "Tracing the Evolution of First Nations Child Welfare in Manitoba: A Case Study Examining the Historical Periods 1979–2006 and 2000–2006." PhD diss. Trent University.

Préfontaine, Darren, Todd Paquin, and Patrick Young. 2003. "Métis Spiritualism." Gabriel Dumont Institute, 30 May 1–46. www.metismuseum.ca/media/db/00727 (accessed 9 January 2015).

Randall, Will. 2011. "Greater Rights for Métis Settlements in Alberta?" University of Calgary Faculty of Law Blog on Developments in Alberta Law, 15 August. ablawg.ca/2011/08/15/greater-rights-for-metis-settlements-in-alberta/ (accessed 19 December 2014).

Razack, Sherene. 1998. *Looking White People in the Eye: Gender, Race, and Culture in Courtrooms and Classrooms.* Toronto: University of Toronto Press.

Razack, Sherene, ed. 2002. *Race, Space, and the Law: Unmapping a White Settler Society.* Toronto: Between the Lines.

Restoule, Jean-Paul. 2004. "Male Aboriginal Identity Formation in Urban Areas: A Focus on Process and Context." PhD diss. University of Toronto.

Rigney, Lester-Irabinna. 1999. "Internationalization of an Indigenous Anti-Colonial Cultural Critique of Research Methodologies." *Wicazo Sa Review* 14, 2: 109–21.

Robinson, Shanneen. 2013a. "The Sundance Ceremony, Part 1." APTN, 14 August. http://aptn.ca/pages/news/2013/08/14/the-sun-dance-ceremony/ (accessed 20 August 2013).

———. 2013b. "The Sundance Ceremony, Part 2: The Buffalo Dance." APTN, 14 August. http://aptn.ca/pages/news/2013/08/14/sun-dance-ceremony-part-2-the-buffalo-dance/ (accessed 20 August 2013).

———. 2013c. "The Sundance Ceremony, Part 3: The Conclusion." APTN, 14 August. http://aptn.ca/pages/news/2013/08/15/sundance-part-3-the-conclusion/ (accessed 20 August 2013).

Root, Maria P.P. 1992. *Racially Mixed People in America.* London: Sage Publications.

Royal Commission on Aboriginal Peoples (RCAP). 1996. *Report on the Royal Commission on Aboriginal Peoples: Final Report.* Vol. 1–5. Ottawa: Supply and Services Canada.

Said, Edward. 1978. *Orientalism.* New York: Vintage Books.

Santin, Aldo. 2007. "Métis Land Claim: Billions Hang in the Balance." *Winnipeg Free Press,* 7 December: A4.

Sawchuk, Joe. 2001. "Negotiating an Identity: Métis Political Organizations, the Canadian Government and Competing Concepts of Aboriginality." *American Indian Quarterly* 25, 1: 73–94.

Schiff, Jeannette Waegemakers, and Kerrie Moore. 2006. "The Impact of the Sweat Lodge Ceremony on Dimensions of Well-Being." *American Indian and Alaska Native Mental Health Research: The Journal of the National Center* 13, 3: 48–69.

Schmidt, Ryan. 2011. "American Indian Identity and Blood Quantum in the 21st Century: A Critical Review." *Journal of Anthropology*: 1–9.

Schouls, Tim. 2003. *Shifting Boundaries: Aboriginal Identity, Pluralist Theory, and the Politics of Self-Government.* Vancouver: University of British Columbia Press.

Sealey, D. Bruce. 1978. "Statutory Land Rights of the Manitoba Métis." In *The Other Natives: The-Les Métis,* edited by Antoine Lussier and D. Bruce Sealey, 1–36. Vol. 2. Winnipeg: Manitoba Métis Federation Press.

Sealey, D. Bruce, and Antoine S. Lussier. 1975. *The Métis: Canada's Forgotten People.* Winnipeg: Pemmican Publications.

Shore, Fred. 1999. "The Emergence of the Métis Nation in Manitoba." In *Métis Legacy: A Métis Historiography and Annotated Bibliography,* edited by Lawrence J. Barkwell, Leah Dorion, and Darren R. Prefontaine, 71–78. Winnipeg: Pemmican Publications.

Siggins, Maggie. 1995. *Riel: A Life of Revolution.* Toronto: Harper Perennial.

Simpson, Leanne, ed. 2008a. *Lighting the Eighth Fire: The Liberation, Resurgence, and Protection of Indigenous Nations*. Winnipeg: Arbeiter Ring Publishing.

_____. 2008b. "Oshkimaadiziig, the New People." In *Lighting the Eighth Fire: The Liberation, Resurgence, and Protection of Indigenous Nations*, edited by Leanne Simpson, 13–22. Winnipeg: Arbeiter Ring Publishing.

_____. 2011. *Dancing on our Turtle's Back: Stories of Nishnaabeg Re-Creation, Resurgence and a New Emergence*. Winnipeg: Arbeiter Ring Publishing.

Smith, Andrea. 2005. "Spiritual Appropriation as Sexual Violence." In *Conquest: Sexual Violence and American Indian Genocide*, 119–35. Cambridge: South End Press.

Smith, David Paul. 2005. "The Sweat Lodge as Psychotherapy: Congruence between Traditional Healing and Modern Healing." In *Integrating Traditional Healing Practices into Counselling and Psychotherapy*, edited by Roy Moodley and William West, 196–209. Thousand Oaks, California: Sage Publications.

Smith, Linda Tuhiwai. 2001. *Decolonizing Methodologies: Research and Indigenous Peoples*. New York: Zed Books.

_____. 2005. "On Tricky Ground: Researching in the Age of Uncertainty." In *Sage Handbook of Qualitative Research*, edited by Norman Denzin and Yvonna Lincoln, 85–107. 3rd ed. Thousand Oaks, California: Sage Publications.

Spencer, Rainier. 1997. "Race and Mixed-Race: A Personal Tour." In *As We Are Now: Mixblood Essays on Race and Identity*, edited by William S. Penn, 126–39. Los Angeles: University of California Press.

Sprague, Douglas N. 1980. "Government Lawlessness in the Administration of Manitoba Land Claims, 1870–1887." *Manitoba Law Journal* 10, 4: 415–41.

Statistics Canada. 2003a. *Aboriginal Peoples of Canada: A Demographic Profile, 2001 Census Analysis Series*. Minister of Industry. http://www5.statcan.gc.ca/bsolc/olc-cel/olc-cel?catno=96F0030XIE2001007&lang=eng (accessed 8 March 2008).

_____. 2003b. *Aboriginal Peoples Survey 2001: Concepts and Methods Guide*. Minister of Industry. http://www.statcan.gc.ca/pub/89-591-x/89-591-x2003001-eng.pdf (accessed 8 March 2008).

_____. 2006 *Aboriginal Population Profile, 2006 Census*. Minister of Industry. 6 December. http://www12.statcan.ca/census-recensement/2006/dp-pd/prof/92-594/Index.cfm?Lang=E (accessed 9 March 2011).

_____. 2013a. 2011 National Household Survey: Aboriginal Peoples in Canada: First Nations People, Métis and Inuit. Government of Canada. http://www12.statcan.gc.ca/nhs-enm/2011/as-sa/99-011-x/99-011-x2011001-eng.cfm#a4 (accessed 14 July 2013).

_____. 2013b. 2011 National Household Survey: Aboriginal Peoples in Canada: First Nations People, Métis and Inuit. Government of Canada. http://www.statcan.gc.ca/daily-quotidien/130508/dq130508a-eng.htm?HPA (accessed 10 May 2013).

Steinhauer, Patricia. 2001. "Kihkapiiv: Sitting within the Sacred Circle of the Cree Way." Unpublished Doctoral Candidacy Proposal, University of Alberta.

Stevenson, Winona. 2000. "Decolonizing Tribal Histories." PhD diss. University of California, Berkley.

Stonechild, Blair. 1986. "Indian View of the 1885 Uprising." In *1885 and After: Native Society in Transition*, edited by F. Laurie Barron and James B. Waldram, 155–170. Regina: University of Regina Press.

Stonechild, Blair, and Bill Waiser. 1997. *Loyal till Death: Indians and the North-West Rebellion.* Calgary: Fifth House Publishers.

St. Onge, Nicole. 2004. *Saint-Laurent, Manitoba: Evolving Métis Identities, 1850–1914.* Regina: Canadian Plains Research Center.

St. Onge, Nicole, Carolyn Podruchny, and Brenda Macdougall (eds.). *Contours of a People: Metis Family, Mobility, and History.* Norman, OK: University of Oklahoma Press.

Stout, Madeline Dion, and Gregory Kipling. 2003. "Aboriginal People, Resilience, and the Residential School Legacy." *The Aboriginal Healing Foundation Research Series.* Ottawa: Aboriginal Healing Foundation. http://www.ahf.ca/downloads/resilience.pdf (accessed 9 November 2011).

Strong, Pauline Turner, and Barrik Van Winkle. 1996. "'Indian Blood': Reflections on the Reckoning of Native North American Identity." *Cultural Anthropology* 11, 4: 547–76.

Struthers, Roxanne, and Valerie Eschiti. 2005. "Being Healed by an Indigenous Traditional Healer: Sacred Healing Stories of Native Americans." *Complementary Therapies in Clinical Practice* 11, 2: 78–86.

Surtees, Robert J. 1986. "The Robinson Treaties (1850)." Treaties and Historical Research Centre, Indian and Northern Affairs Canada. Aboriginal Affairs and Northern Development. http://www.aadnc-aandc.gc.ca/eng/1100100028974/1100100028976 (accessed 15 April 2012).

· Sweetgrass, Shari Narine. 2011. "Supreme Court Rules Métis Can Control Own Membership." *Alberta Sweetgrass* 18, 9: n.p. http://www.ammsa.com/publications/alberta-sweetgrass/supreme-court-rules-m%C3%A9tis-can-control-own-membership (accessed 4 April 2012).

TallBear, Kimberly. 2003. "DNA, Blood, and Racializing the Tribe." *Wicazo Sa Review* 18, 1: 81–107.

Teillet, Jean. 2013. *Métis Law in Canada.* Pape Salter Teillet. http://www.pstlaw.ca/resources/Metis-Law-in-Canada-2013.pdf (accessedAccessed 26 August 2014).. http://www.pstlaw.ca/resources/Metis-Law-in-Canada-2013.pdf.

Thornton, Russell. 1997. "Tribal Membership Requirements and the Demography of 'Old' and 'New' Native Americans." *Population Research and Policy Review* 16, 1–2: 33–42.

"A Timeline of Residential Schools, the Truth and Reconciliation Commission." 2011. CBC News, 11 June. http://www.cbc.ca/news/canada/story/2008/05/16/f-timeline-residential-schools.html (accessed 5 September 2011).

"Tribal Directories." *U.S. Department of the Interior, Indian Affairs.* http://www.bia.gov/WhoWeAre/BIA/OIS/TribalGovernmentServices/TribalDirectory/ (accessed 23 May 2013).

Urban Aboriginal Peoples Study (UAPS). 2010. *Main Report.* Environics Institute. http://uaps.ca/wp-content/uploads/2010/03/UAPS-Main-Report_Dec.pdf (accessed 30 June 2011).

Van Kirk, Sylvia. 1980. *Many Tender Ties: Women in the Fur-Trade Society, 1670–1870.* Winnipeg: Watson and Dwyer Publishing.

____. 1985. "'What if Mama is an Indian?': The Cultural Ambivalence of the Alexander Ross Family." In *The New Peoples: Being and Becoming Métis in North America,* edited by Jacqueline Peterson and Jennifer Brown, 207–17. Winnipeg: University of Manitoba Press.

Vickery, Paul. 2006. *Bartolomé de las Casas: Great Prophet of the Americas*. New Jersey: Paulist Press.

Waldrum, James T. 1986. "The 'Other Side': Ethnostatus Distinctions in Western Subarctic Native Communities." In *1885 and After: Native Society in Transition*, edited by F. Laurie Barron and James B. Waldram, 279–95. Regina: University of Regina Press.

Weaver, Hilary N. 2001. "Indigenous Identity: What Is It? Who Really Has It?" *American Indian Quarterly* 25, 2: 240–55.

Weber-Pillwax, Cora. 2001. "What is Indigenous Research?" *Canadian Journal of Native Education* 25, 2: 166–76.

Wesley-Esquimaux, Cynthia, and Magdalena Smolewski. 2004. "Historic Trauma and Aboriginal Healing." *The Aboriginal Healing Foundation Research Series*. Ottawa: Aboriginal Healing Foundation. http://www.ahf.ca/downloads/historic-trauma. pdf (accessed 9 November 2011).

Widder, Keith. 1999. *Battle for the Soul: Métis Children Encounter Evangelical Protestants at Mackinaw Mission, 1823–1837*. East Lansing: Michigan State University Press.

Williamson, Tara. 2013. "Of Dogma and Ceremony." *Decolonization: Indigeneity, Education and Society*, 16 August. http://decolonization.wordpress.

com/2013/08/16/of-dogma-and-ceremony/ (accessed 20 August 2013).

Wilson, Shawn. 2001. "What is Indigenous Research Methodology?" *Canadian Journal of Native Education* 25, 2: 175–81.

_____. 2003. "Progressing Toward an Indigenous Research Paradigm in Canada and Australia." *Canadian Journal of Native Education* 27, 2: 161–71.

_____. 2008. *Research is Ceremony: Indigenous Research Methods*. Winnipeg: Fernwood Publishing.

Wilson, Terry. 1992. "Blood Quantum: Native American Mixed Bloods." In *Racially Mixed People in America*, edited by Maria P. P. Root, 108–25. London: Sage Publications.

Womack, Craig. 1997. "Howling at the Moon: The Queer but True Story of My Life as a Hank Williams Song." In *As We Are Now: Mixblood Essays on Race and Identity*,

edited by William S. Penn, 28–49. Los Angeles: University of California Press.

Woodley, Edward. 1953. *The Bible in Canada*. Toronto: J. M. Dent and Sons.

Wookey, Janelle, dir. 2008. *Mémère Métisse/My Métis Grandmother* (documentary). The Winnipeg Film Group.

Yellow Bird, Michael. 1999. "What We Want to be Called: Indigenous Peoples' Perspectives on Racial and Ethnic Identity Labels." *American Indian Quarterly* 23, 2: 1–21.

York, Geoffrey. 1990. *The Dispossessed: Life and Death in Native Canada*. London: Vintage UK.

Zack, Naomi. 1993. *Race and Mixed Race*. Philadelphia: Temple University Press.

_____. 1995. *American Mixed Race: The Culture of Microdiversity*. Toronto: Rowman and Littlefield.

_____. 1998. "My Racial Self over Time." In *Miscegenation Blues: Mixed Race Women's Voices*, edited by Carol Camper, 20–27. Toronto: Sister Vision Press.

Index